The International Committee of the Red Cross

The Graduate Institute of International Studies – Geneva
Società Italiana per la Organizzazione Internazionale – Roma

INTERNATIONAL ORGANIZATION AND THE EVOLUTION OF WORLD SOCIETY
Volume 2

The International Committee of the Red Cross

by Georges Willemin and Roger Heacock
under the direction of
Jacques Freymond

1984 **MARTINUS NIJHOFF PUBLISHERS**
a member of the KLUWER ACADEMIC PUBLISHERS GROUP
BOSTON / THE HAGUE / DORDRECHT / LANCASTER

This research was carried out with the
financial assistance of the Swiss National Foundation for Scientific
Research and the Italian Research Council.

ISBN 90-247-3064-3

The Graduate Institute of International Studies – Geneva

Società Italiana per la Organizzazione Internazionale – Roma

To be published in the same series:

- The Food and Agriculture Organization
- The International Labour Office
- The World Health Organization

Preface

The phenomenon of the international organization, the first hesitant signs of which appeared in the second half of the nineteenth century, made more noticeable progress in the inter-war period, and developed most rapidly and strongly in the years immediately following the Second World War to become the most salient and characteristic aspect of modern international society.

Yet the fundamental structures of the different institutions–which nonetheless had been created on a more or less uniform model–and the division of duties between organizations with general interests and functions and others concerned with particular sectors, as well as between organizations with a universal calling and those more regionally oriented, had been conceived in accordance with criteria which corresponded to the nature of the international society and to the needs for cooperation which existed at the time these organizations were created, and which seemed would last for ever without any great changes.

Yet in the decades which followed, the inter-state society and above all the underlying human community of the world, underwent multiple and profound transformations. Among the causes for this we can mention those which are self evident and those which have had important consequences:

a) the formation of an impressive number of independent States spread over large areas of the globe which had previously been in a dependent position vis-à-vis a limited group of pre-existing States;
b) the growing diversification at different levels between the components of the international society;
c) the redistribution of the balance of power, due to a group of complex factors and the formation, still unfinished and mobile, of a plurality of rallying centres;
d) the multiplying causes of tension and the ever increasing supervention of conflicts, as much international as internal, which are often so embroiled that it is impossible to establish clearly their origins, nature or limits.

To these, if you will, more immediately understandable factors can be added others, less direct and less apparent, but no less important to the ends being considered here. We should consider for example:

a) the impressive progress in science and technology which has had repercussions on the possibilities for using human and material resources; and at the same time the new distribution of these resources, which has had ensuing consequences on the balances and mecanisms of trade;

b) the appearance of new needs for cooperation–political, military, economic, health, cultural, scientific, and technical, etc.–the nature and proportions of which are no longer comparable to those which existed previously;

c) the development of very complex transnational human relations side by side with traditional type of international relations, their overlapping, and the reciprocal influence which has derived from such contact;

d) the demographic growth, its unequal distribution, and the problems arising out of disparities in population density in different regions, living conditions and needs which are at times the most basic ones;

e) the fact that world attention has focused increasingly on the human person, on his condition, the respect for his fundamental rights and his demands for progress, and consequently the tendancy of protection agencies either already created or envisaged, to overcome the obstacles posed by a continued reaffirmation by sovereign States of the principle of State sovereignty.

One quickly realizes that this enumeration is not exhaustive.

All these factors and many others as well, have had and are having growing repercussions on the phenomenon of the international organization, which at times bring it to the verge of a state of crisis. On the one hand, these factors have provoked the creation of new agencies which has given rise to numerous demands for collaboration, rationalisation, redistribution of duties, competition in the search for resources, and the perfecting of means for avoiding duplication. On the other hand, these factors have highlighted the inflexibility of the structures and of the original methods of implementation, and they have often threatened the old balance between the different agencies. Serious tensions are evident between the need for change on the one side and for preservation on the other. Serious conflicts at times arise within such and such an organization, and it is not always easy to discover the real causes which are often hidden behind other factors. With particular respect to the objectives of international activity, we know only too well the recurring difficulties of establishing priorities between political and civil rights, and economic and social rights. And again, more generally, the problem between the protection of the rights of man in its entirety, and political or ideological preoccupations as well as economic preoccupations, such as the demands for a new international economic order. Finally, these different factors have highlighted the changes which have taken place in the participation of member States in the activities of international organizations

–the attitudes taken by these States and the demands which they have manifested therein–in the new characteristics of "multilateral diplomacy" and in the role of large united organizations on the development and transformation of structures and methods of practise of international organizations. Here too this rapid overview is by no means exhaustive.

The impact of these transformations which occurred in the life of the international community on the manner of being of the international organizations and on the activities required of them, inevitably draws the attention of those scientific institutions which are concerned with the study of international relations. It is indeed their role to provide theoreticians, practitioners, and above all new generations of students who receive their teaching, with an overall picture of the phenomenon of the international organization which is not–or at least which is no longer–based only on a reading of the constitutional texts, and the description contained therein of the objectives, structures and activities originally envisaged. The performance which is expected from these scientific institutions ought rather to aim at bringing alive the reality and actuality of the organisms which they are studying, the evolution which has taken place in their structures and in their functioning, the ability of the means which they employ to respond to the aims to which they aspire, and the effective impact of their activities on the needs and relations of their members. It must also demonstrate the demands which are manifested and the possibilities for further adaptation and transformation.

The Italian Society for International Organization in Rome, and the Graduate Institute of International Studies in Geneva, have for some time been convinced of the affinity of their aspirations and of their programmes. Being aware of the interest of these aspects of current international life, they have undertaken to unite their efforts, human and material resources, and work tools, in order to devote themselves to a series of in-depth studies on the subject, which will be linked together by an organic overall programme. To this end, the two institutions sought and obtained the contribution of *Consiglio Italiano Delle Ricerche* and the Swiss National Fund for Scientific Research and, with this support, they set up four initial and parallel research programmes having as their specific subject three distinct inter-governmental organizations: the United Nations Food and Agriculture Organization, the International Labour Organization, and the World Health Organization. To these was recently added an organization which although not having an inter-state origin and structure is no less international with respect to its sphere of activity, namely, the International Committee of the Red Cross. The presence of the headquarters of these four organizations in Rome and Geneva has no doubt influenced the priority of the choice, considering the facilities which derive from carrying out a thorough study of all necessary information at the source. This now being underway, the two founding institutions have already planned a second series of research programmes which will concern three other specialized institutions and an autonomous agency of the United Nations. The analysis might thereafter be extended to cover other organizations and, at the end, a final study is envisaged, to demonstrate the shared aspects arising out of such individual researches.

The volume presented here concerning the International Committee of the Red Cross is No. 2 of the first series. The promoters of the initiative hope that this work, as well as the others whose publication will follow, will arouse the interest both of specialists in the field, and of the numerous individuals involved in international organizations. They are happy to take this opportunity to thank those who in different ways have contributed in these works and those who, in the institutions concerned, have lent them moral and material support.

Christian Dominicé
Director of the
Graduate Institute
of International
Studies

Roberto Ago
President of the Società
Italiana per la Organizzazione
Internazionale

Foreword

This study of the ICRC is part of a broader research project undertaken on the initiative of Professor Roberto Ago. Its purpose is to determine the impact of transformations in the international system since 1945 on international organizations and the latters' reaction.

The ICRC was chosen along with intergovernmental organizations like the ILO, the WHO and the FAO, because it represented an interesting case of a uninational international organization, a Swiss private association, which is nonetheless recognized as a subject of international law and is therefore situated at the level of State actors in the international system.

There was no question, for this study, of reconstituting the history of the ICRC from 1945 to the present. Such a goal would have been too ambitious, and impossible to realize in the time alloted. We therefore limited ourselves to studying the reaction of the ICRC to changes in the international system by observing, on the one hand, the evolution of its activities and, on the other, the institutional and political measures it takes to pursue them.

This deliberately succinct report therefore aims at furnishing precise indications, to the extent possible, concerning the geographic extension of the ICRC's activities, their increase in volume, their diversification, as well as changes which have taken place in the structure of the ICRC and in its relations with the League and with the States. This explains the importance of the *Tables,* of which the text of the report is essentially a commentary.

The bulk of the research rested on the shoulders of Mr. Georges Willemin, former ICRC delegate, who conceived and drew up the Tables, and wrote much of the commentary. Having been called upon once again to serve the ICRC, Mr. Willemin was unable to finish the report, whose final text was revised by Mr. Roger Heacock, in agreement with the research Director, who has revised the whole manuscript.

Let us note, finally, that the research was undertaken and carried out with the authorization of the ICRC, which is in no way responsible for the present text. Access to documents, none of which may today be considered confidential, was greatly and openly facilitated by ICRC employees, to whom we are grateful.

Jacques Freymond

Table of Contents

List of Graphs and Tables

List of Abbreviations

AR	Annual Report
CPWA	Central Prisoners of War Agency
CTA	Central Tracing Agency
EEC	European Economic Community
GIM	Group for International Missions
ICRC	International Committee of the Red Cross
IHL	International Humanitarian Law
Indsec	Indochina Bureau
IOG	Indochina Operational Group
IOR	International Organization for Refugees
IOs	International Organizations
IPWA	International Prisoners of War Agency
IRC	International Red Cross
IRCA	International Red Cross Action in Indochina
IRRC	International Review of the Red Cross
ITS	International Tracing Service
League	League of the Societies of the Red Cross and Red Crescent
NSs	National Red Cross Societies
OAS	Organization of American States
OAU	Organization of African Unity
POWs	Prisoners of War
RIIC	Revue internationale de la Croix-Rouge
UN	United Nations
UNHCR	United Nations High Commissioner for Refugees

Introduction

INTRODUCTION

1. Sources

1.1. The Choice of Sources

The main sources of information for this study, whose purpose is to analyze the activities of the ICRC and their impact on the institution, were the public documents of the ICRC. Research was initially based on the ICRC's Annual Reports (AR's)[1].

The Annual Reports are regularly presented to the Red Cross International Conferences. From the 17th (1947) to the 21st (1969), they came together with a "Summary Report, X-Y". Together they are a continuation of the ICRC "General Reports on its activities from X to Y", presented at international Conferences from the 10th (1921) to the 17th (1938). Whatever the precise legal function of those reports within the International Conference[2], they are for the ICRC a means of informing the members of the International Red Cross of its activities. It is interesting in that respect to note that the Annual Reports go forward chronologically from the three-volume report (1700 pages) on the activities of the ICRC during the Second World War (September 1, 1939-June 30, 1947)[3]. They reflect the ICRC's concern at the end of the war and through the middle of the 1950s with justifying itself before the international Conference[4] and responding to the accusations levelled against it.[5] In addition to being the main source of

---

[1] As of 1954. From 1947/1948 to 1953, they were entitled *Report on General Activities.*

[2] The reports, like those of the other members of the IRC, are "submitted to the examination" of the General Committee and are then the object of a resolution of the Conference in which the Conference either "takes into account" or "takes note of" the information supplied by the ICRC, or "accepts" or "approves of" the activities of the ICRC. Since 1965 (20th Conference), the first variant has been adopted. (*Cf.* PERRUCHOUD, Richard. *Les résolutions des Conférences internationales de la Croix-Rouge.* Geneva, Henry-Dunant Institute, 1979, p. 140 f.)

[3]. The first *Annual Report* covers the period from July 1, 1947 to December 31, 1948.

[4] In 1948 and 1952, the ICRC *requests* the approval of the Conference (PERRUCHOUD, *op. cit.*).

[5] *Cf.* the document "Réponse du CICR à certaines accusations concernant ses activités" (Toronto, 1952). The ICRC refers those who would evaluate its activities to the reports on its activity during World War Two and to the Annual Reports. *Cf. AR,* 1952, pp. 95 ff.

information on the activities of the ICRC, the Annual Reports possess the formal quality of regularity and thus a certain continuity in presentation and chronology (covering the entire period). We will briefly discuss their limitations in the section "Evaluation".

Analysis of the *International Review of the Red Cross (IRRC)* is a useful complement to that of the Annual Reports, since the *Review*, in addition to regular coverage of the activities of the ICRC, contains extracts of presentations, speeches, articles by leaders of the organization. But for a global approach such as ours, the *Review* has certain drawbacks. As a monthly publication (bimonthly beginning in 1978) it covers brief periods. It is closer to an information bulletin[6] than to an official account, and does not strive to be systematic in dispensing information. The *IRRC* nonetheless contains a great deal of valuable data which complement the yearly reports. It is useful if one is interested in a particular conflict, in a single activity or in a brief period, but not, without an effort exceeding the value of the result, if one is seeking a global approach. It would be necessary to establish a largescale graph with numerous entries and, after analysis, condense the practical information (there could theoretically be more than 400 entries concerning a single item[7]). But even then, since the information is not provided in a systematic manner, the result obtained would only have approximate value.

Other sources used were the occasional reports on certain actions (see Bibliography). Their informative value varies. There are very detailed reports (example: Palestine), and narrative brochures destined for the "general public". Some do nothing more than assemble texts already printed in Annual Reports (example: Yemen).

A fourth category of documents we studied for certain quantitative aspects of operational activities is constituted by the reports drawn up by Peat, Marwick, Mitchell & Co. They are useful in verifying the information contained in Annual Reports whose figures, especially during the period 1968-1973, are not very transparent concerning the volume of relief distributed in the course of certain major actions, and which are sometimes even incomplete.

Nor have we neglected, concerning this period which has not been subjected to the same kind of systematic scrutiny as the earlier years described by Pierre Boissier[8] and André Durand,[9] the accounts of former

---

[6] Originally (as of 1869), the ICRC edited a "Bulletin international des Sociétés de secours aux militaires blessés". The present title was chosen in 1919.

[7] More than 400 issues of the *IRRC* were published between 1946 and 1980.

[8] BOISSIER, Pierre. *Histoire du Comité International de la Croix-Rouge, de Solférino à Tsoushima.* Geneva, Henry-Dunant Institute, 1978; 512 p.

[9] DURAND, André. *Histoire du Comité International de la Croix-Rouge, de Sarajevo à Hiroshima.* Geneva, Henry-Dunant Institute, 1978; 590 p.

delegates,[10] the numerous articles published by members of the Committee or by attentive and informed observers, theses and scientific works based on sometimes very thorough research in the ICRC archives. In fact, the history of the International Committee of the Red Cross is much more transparent than is usually claimed and it is in the interest of the institution that this should be the case. The historian can in the final analysis dispense with reading notes taken at the internal sessions of the Committee and its organs. These must remain confidential so as to preserve the freedom of action of the ICRC in activities underway and, even more importantly, so as to leave to it alone the task of evaluating given actions in the light of principles, and thus adjust tactical measures to the needs of a chosen strategy and establish from case to case the limits of discretion in the conduct of its diplomacy.

1.2. Evaluation of the Sources Chosen

1.2.1. The Questions Which the Sources Do Not Answer

One must be conscious that, in limiting ourselves to the published documents of the ICRC, we could only deal with certain aspects of interest to our research in an indirect and incomplete manner. As is well known, the ICRC differs from international organizations in that it is uninational. Whereas the international organizations are directly affected in their internal structures by the emergence of numerous new States in the 1960s, the ICRC is first of all influenced by its activities, as they are perceived by the delegate in the field. It must however be noted that its make up changes, that little by little older delegates are replaced by younger ones, and that this slow but continuous renewal contributes to the rising consciousness of the evolution of the international system. It is to the extent to which the Committee becomes aware of that evolution of the international community that its policy is modified.

The Annual Reports tell us at what moments the ICRC displaces its activities towards the third world and at what moments it increases its involvement there. But we cannot really affirm, based on our sources, that the evolution of the action of the ICRC was optimal in view of the conflict situations in which it should or could have intervened. In order to answer that question it would be necessary first of all to establish the complete list of the offers of service made by the Committee. On that basis one could evaluate to what extent it was the States which impeded the action of the ICRC. One would also need to analyze certain internal documents, among them the minutes of the Executive Committee[11] and the Assembly, the two

[10] HENTSCH, Thierry. *Face au blocus, Histoire du Comité International de la Croix-Rouge dans le conflit du Nigéria*, 1967-1970. Geneva, Droz, 1973; 307 p.

[11] As of 1974; previously called Counsel to the Presidency.

organs which determine the policy of the institution. Those documents would be infinitely more revealing than the Annual Reports as to the level of consciousness of the Committee which is, along with the attitude of the States toward the institution, one of the decisive factors in the action of the ICRC.[12]

The development of the action of the ICRC from 1949 to 1980 and its expansion furnish valid proof that the ICRC *reacted* to the evolution of the international system, as we describe it below. That is what we strive to demonstrate in the first part.

A second type of questions, similar to the above, concerns the relations between international humanitarian law and the (operational) activities of the ICRC. Of all the neutral intermediaries which intervened in post-war conflicts, the ICRC was probably, both in frequency and in intensity, the most active. In this sense, the Annual Reports make it possible to establish an impressive list of protection activities which the ICRC was able to carry out in favor of victims in the framework of international law and humanitarian principles. They do not, on the other hand, provide a sufficient basis for evaluating the effectiveness[13] of international humanitarian law, nor even the effectiveness of the protection accorded by the ICRC.

1.2.2. "Yield" of the Sources, Gaps.

Public documents make it possible to consider in a global manner the action of the ICRC over a period of approximately thirty years. The major lines of its evolution are thus traced. But, since it is not possible to follow the daily action of the ICRC, we had to limit ourselves to its Annual Reports which could only give a general picture, because the Committee wishes to retain control over the information and also, perhaps, because it is not equipped to register all aspects of its activities. It would therefore be necessary to have a system permitting the systematic recording of all data considered important.[14] Since this is not the case, it is not surprising that there should be few constants through the thirty or so Annual Reports.

---

[12] A thesis on the functioning and mechanisms of the ICRC thus had to be abandoned for lack of documents.

[13] *Cf.* Bosshardt, Werner. *Zur Effektivität des Kriegsvölkerrechts. Möglichkeiten empirischer Forschung,* in the collection "Kleine Studien zur politischen Wissenschaft», No. 21, Zurich University, 1973, 34 p. Bosshardt, on pp. 27-29, sets out what in his view would be a systematic analysis of conditions necessary for the success of the ICRC's action. The project was not realized, probably due to difficulties, mentioned by Bosshardt (p. 28), in assembling the required information.

[14] Certain collaborators would like to dispose of a data bank, which would imply that the ICRC knows what it considers to be essential in its activities to an understanding of its functioning and in terms of information.

An important consequence results from this situation, in terms of research: we had to adopt an inductive method, and inventory activities where it was possible to do so.

1.3. Utility of the Study

One should refrain from extrapolating future tendencies from the observation of the evolution of activities. The graphs should not be seen as "humanitarian" productivity or yield curves. The ICRC, by its very nature, acts from time to time and in case of an emergency. The activities of the ICRC directly depend on the unpredictable course of history.

The permanent reference to tradition ensures a certain continuity. But tradition is not a given, it is only a source of inspiration to the extent to which it is alive. Historical consciousness based on the knowledge of tradition is a means for defining and maintaining its identity. It can happen that the ICRC "forgets" what it has done and suddenly rediscovers it under the impact of events. This was the case in the area of medical activities, which were of capital importance during the Second World war and in Palestine (1948-1950) and which practically had to be reinvented during the 1970s, notwithstanding sporadic actions in between. Likewise the Central Tracing Agency, long absorbed by the results of World War Two, had forgotten that its tradition was precisely to be at the forefront of the operational activities of the ICRC.

It can also happen that the Committee does not have a sufficiently clear idea of some of the activities which are taking place in the field. This was the case during the repeated intercessions of delegates on behalf of political detainees, which occurred at the very same time as strong resistance was being manifested in the Committee to intervening in matters affecting the internal security of States.

The study we have undertaken therefore seeks, within the limitations imposed on a research project, to reestablish dialogue between an evolving world and an institution, and help in illustrating, over and beyond efforts at adaptation, the remarkable continuity of its action.

2. HISTORY OF THE ICRC, 1863-1945

Although the history of the ICRC is known and was described in detail in the works of Pierre Boissier and André Durand, not to speak of numerous studies on the action of the organization, it seemed useful to us briefly to recall the stages in the institution's life. What is important here is, in essence, to clarify the perspective in which the ICRC approached the world system during the second half of the twentieth century. It already had, in 1949, a long history behind it, a history rich with experiences from which it drew conclusions and rules for action.

2.1. The Creation

The circumstances are well known, in which a group of five Genevan personalities, among them Henry Dunant, author of the galvanizing book, *Un Souvenir de Solférino*, established itself as an "International and Permanent[1] Committee for Relief to Wounded Military Personnel" in 1863. The program of the Committee was contained in the name it chose. The objective can be summed up in a single gesture, that of the Good Samaritan. By the choice of the adjectives "international and permanent", the Committee displayed, from the time of its creation, the will to enlarge the framework, fortuitous in terms of time and space, of that gesture, and to lay down the bases of a universal and durable movement. For the Committee, if one wished to provide relief without distinction to the wounded of war, one had to engage in a concerted international activity composed of two facets:

- on the one hand, national relief Committees should be created in each country and
- on the other hand, States must commit themselves to respecting a certain number of dispositions aimed at favoring the realization of the objective (bringing relief in time of war).

On August 22, 1864, thanks to the initiative of the International Committee, the first of the so-called Geneva Conventions–the first international humanitarian Convention of modern times–was adopted. Assistance to the wounded was placed under a protective sign, the red cross on a white field. Actors (nursing personnel, sanitary services, chaplains and anybody

[1] "Comité international et permanent de secours aux blessés militaires". The designation "permanent" is adopted in 1875.

bringing relief) and beneficiaries (sick and wounded military personnel), as well as the locations (ambulances, military hospitals and any shelter housing the wounded), were recognized as neutral in combat and protected thanks to the sign.

As of its creation, the International Committee of the Red Cross (ICRC or Committee) defines its objectives and the scope of activities. The ICRC sees itself as an institution with an international vocation, possessing a private and national base.

It considers itself as:

- The founder of the International Red Cross Movement (IRC). Due to the moral authority which this quality confers upon it, it recognizes Red Cross National Societies (NSs);[2]
- promoter of international humanitarian law. As such, it is its guarantor and it concerns itself with its development, its reaffirmation and its propagation;
- coordinator of relief organized by members of the IRC. In 1870-1871, it creates and manages the first "International Agency for Relief to Sick and Wounded Military Personnel" (the so-called Basel Agency);
- as an actor in the theater of conflicts, it acts in the area[3] of the protection of and assistance to victims. First actions: the intervention of Henry Dunant at Solferino (1859), and that of the Committee during the Franco-Prussian war (1870-1871).

2.2. Evolution to the End of the Second World War

The institution has not fundamentally changed. It has remained a private institution, governed by Swiss law,[4] whose members are elected by cooptation among Swiss citizens. The number of members has been increased from five to between fifteen and twenty-five. Although it is national in character, the legal status of the ICRC leaves it free to act in the international field, given the fact that "Swiss law is not interested in the international activity of the ICRC".[5]

The ICRC drafted its first Statutes in 1915. It modified and revised them four times before 1945 (in 1921, 1928, 1930 and 1939).

[2] The first to take this name is the Netherlands Red Cross in 1867. *Cf.* Ruegger Paul. "L'organisation de la Croix-Rouge internationale sous ses aspects juridiques". *Recueil des Cours de l'Académie de droit international de La Haye*, Vol. 82, I, 1953, p. 387.

[3] We prefer to use the singular. *Cf.* Moreillon Jacques. "In conflictual situation, protection and assistance cannot be fundamentally separated..." *IRRC*, 1981, vol. 63, p. 268:

[4] Perruchoud, *Les résolutions des Conférences,* p. 19.

[5] *Ibid.*, p. 20.

The organization has evolved, however. The founding members of the Committee fulfilled all of its functions as a group. They were simultaneously the assembly responsible for the general conduct of affairs, the administrative infrastructure and the delegates in the field. With time, three distinct levels of decision making were formed.[6]

2.2.1. *Towards the Universality of the IRC.*

While it was at the outset a European creation,[7] the IRC as a movement is open to all the world's nations. The Committee is prepared to recognize the National Society of any country on condition that its government has first recognized it and signed the Geneva Conventions. Among the first non-European National Societies were the Ottoman Society (1868), the Peruvian Society (1879) and the Japanese Society (1886). The Movement's expansion is quite rapid. There are seven National Societies when the Convention is signed in 1864, 21 in 1869, 37 in 1899 and 62 in 1939. These National Societies are not simply national groupings pursuing an identical goal. One of their essential objectives is to maintain mutual relations and to respond to requests for assistance on the part of sister Societies.[8] The universality of the IRC is reinforced by that international solidarity.

The sign adopted by the Movement is a symbol which comes from European culture. Although in the minds of the founders,[9] the sign was simply the inversion of the Swiss flag, the red cross on a white field is a cross. The Committee is conscious of this fact since, while recognizing the latent religious nature of the sign, it declares as early as 1876 that "one could even accept the modification of the red cross for non-Christian States". Humanitarian principles must, it feels, take precedence over religious beliefs.[10] The Red Crescent is not, however, officially recognized until 1929. In fact, the Red Cross Movement and the Committee preserve their European imprint, and this in turn reflects the 19th century international system.

International Conferences of the Red Cross are convened in Europe and North America. The first move outside the European cultural sphere takes place in 1934 (Tokyo, 15th Conference). But it is not until the period following the Second World War that the recognition of the universality of

---

[6] *Cf.* FREYMOND Jacques. *Guerres, Révolutions, Croix-Rouge. Réflexions sur le rôle du Comité international de la Croix-Rouge.* Geneva, IUHEI, 1976, pp. 3-35.

[7] With an eye to preparing the 1864 Diplomatic Conference, the Committee undertakes a "European survey" (Moynier in BOISSIER. *Histoire du Comité,* p. 116).

[8] *Cf.* DURAND André. *Le Comité international de la Croix-Rouge.* Lausanne, Centre de Recherches Européennes, 1980, p. 21.

[9] BOISSIER, *op. cit.,*, p. 105 ff.

[10] Moynier in BOISSIER, *op. cit.*, p. 402.

the Movement and the will to express it concretely, motivates the leaders to organize the Red Cross Conferences more and more frequently outside of Europe: the 19th Conference takes place in New Delhi in 1957. Then, after the centennial celebration of the ICRC in Geneva in 1963 and the International Red Cross Conference held in Vienna in 1965, Istanbul (1969), Teheran (1973), Bucharest (1977) and finally Manila (1981) successively host the Movement. The fact that meetings should now be held any place in the world and that the participants come from the four corners of the globe is essential if the principle of humanity is to aspire to universal respect. It allows one to presume that general agreement exists concerning that principle.

2.2.2. *The ICRC as Promoter of International Humanitarian Law*

The moral principles on which the founders of the Red Cross based their initiative were not explicitly defined from the outset. It was probably not considered necessary in the relatively homogeneous Western society in whose bosom the movement was taking shape. The reference made to them in the first Convention were intended to suffice: "Humanity", "Neutrality" under article 5; "Impartiality" under article 6. Matters are clear enough for the ICRC to be charged as of 1869, during the second Conference, with assuring the propagation of the principles whose guardian it is. It will accomplish that task with a consciousness permanently sharpened by the confrontation with daily reality. As soon as it is engaged in the protection of victims of conflicts and has formulated a few basic principles in the name of which it intervenes, it is forced by circumstances to define norms and set up an international legal instrument.

Gaps were revealed in the first Convention concerning maritime conflict. These gaps are filled by the First Hague Peace Conference (1899) which drafts a Convention adapting the 1864 Geneva Convention to sea warfare. A few years later, a new Convention is adopted which does not significantly enlarge the field of application of the existing Conventions which, for their part, are intended to ensure the protection of sick and wounded military personnel in conflicts between States. New points are introduced, for example the protection of "the personnel of voluntary relief societies"–the first recognition of the Red Cross as an actor in conflicts, aimed at expanding "moral" protection:[11] the lists of the wounded and the dead who have been buried must, once drawn up, be passed on to the adversary.

During the First World war, the Geneva and The Hague Conventions were shown to be insufficient. The ICRC, in September 1917, convened the National Societies of the neutral countries of Europe. It felt as of that time

[11] Meaning that which is related to the "principle of humanity".

that protection should be extended to prisoners of war (this was the intent of the 1921 Convention) and to civilians who have come under the control of the enemy (a concern voiced in the 1923 draft Convention). The 1929 Diplomatic Conference was to adopt a Convention governing the treatment of prisoners of war, but would not follow the ICRC on the question of civilians.

The First World war also witnessed the appearance of new arms among them chemical weapons. As of 1918, the ICRC favored their banning. Its campaign resulted in the adoption of the Geneva Protocol of June 17th, 1925, concerning the prohibition of the use in war of axphyxiating toxic and similar gases and of bacteriological means. It was the organization's first direct intervention in the reserved legal area of The Hague. The ICRC, however, thanks to its first President, Moynier, had always been interested in the laws and customs of war. Despite the emergence of the law of The Hague, its interest did not abate, so that it progressively covered the entire field of humanitarian law, furthering "Geneva law" while maintaining its interest in the "law of The Hague". The roots of that dynamism are to be found in the ICRC's experience in conflicts. It is in this areas that the limits of the Convention's prescriptions appeared and that the necessity of a broader application of humanitarian principles was most strongly felt.

2.2.3. The ICRC as an Actor in Conflicts

The Committee could not afford not to take into account the political views of the European powers in defining the applications of the principle of humanity. It probably did not itself at first think in terms of a broader application guided as it was by the experience of Dunant at Solferino. But Dunant, like the other members, was soon interested in extra-conventional situations. History shows that, in those cases, they displayed humanitarian pragmatism by seeking to promote the "development of the principles of humanity", to use Moynier's expression. So it was that, as of 1870, the Committee defended the need for the Red Cross National Societies to act in the framework of colonial "expeditions" and "internal struggles".[12]

At the outset of its existence the Committee as such was not present in the theaters of conflicts. Dr. Appia, member of the Committee, left on his own initiative in 1866 and 1870 to join the Prussian ambulances, and was disavowed by the Committee. Henry Dunant, who was in Paris in 1870 in the midst of combat, was not supported by the Committee either. According to the Committee, the presence in the field had to be limited to National

[12] Eleven examples for each of the two types of conflicts are given for the period 1863-1895 in the *Manuel chronologique,* p. 285, under "Prises d'armes dans lesquelles la Croix-Rouge est intervenue" ("Arms Seizures in Which the Red Cross intervened").

Societies (Central Committees) of belligerent countries. And the first mission dispatched by the Committee was logically sent to bring assistance to a National Society created in an emergency situation: the Montenegrin Red Cross (1875-1876).[13]

It was apparently in 1912, during the Balkan war, that the ICRC was for the first time to send delegates to the theater of a conflict. But it was to acquire its experience during the First World war, an experience which was used between the wars (Sino-Japanese war, 1932 and 1937, and Ethiopian war), as well as in internal conflicts (Hungary 1919, the USSR 1921 and, especially, the Spanish Civil war 1936 to 1939). This list is not exhaustive, but it shows how the ICRC, by the pressure of circumstances, was progressively brought to intervene directly on the operational front.

The Committee had developed its firsts operational activities in 1870-1871, by creating in Basel an Agency for information and relief to the sick and wounded of the French and Prussian armies.[14] That office was designed simply to organize the exchange of information among National Societies and a Center for relief transmission, but it took the initiative of extending its activities to military personnel not protected by the Convention by organizing the exchange of correspondance between prisoners of war and their families. The ICRC, in that way, instituted a type of activities aimed at the "relief of the moral suffering of victims of war", which it continuously developed (1912, Belgrade Agency; 1914, creation of the International Prisoners of War Agency; 1936, creation of the Spanish Service; 1939, creation of the Central Prisoners of War Agency). During the First World war, it improved its methods and increased its activities in this area. Its experience was to serve as the basis for the international ordering of this type of protection (1929 Convention). By its successive initiatives, the ICRC created a working instrument designed as far as possible to preserve the identities of victims of conflict and protect their family ties.

Organizing the transmission of relief was the other type of activity which the Committee developed from its inception. Since the problem of assistance was not only posed for sick and wounded military personnel in the hands of the enemy, but also for healthy prisoners of war, the Committee favored the creation of an International Committee for Relief to Prisoners of War (which was to take as its emblem a green cross on a white field), and likewise created a Central Relief Agency for military personnel interned in Switzerland (the Bourbaki army). These two organs owed their existence to the justified concern with keeping the ICRC within the limits of its original mandate, thus avoiding its having to take on these tasks directly. But their

---

[13] During the uprising of Herzegovina against the Ottoman Empire, neighboring Montenegro was submerged with refugees.

[14] *Cf.* Djurovič, Grodomir. *L'Agence Centrale de Recherches du Comité international de la Croix-Rouge*. Geneva, Henry-Dunant Institute, 1981, p. 95.

independence was something of a "legal fiction". In 1912, there was no longer any question of separate organizations. The Belgrade Agency set up by the ICRC took on the task of transmitting relief, not only to healthy prisoners of war, but also to civilians.[15] During the two world wars, the transmission of relief was to take on gigantic dimensions for an institution of the ICRC's size.

Unlike the transmission of relief, that of medical assistance (Montenegro action, 1875-1876) was not soon renewed. For the ICRC, it was up to the National Societies of neutral countries to show their solidarity. It limited itself to keeping informed of needs. Medical assistance was developed later, through visits to prisoners.

The passage from the simple transmission of relief materials to their distribution by the ICRC also took place during the First World war. Prisoners of war were the first beneficiaries. Between the two wars, the ICRC also organized several relief distributions in favor of civilians, among which the Spanish Civil war action (1936-1939) is the most important.

But the 1914-1918 war and the numerous civil wars which followed had bankrupted most countries in Europe. The aid needs of civilian populations were such that they required an international relief organization. The ICRC actively participated in efforts at coordination. It adhered to the International Union for Relief to Children whose patronage it accepted (1919). The ICRC was likewise prepared to assume, along with the League, certain responsibilities, among them "the execution of the task of relief[16]" in the International Relief Union, an organism created by the League of Nations (it was inoperative for urgent relief actions).

Visits to prisoners of war (POWs), and to interned civilians, were, in chronological order of their emergence, the third type of ICRC activities. It was through the distribution of relief that the ICRC was brought, not to take charge of prisoners, but physically to go towards them. At the beginning of the First World war, "the Committee... is primarily concerned with the transmission and distribution of relief packages which imply its presence in the camps and its knowledge of the needs of prisoners[17]". With its visits to prisoners of war the ICRC initiated an activity which it extended to other categories of detainees (civilian internees, foreigners, political detainees), before visits to POWs had even become "conventional" (1929 Convention). During the Second World war, visits to POWs and civilian internees took on such proportions that they have since been considered the most important "traditional" activity of the ICRC.

---

[15] DJUROVIČ, *op. cit.*, p. 36.

[16] DURAND, 2, *Histoire du Comité*, p. 142.

[17] *Ibid.*, p. 52.

2.2.4. *The International Committee as the Central Organ of the IRC Movement.*

"In 1863, the ICRC is entrusted with the mission of functioning as the central agency for the exchange of information among National Societies..."[18] Four years later, the ICRC was charged with creating a journal (the future "International Bulletin"), exchanging communications and transmitting relief in case of war. In the years which followed, the International Red Cross Conferences, which included National Societies and States parties to the Geneva Conventions, were to bestow ever more numerous mandates on the ICRC and to confirm traditional mandates. The ICRC nonetheless maintained its independence, as specified by the IRC statutes, within the framework of the basic principles of the Red Cross (as well as in the framework of the resolutions adopted by the IRC and its mandates, which are in accord with the principles).

The creation of the League of National Red Cross Societies, in 1919, inaugurated a brief period of confusion. The very circumstances under which the League was created, the widespread belief that the end of the global conflict announced the coming of an international community, caused the promoters of the League to believe that it was up to them to take over the mission of the ICRC. That was not to be the case, and inevitable tensions arose which both sides attempted to reduce by arriving at a division of labor. It was not until 1928 that relations between the two international organizations, one "multinational" and one "uninational", were defined by the adoption of the statutes of the International Red Cross. They were relations among equals (which had not been evident at first) which were to divide up areas of competence within the overall domain of the IRC. The ICRC, in principle, preserved all of the functions which had previously been ascribed to it by the Conferences and, in any event, the essential ones, those traditional tasks which we have enumerated above.

The League developed new sectors of activity, among which sanitary education, recruitment and training of nurses, the promotion of the Junior Red Cross became permanent mandates before 1945.

In certain sectors of activity, however, a clear distinction between the areas of competence of the ICRC and the League is difficult to make. In those cases, the Conference attributes joint mandates to the two organisms and leaves to them the task of working out in practice a judicious division of labor. For the period 1928-1945, that division of labor bore on the "promotional"activity of the Movement, that which aims at "favoring the creation of National Societies",[19] and the propagation of Red Cross

[18] PERRUCHOUD, *Les résolutions*, pp. 146-157.

[19] *Ibid.*, p. 153.

principles among young people (drafting a manual). But the most delicate problem concerns the coordination of Red Cross aid. The distinction between relief actions in times of peace (League) and times of war (ICRC) might help in orienting the efforts of each one of the institutions, but could not, in numerous instances, be strictly followed. During the Spanish Civil war and the Second World war, the ICRC and the League were led to cooperate. Special accords were then concluded among them in order to delimit the distribution of tasks. Two fundamental reasons impose upon them constant cooperation in relief matters: the degree of need in certain obvious cases of war requiring the total mobilization of the Red Cross system and–especially after 1945–the increasing difficulty in distinguishing between times of war and of peace.

3. Conflicts and Transformation of the International System, 1945-1980

If war is as old as the history of humanity, it is not an immutable phenomenon like natural catastrophes. The nature of conflicts evolves with the transformation of relations among communities. Modern conflicts are determined by the international system, and they in turn affect it.

The Second World war was due to the profound transformation of the international system which the First had brought into existence. Before 1914, Europe was the center of the international system. Its main Powers often behaved as though they ruled the world. After the Second World war, Europe was divided into two zones, whose poles, the USSR and the USA, are no longer "European" in the strict sense, although they remain historically and partly geographically linked to Europe.

The antagonism of the two superpowers brought about the bipolarization of the international system which dominated the international political scene of the 1950s and early 1960s. Without ever degenerating into direct confrontation, several dramatic crises–among them the Berlin blockade (1948), the Hungarian (1956) and Cuban crises (1962)–punctuated the "cold war" which the two superpowers had been waging since the end of the "universalist dream". That dream, whose instrument the UN is, created an illusion only briefly, if at all. The UN rapidly became a place of synthesis between the ideal of a community among States which were in every respect equal and the *Realpolitik* of the superpowers. Within the UN, the latter are the "primi inter pares."

But since the new interstate system established in 1945 by the international community was to operate according to the democratic, and no longer the feudal, model, a new and irreversible movement had been set in motion which the cold war could only slow down: decolonization.

Twelve Asian States, among which two in the Middle East, achieved their independence between 1946 and 1949, and only seven (among which six were African States) in the 1950s. But the example of the Asian States strengthened the will to independence of the other, essentially African, colonies. As different as their ideological and political aspirations may have been, they all had a common goal: their integration as equals into the international system, which was ensured by their admission to the UN.

Independence was not achieved without struggle, always political, sometimes armed. The European powers–except Great Britain with respect to the Asian countries–which had survived the Second World war, attempted to preserve their privileges. They thought they could ignore the letter and the spirit of the United Nations Charter in which the right of peoples to self determination (Article 1 and Article 73) had been stated. But Europe, which in 1939 still controlled nearly a third of the surface of the globe and a third of the world population under colonial dominion, was in 1945 no longer the absolute master of even its own.

It could no longer keep its colonies against the combined will of the international community and the two superpowers. France and the Netherlands thus had to give up Indochina and Indonesia. But American concern with containing the communist threat definitively carried the day over universalist considerations as witnessed by the Korean war. (Other examples of the American containment policy: intervention in Iran in 1953 and in Guatemala in 1954.)

France was therefore able to continue conducting wars against its overseas territories (Indochina, Morocco, Tunisia, Algeria) without being opposed by the US.

Between 1960 and 1962, the international community increased by approximately thirty States, by 44 through the 1960s. The multiplication of States was in and of itself a potential source of growing strife, for the construction of a new State was based on the exogenous base of the colonial heritage and the fragmented base of an authentic cultural tradition. This almost inevitably produced internal tensions which could easily become internal conflicts, or even open civil wars. The most striking examples are those of the Congo-Zaïre (1960-1964), Cyprus (1964), Nigeria (1967-1970) and, more recently, Angola (1975).

From a mathematical point of view, the multiplication of States also dramatically increases the risk of war among two or several States. There is no lack of objects of contention, since the borders were imposed by colonial powers, often without taking into account local configurations. Examples are the wars between India and Pakistan over Kashmir (1948-1949) and Bengal (1970), Morocco and Algeria (1962-1963), Rwanda-Burundi (1962-1963), Niger-Benin/Dahomey (1963-1965), etc. To that list must be added the particular case of the Middle Eastern conflicts (1948-1950, 1956, 1967, 1973).

But by and large, it must be noted that there has been a relative absence of interstate violence since 1945 in the international political system. One should not however conclude that violence has diminished and that the present period has been particularly calm ever since the Second World war.[1]

[1] JACOBSON, Harold. *Network of Independence: International Organizations and the Global Political System.* New York, Alfred A. Knopf, 1979, pp. 208 and 214.

While it is true that there have been few so-called classical wars among States in the post-war period, one can nonetheless count several hundred conflicts or conflictual situations between 1946 and 1980. There were 224 according to Casadio,[2] to which one can add 156 coups d'Etat. The essential question is not to know whether the evolution of the present international system is characterized by the multiplication of conflicts or their diminution. It is not a simple question of numbers.

A brief comparison with the second half of the 19th century should make it possible to bring out the particular characteristic of the present international system. Between 1863 and 1895, one counts at least 198 wars, international conflicts and civil wars.[3] The number of conflicts is therefore approximately the same.

a. The European States alone "supported" (by being directed implicated in) 117 wars, of which 86 were outside of Europe.[4] In other words, a dozen powers to a great extent decided issues of war and peace in the world. Only Latin America and North America could, to a certain extent, conduct wars, internal ones or the most part, without precipitating the direct intervention of a European power. In the contemporary international system, the decision-making centers have increased more than tenfold due to the multiplication of States. The decision to settle an internal or external conflict by force belongs to a large number of States. The diplomatic field has been extended to the entire world and alliances are no longer simply made within the European sphere (with or against a superpower).

b. When Professor Chaix, in 1896, drew up his "list of wars", he noted the difficulty in gathering complete information concerning non-European conflicts: "It is therefore only since 1880 that one finds numerous references to Africa. What had happened there until then? There was clearly fighting everywhere, *but incognito*.[5]

With the development of telecommunications, the international community disposes of rapid and virtually universal elements of information. States in conflict or wishing to enter into conflict must take into account the fact that their decisions and doings will be made public in a far stronger sense than during the 19th century.

The circulation of information educates public opinion which develops a universal sensibility. An event deep inside Turkey no longer leaves one

---

[2] *Cf.* footnote 1, p. 46.

[3] Chaix, Emile. "Le théâtre des guerres contemporaines de la Croix-Rouge". *Bulletin international des Sociétés de la Croix-Rouge,* No. 107, July 1896, p. 176.

[4] *Cf. Manuel chronologique pour l'histoire générale de la Croix-Rouge,* 1863-1899. Geneva, ICRC, 1900, 30 p..

[5] Chaix, *op. cit.*, p. 170.

indifferent. This is an undeniable fact, even if the sensibility of public opinion remains gradual, selective and emotionally manipulable.

c. So-called classical warfare–that which takes place on a clearly defined battlefield–has probably never existed. War knows no frontiers. It affects people other than the combatants. It does not only implicate their governments and their soldiers. It breaks out independently of their will.

If a good number of conflicts during the 19th century in Europe were classical wars, there were also insurrections and uprisings and, most of all, colonial expeditions. The 19th century therefore already knew a "multiplicity" of types of conflicts–and the Committee in 1896 expressly referred to them.

Types of conflicts can more easily be defined for the nineteenth century than for the present period because the great powers of that time were directly implicated in almost two thirds of the conflicts and they did not make any bones about defending their policies. "Internal struggles", on the other hand, take place more "within the family", away from the curiosity and therefore the pressure of international opinion. "One often is unaware of their beginning and their end".[6] For these reasons nineteenth century conflicts can more easily be identified and classified.

But in the contemporary international system, the great powers have considerably enlarged the range of interventions and they prefer indirect and if possible camouflaged ones. Hence the very clear predominance of "non-international conflicts" as compared to international conflicts.

Governments as well as opposition groups, furthermore, must take into account the international community (its organization, other States, opinion, etc.). Whereas governments will do everything to diminish their opponents in the eyes of international opinion and to minimize their representativeness, the latter apply all their imagination to attracting the attention of the international community. For victory is at present achieved just as much if not more in that forum than on the battlefield.

The use of force and violence are thus modified. States develop new methods for hiding their moves from international opinion. Disappearances and torture leaving no physical traces are specific products of that will to hide. For adversaries, there is no longer any imperative necessity to defeat the enemy. Attacks can be directed anywhere against anyone, as long as they are accompanied by an "explanatory note" directed at international opinion. Thus does terrorism develop.

d. The appearance of the atomic bomb and the development of nuclear weapons have also modified the nature of conflicts. Previously, international warfare between great powers was conducted with the most modern arms

[6] *Ibid.*, p. 171.

they disposed of. The German cannons in 1870 and the British tanks during the First World war were decisive elements in victory.

Since Hiroshima and Nagasaki, the great powers have been obliged to avoid direct confrontation. Risks have become incalculable. Nor can they any longer attack a smaller State without the minimal accord of others, if only negatively in the sense that others do not see in it a "casus belli". Great powers, furthermore, for the first time in history, cannot put to use the totality of their panoply during an engagement with a small State (Vietnam).

Great powers are to a great extent paralyzed by their atomic weaponry during conflict. They are therefore less inclined than were the old colonial powers to defend their interests through open force. They also have an interest in favoring diffused conflicts and in making their presence impossible to perceive, to prove.

e. Finally, the presence of international organizations during conflicts is an essential characteristic of the present international system. It is not an absolute novelty since the ICRC had been called upon to intervene in conflicts during the second half of the 19th century. But the number of international institutions intervening in present conflicts, their multinational character, their pacifying role, and the frequency of their interventions are specific elements of the post-war system.

The UN, the OAS, the OAU, the Arab League and the Council of Europe have been called upon to attempt to settle conflicts 146 times between 1946 and 1970.[7] In other words, in the majority of conflicts, the States manifested their will to turn to an international institution and have it propose peaceful solutions to their differences.

The fact that States in conflict only see this approach as one of their options and that they try, often simultaneously, to reach their goals through force, does not mean that they contest the role of the international organizations in assuring the cohesion of the international system. But the attitude of the States seriously impedes the initiatives of the international organizations (IOs). One can thus not know, according to the specialists, whether the IOs on the whole contribute in a *decisive* manner to the maintenance of security in the world.[8]

To sum up, the best definition of post-war conflicts is probably negative: conceptual categories making it possible to establish clear distinctions no longer correspond to the international community's perception of conflicts. If the perception has been modified, it is because the structures of the international community have changed. The dispersion of decision-making

---

[7] BUTTERWORTH, Robert. *Managing Interstate Conflict, 1945-1974.* Data with Synopsis, Pittsburgh, UCIS, 1976; 535 p.

[8] JACOBSON. *Network of Independence,* p. 212 ff.

centers which took place with the multiplication of States goes hand in hand with a dilution of the "truth". The conflictual reality elicits divergent, opposed interpretations. A combatant is a terrorist and vice versa. An internal affair is an international conflict and vice versa. This divergence of views is not only the expression of a voluntarist interpretation elaborated for political ends. It is also the product of a phenomenon which is more and more influential in the international system: the dissolution of societies which brings about a dilution of power.

The reality of conflicts has itself been diversified. Conflictual events, actors, means used, are no longer to be described according to traditional categories; hence the need to proceed to a "descriptive analysis of conflicts", such as that which Franco A, Casadio, assisted by Marina Cerne, has completed. This book[9] will no doubt establish a useful base for his projected study on *the evolution of international relief action.*

[9] CASADIO, Franco A. *Conflittualità mondiale e relazioni internationali, 1945-1982*. Publicazioni della Società italiana per l'Organisazzione internazionale, Padova, CEDAM, 1983; 298 p.

PART ONE

THE REACTION OF THE ICRC TO THE EVOLUTION OF THE INTERNATIONAL COMMUNITY SEEN THROUGH THE OBSERVATION OF ITS ACTION

CHAPTER I

Extension of the ICRC's Presence in the World

One cannot escape the conclusion that the dominant conception and the practice of humanitarian law, until 1945, remained European-centered, even though the ICRC had undertaken worldwide efforts. When speaking of Europe at that time, one must recall the colonial relations which still characterized large parts of the globe, especially in Africa and Asia. As indicated by André Durand,[1] the ICRC's actions, between 1911 and 1945, took place over a period marked by 15 wars. Among those, the only colonial-type conflict in which it offered its mediation was the Rif war, and only because it involved military operations led by enemies each of which controlled a part of the contested territory. The independence and liberation wars of the period were still experienced even more than they were defined as internal conflicts exclusively concerning the colonial power, and in which the ICRC had to avoid becoming embroiled.

None of this negates the fact that the ICRC had fully participated in humanitarian actions during the Second World war, with more or less success depending on the area of intervention. And it entered the post-war period strengthened by the lessons of the world conflict. The rising consciousness brought about by the conflict which ended in 1945 could not help but undermine the European-centered conception and set off a kind of slow "decolonization" of the conceptions of the Committee itself.

Barely one year after the end of hostilities, it circulated a draft project for the revision and extension of the Geneva Conventions, which is presented, first to the Red Cross Societies, then to governments. The project was finally embodied in the four Geneva Conventions signed by the States in 1949. If these new Conventions "are clearly to be situated in the historical continuity of the Conventions which came out of the first Geneva Convention"[2], their

[1] DURAND 2, *Histoire du Comité*.

[2] DURAND André. *Le Comité International de la Croix-Rouge*. Lausanne, Jean Monnet Foundation, 1980, p. 42.

role was mainly to fill in gaps which had been observed during the war. They innovated in areas covered little or not at all, through the extension of the categories of persons protected,[3] through the affirmation of rules of treatment having an absolutely prohibitive character and, for the first time, through the reference to non-international armed conflicts (Article 3 common to the four Conventions). This is the period when the Information Agency on Prisoners of War, created in 1939, had its activities confirmed by its mention in the Conventions.

It was of course at the moment when international relations, peaceful or warlike, underwent a worldwide geographic extension, that conflicts not having a legally international character gained in importance. It was also evident that the involvement of civilian populations in combat (as victims or participants) had become a market characteristic of various wars, given the quality of weapons and the intensity of the engagement of entire populations in certain struggles.

One must nonetheless recognize that the 1949 Conventions reflected an incomplete vision of the new international system. This is why they were not adequate in terms of the practical needs of the ICRC; it became necessary to convene a new conference on humanitarian law. The perception of the nature of the post-war era was, in 1949, still rather confused. True, the cold war was gaining in intensity (Greek Civil war, Marshall plan, Berlin blockade, creation of the Chinese People's Republic), but it had not yet degenerated into the East-West armed conflict which would, one year later, expose the workings of the system while revealing its limits and its complexity: the Korean war. In 1949, it was still possible to dare to think, at the ICRC as elsewhere, that peoples, or at least States, would as far as possible use the channels of the United Nations in order to settle major differences, and that they would avoid the recourse to arms of massive destruction.

The Korean war destroyed military and political illusions: the country in question came out of the war devastated, mainly by bombing and heavy artillery concentrated on all large cities. The UN had become the tool of a majority coalition within it and therefore itself an actor (and not a mediator) in a conflict.

But in 1949 already, at the time of the signature of the four Conventions, the awareness of the fragility of the collective security system existed. Anti-colonial wars were well underway, thus posing humanitarian problems and placing the ICRC under the obligation of intervening in an area and in conditions which it did not yet know well.

It must clearly be stated that we are not here tracing the history of a "humanitarian expansion". The ICRC is not omnipresent in a tumultuous

[3] An extension which the 1929 Geneva Diplomatic Conference had already called for.

world. It offers its services essentially in case of conflicts, which can take on very diverse forms. Its presence is therefore necessarily limited in time and variable according to the international situation. Conflicts, depending on their nature and intensity, set off or do not set off ICRC actions. And, although there is an obvious concordance between the nature of the conflict and that of an ICRC action, a certain number of factors cause the evolution of the presence and the commitment of the ICRC not to be *a priori* parallel to evolution of conflicts. Among those factors there is above all the political will of States to accept or to refuse the offers of service of the ICRC and the decision of the Committee to offer or not to offer its services. In other words, the image of the ICRC in such and such a sector of the international community and the prevailing vision of the world in the Committee at such and such a moment are factors which, above and beyond the strictly mechanical nature of a conflict and its progression, are in the final analysis responsible for the ICRC's involvement, and once such an involvement exists, of its characteristics. These two complementary factors considerably modify the idea of a more or less parallel evolution of ICRC activities and conflicts. In other words, to use a metaphor, the ICRC is surely an image of international crises, but the image it reflects is made up of shadows and lights, of non-action and action.[4] Our analysis is therefore not that of crises and conflicts in the international system itself, but that of actions undertaken by the organization.

1.1. The Delegations

During the Second World war, the ICRC was to extend its presence to the entire world. It was of course not the first time it acted outside of Europe, but never before had its engagement been as massive and intense. At the end of the war, the number of delegations and sub-delegations exceeded eighty. Half of them were in Europe and the other half on the other continents.[5]

Since then, the ICRC has never "disarmed". The conflict of 1939-1945 having forced it to extend its presence throughout the world, the ICRC feels that it is its duty not to demobilize right away. The introduction to the 1949 Annual Report drafted by the Committee specifies the policy it intends to pursue.[6]

---

[4] In the Annual Reports, mention is occasionally made of a refusal of the ICRC's services on the part of a State.

[5] *IRRC,* vol. 30, 1948, p. 44-63. (The *International Review of the Red Cross* has been published in English since 1961.)

[6] *AR,* 1949, p. 5 f. In this, it was following the general evolution of State practice. "Since 1940, there have been neither declarations of war nor treaties of peace." BOUTHOUL, Gaston and CARRERE, René. *Le défi de la guerre, 1740-1974.* Vendôme, PUF, 1976, p. 133.

"The present state of international relations compels the Committee to maintain an intermediate position between war mobilization and the peace-time conditions that existed before September 1939."

This is why the Committee decided to maintain its representational network and only scaled it down very slowly. The system of "honorary delegates" recruited on the spot, among members of the Swiss expatriate community who lend their aid without pay, made it possible for the ICRC to prolong its presence at a constant level despite serious financial difficulties which it experienced in the early 1950s.[7]

These delegations were, however, mainly "mail boxes" with a purely representative role. They did not undertake major actions. Starting in 1960, the ICRC, conscious of what were mainly qualitative limitations in this system, set up delegations whose first task was the organization of activities and not representation.[8] One can therefore not really compare the 30 delegations of 1954 with the 15 delegations of 1971, for example. Whereas there are in 1954 more representational delegations, in 1971 they are essentially operational, so that the level of activities in 1971 has increased more than tenfold as compared with 1954.

One likewise notes an evolution in the conception of representation, leading in 1970-1971 to the opening of three permanent regional delegations, in Ethiopia, in the Cameroons and in Venezuela, from which the delegates, who are now professionals, travel into the neighboring countries.

But the great turning-point of the post-war era which came with the Nigeria-Biafra war (1967-1970), made it necessary to gather information on the spot, to disseminate humanitarian principles in the field and to intensify the action of the ICRC in the area of protection and assistance to victims.[9]

---

[7] In 1949, the ICRC had 35 paid and 38 unpaid delegates whereas in 1954, 30 out of 34 are unpaid. At the same time, the number of delegations drops from 35 to 30 (*AR*, 1949, p. 15 and *AR*, 1954, p. 10 f.).

[8] In 1960 in the Congo, in Laos and in Nepal; in 1962 in North Yemen.

[9] "Beginning in the late 1960s and early 1970s, the international community became increasingly aware of the shortcomings and inadequacies of the then-existing mechanics of international relief assistance. The magnitude of suffering, the evident waste and duplication, the use of disaster aid for political ends, and the often embarrassing publicity in such disaster situations as the Nigerian civil war, the 1968 Peruvian earthquake, and the 1970 cyclone of East Pakistan resulted in the first major efforts at reorganizing the international relief system in the postwar era." STEPHENS, Thomas W. "Between Expectation and Endeavour: UNDRO and the Problems of International Relief Coordination". *Disaster Assistance. Approach, Reform and New Approaches,* New York, Lynn, H. Stephens and Stephen J. Green, eds., New York University Press, 1979, p. 29. The text here quoted reveals the rising consciousness which at the end of the 1960s concerned all organizations involved in bringing aid to victims. Of the three examples given, it is the Nigerian conflict which directly challenged the ICRC.

Whether in practice or in the legal sphere,[10] the experience of the Nigerian conflict is very important. The work which, shortly after the events, was devoted to the conflict from the point of view of ICRC's efforts, observes that there is indeed an important lesson to be drawn for the future. Estimations, figures, budgets, this is the clear language which governments can understand. To the romanticism of the appeal must now be substituted the logic of the investment plan. The profits to be derived cannot be given monetary value, but they are nonetheless real: lives saved, a catastrophe avoided. In sum, a less costly operation than the immense, hasty and desperate relief to operation to the financing of which one would have to resolve oneself later, under the pressure of a public opinion scandalized by the extent of irreparable disaster which one had allowed to happen.[11]

These recommendations correspond perfectly to the changes made after 1970, which went towards an intensification of the engagement in terms of presence, prescience and appeals for funds.

Since 1954, then, due to the international political situation, the ICRC feels obliged to maintain its presence in all regions of the world. That nearly constant presence is also intensified, as witnessed by the repeated opening of operational delegations as of the beginning of the 1960s and then by the opening of several regional delegations in the 1970s.

The extension of the presence of the ICRC in the world can be grasped in its broad outlines through the description of the opening of delegations. But since the delegation of 1949 and that of 1980 are not truly comparable, one must use criteria other than the opening of a delegation if one is to have a more concrete idea of the reality of the presence of the ICRC in the world.

1.2. Visits to Places of Detention and Distribution or Transmission of Relief

These two types of operations cover a large part of the main field of activity of the ICRC, namely protection of and assistance to victims of conflicts. We can therefore hypothesize that any country having opened the doors of one or several places of detention and any country having received aid, whatever its value, has experienced an "ICRC presence" during a given year (cf. Table 1). This definition of presence does of course amount to a reduction in the area of activities considered external. We have adopted it

[10] "The proposals made by the ICRC at the Diplomatic Conference, in favor of delivering aid to civilian populations in case of armed conflict, take into account the Nigerian experience." FREYMOND, *Guerres, révolutions, Croix-Rouge*, p. 101.

[11] HENTSCH, Thierry. *Face au blocus. Histoire de l'intervention du Comité international de la Croix-Rouge dans le conflit du Nigéria, 1967-1970*. Geneva, IUHEI, 1973, p. 238.

because it furnishes a comparative base,[12] and we have thus been able to trace tendencies in the presence in the field of the ICRC (cf. Tables 2-6). Protection actions without any visit and assistance actions without any material distribution are exceptions.[13]

1.2.1. Overall Analysis (Table 2)

The analysis of the ICRC's presence reveals that it was more or less stationary for twenty years (1949-1968), with the number of countries concerned by an ICRC activity fluctuating between 20 and 30. The Committee probably needed time to translate into acts its perception of changes in the world system. The international climate, further, is not favorable to a significant progression in its activities: the intensity of the cold war and the armaments race does not encourage governments to increase their donations, be it to National Societies or to the ICRC.

It is for this reason that the ICRC, after having terminated its main activities resulting from Second World war commitments in 1947, undergoes a decrease in its ordinary budget from 1949 to 1953 and it is not until 1960 that it once again reaches its 1949 level.

Governments are difficult to mobilize for humanitarian actions and the Committee, conscious though it may be of its obligation to intervene more, is still divided in the face of risks–including financial risks–which it would have to assume. The budgetary obstacle remains all the more difficult to overcome since there is a lack of technical know-how in the area of fundraising. It is not until 1970 that a fundraiser's position is created. In 1980, half a dozen persons do nothing else.

As already indicated, it is the Nigerian conflict which unblocks the situation after 1968 and there is in the space of five years (1968-1973) a rapid extension: the number of countries concerned by an ICRC activity has tripled. The awareness becomes acute (even if, as we will see later on, it has already existed within the Committee from the beginning of the decade) that the world which lies outside of the industrialized areas is little known, despite or because of the preponderance of the system of honorary delegates. It is necessary to be constantly on the spot, given the limited means which lie

[12] The sources give regular information of sufficient detail concerning these two activities, which can be compared over a period of thirty years. A visit and a distribution remain essentially unchanged.

[13] Among these exceptions one must note repatriations of persons and family reunions organized by the ICRC. The other cases of a presence not corresponding to the two criteria are in general cases of "logistical" delegations. Concretely, one can cite for example repatriations from Uganda (1965), Zaïre (1968), Kenya (1971), Japan (1959-1967), the People's Republic of China (1974), Iraq (1969), etc. Other repatriations took place along with a simultaneous visit/relief action in the country of origin.

at one's disposal. The regional delegates are to make contact with governments, diffuse international humanitarian law among civil and military authorities. In 1970, a school manual is written, translated into 36 languages, and distributed everywhere in the world where governments give their permission.

From 1973, the extent of the presence progressively retracts. The Committee has decided to define, to narrow down, criteria for intervention, be it in the area of protection or of assistance.

The strong extension of the presence of the ICRC which one can observe between 1969 and 1973 is due more to the increase in the number of States than to the number of conflicts. 1973 is not any more than 1955 a year of widespread conflict. And neither year is, by any standard of measurement, a year in which ICRC activities are most intense. It is in 1949-1950 (Palestine), 1956 (Hungary and Suez), 1967-1969 (Middle East and Nigeria) and 1978-1980 (Middle East and Kampuchea) that the ICRC appears to be most strongly engaged, during years where the curve of conflicts tends to *decline* (cf. Table 2).

The geographic extension of the ICRC therefore tends to be inversely proportional to the intensity of its activities in the case of conflict, because the organization must then reduce the number of its engagements and make a more selective evaluation of needs. One must not however forget that the freedom of the ICRC to become involved or not is significantly reduced and that it will, in the 1970s, have to work to strengthen its means so as to ensure its presence in a greater number of conflicts.

1.2.2. Comparative Evolution of Conflicts and ICRC Interventions (Table 3)[14]

As stated above, such a comparison is not the purpose of our research. It is nonetheless interesting to see if there is a relationship between the curves of conflicts and ICRC interventions.

Since a list of conflicts cannot claim to be perfect, we have found it useful to choose several. The Casadio list[15] includes violent conflicts, having caused human suffering, but does not include all international or internationalized tensions, or coups d'Etat. The Zacher list[16] is based on the limitative conception of "international conflict".

---

[14] Thus, Table 3 represents rather rough comparisons in that we are comparing a number of *conflicts* involving several countries with a number of *countries* concerned by ICRC actions. We do not think, however, that the tendency of conflict curves would be notably altered if one were to take countries as the unit.

[15] Not published.

[16] ZACHER, Mark. *International Conflicts and Collective Security, 1947-1977:* the United Nations, OAS, OAU and Arab League. New York, Praeger, 1979; 297 p.

And finally, the Butterworth list[17] includes conflicts which were brought before certain international organizations seeking their intervention in favor of peace, namely the UN, the OAS, the OAU, the Arab League and the Council of Europe.

Depending on the criteria which one adopts, one obtains strongly divergent representations of the conflictual evolution of the international system. The intensity (number of conflicts) varies from the simple to the quintuple. Periodizations do not concord at all either.

For Casadio, the number of conflicts, since 1955, has always been on the increase. Zacher, on the basis of his criteria, arrives at a division of the post-war period into two sections: a first, calmer one (until the beginning of the 1960s) followed by a second more agitated, but remarkably constant one in the 1970s. The Butterworth list, on the other hand, somewhat illustrates the proverb, "the sum of all vices is constant". It also indicates a slight growth during the 1950s, a stabilization in the 1960s and a diminution of conflicts from 1970 to 1974.

The three lists (Table 3) agree on only one point: the period from 1950 to 1955 is relatively the calmest. Otherwise they contradict one another too strongly to make it possible to conclude that there was an increase in conflicts during the post-war period.

Since the three representations differ so much, and since none of them runs parallel to the curve of ICRC actions, the main conclusion has to be negative: there is no clear relationship between the *evolution*[18] of conflicts and that of ICRC actions. Therefore, and this seems to us to be the most interesting point, the rapid extension of the presence of the ICRC in the world at the beginning of the 1970s is at any rate not a response[19] to a hypothetical intensification of the permanent crisis of the international system.

The only parallel which we would be tempted to establish is the relative constancy of evolutions during the 1950s and 1960s.

One should, however, add two remarks which are important: conflicts tend to prolong themselves. Many become endemic. They also undergo changes in character because of the very fact that the international system has become transnational, which makes the application of criteria for intervention as defined by the Conventions and the recent Protocols very difficult. Since 1970, for these reasons, the task of the ICRC has become constantly more burdensome.

---

[17] BUTTERWORTH. *Managing Interstate Conflict, op. cit.*

[18] There is of course a relationship between a conflict within a country and an ICRC action in the same country. But, as stated above, it is a complex relationship involving a variety of non-measurable factors.

[19] Even with reference to the Casadio curve.

1.2.3. Relationship Between the Activities of Protection and Assistance

As for the distribution of ICRC activities, by which is meant the division of effort between protection, its primordial mission, and assistance, one can note variations over the entire post-war period.

At the beginning of the 1950s, relief actions are significantly more numerous than those of protection. There follows a period going from 1956 to 1968, during which the distribution is balanced (with, beginning in 1963, a few years in which the protection actions are more numerous).

In the period 1969-1972, the two types of activities developed together, protection sometimes even preceding assistance, while from 1972 to 1978, assistance clearly exceeded protection, although one must stress, the fact that the protection of victims through visits has never, since the Second World war, been as extensive as during the 1970s. One might therefore conclude that the ICRC undertook equivalent and simultaneous efforts in its areas of competence. As we have previously stated, the gesture of many travelling delegates, consisting in "peppering" the countries of their region by offering the relief packet, usually to the National Red Cross, is mainly responsible for the fact that, in 1973, one country out of two benefited from an ICRC action. A corrective policy, through which the ICRC once again concentrates its activities on conflictual situations, is followed from 1974. The nineteen seventies are, furthermore, a decade in which one registers a slight increase in the number of conflicts.

Delegates begin to demand the right to visit political detainees (often called "administrative" or "security" detainees), and prison doors begin to open. At the beginning of this new phase, the approach is global: the ICRC asks to visit all prisons. The marked increase in distributions (whose apogee is situated in 1973) also results from this global approach: delegates depart on a tour, a relief case (often of minimal value) in hand. And the ICRC, as of 1970, disposes of its own stores for distribution, whereas it previously had to depend on annual accords concluded with the EEC or the Swiss government.

In the first case, the ICRC becomes aware of the impossibility of visiting every detainee being held under any type of circumstance. Visits must serve the practical and immediate goal of protection. As for assistance, the accord concluded with the League in 1974, which specifies the aid brought to National Societies, reveals the Committee's wish to limit its engagements in the area of assistance. Bilateral aid to countries continues long after 1974, but it is of a lesser volume when there is no conflict. Since this aid is much more important than before in case of conflict, it results that, despite the reduction in the volume of activities, it is much more efficient.

The organization is therefore to remain faithful to its traditional vocation, which is to preserve a balance between protection and assistance. No matter what may be said by those who are nostalgic of the past, never, since 1945, has the ICRC been so close to its tradition (and on a much larger scale) than during the years 1979-1980 (cf. Table 5).

It is striking based on this overview, to note that the first and the last periods have in common the engagement of a greater number of actions of assistance than of protection. But it must be noted that, in the most recent period, there are nonetheless a considerable number of protection actions, while after the end of the Second World war, there were not very many.

1.2.4. Comparative Analysis of Activities by Zones[20]

During the 1950s, the sequels to the Second World war and a few current European wars take up good part of the activities of the ICRC (cf. Table 4). But the ICRC is also active in Asia, in the Middle East and in North Africa. Those are the conflicts which preoccupy it and in which it encounters the greatest resistance on the part of the belligerents. The intransigence of the adversaries in the cold war and the pride of the colonial powers prevent the ICRC from undertaking impartial and balanced activities outside Europe.[21] Activities in Africa constitute the new element of the 1960s; surprisingly, protection activities are more numerous.

1.3. A Case Study: the Gonard Report on Africa (1962)

The geographic extension of the ICRC's activities, rapid though it may have been during a period whose revolutionary dimension Europeans did not understand, often forced it to improvise. But one would be wrong to believe that it allowed itself to be overtaken unprepared, by events.

One of the most important tasks of the Committee is to observe the international political scene so as to define conditions in which it might be led to plan and conduct its humanitarian mission. This constant reflection on a world in flux, which occurs in plenary sessions or in the dialogue between the President and his collaborators, can only be grasped through the analysis of minutes and internal correspondence. But we do not think we

---

[20] Since 1970, external activities have been divided into five geographic zones, whose confines have since then only been very slightly altered. Today, the zones are drawn up as follows:

- Europe: Europe and North America;
- Latin America: Latin and Central America and the Caribbeans;
- Africa: excluding North Africa (Egypt, Libya, Tunisia, Algeria, Morocco, Mauritania);
- Middle East: North Africa and the Middle East including Iran;
- Asia: from Afghanistan to the Far East.

[21] The Kashmir (1949) and Bengal (1950) actions, and most of all the Palestine action (1949-1950) are exceptions.

are violating the obligation of discretion by giving an example which illustrates the contingency planning of the institution. It concerns Africa.

At the end of 1961, Léopold Boissier, President of the ICRC, took the initiative of entrusting one of his colleagues, Samuel Gonard, with an information mission in Equatorial and Central Africa. The decision is motivated by the evolution of the political situation in Africa and, more specifically, by the problems which the Congo crisis caused the Committee. The mandate given Samuel Gonard is explicit:[22]

"To gather information on what the ICRC might usefully undertake in order to ensure a certain protection for military and civilian victims of all sorts of conflicts and unrest which might break out in Africa as well as the possibilities for action by the Red Cross in favor of those victims" (p. 4).

The importance and extent of the task are revealed by the length foreseen for the mission, two months, considered essential to its success.

Three groups of countries are included in the list of places to visit, "three worlds profoundly marked by strong colonial particularism and traditions even more accentuated there than on our own continent" (p. 6). The areas involved are British, Belgian and French colonies and ex-colonies.

Success, at least in the diplomatic field, is guaranteed in advance for the conversations which are to take place with several hundreds of officials and private persons from all walks of life, since "the ICRC's will to be present has been vigorously approved by those personalities, who fear abandonment" (p. 13). In those times of the defeat of colonialism, it is not clear, especially in the eyes of the Africans, that an essentially European organization will be independent enough to allow itself not to be influenced by the wave of bitterness and revenge carrying certain public opinions and governments. The report, in point of fact, reveals the self-critical capacities of its author and therefore of the institution he represented. It expresses the constant will to correct preconceived ideas: "The problems of each one of those countries are revealed on the spot in their immediate, practical, sometimes unexpected aspects. We came to realize this in relation to the baggage of preconceived notions which we had brought with us." (*Ibid.*).

Prejudices accumulated through centuries of colonial domination could not of course be totally dropped. One does not from one day to the next escape the mentality of the "bearer of civilization". But an essential process of reevaluation of Africa and the Africans seems to have begun, which will make it possible to carry out various activities on that continent. Even if Samuel Gonard, as he himself admits, had no contact "with the so-called middle and lower classes..." (p. 23), he understands the potential effects of both African tribalism and nationalism (p. 20), with their implications for

---

[22] We based ourselves for this brief account of this mission on the (unpublished) report by Samuel Gonard.

entire regions such as Southern Rhodesia which is, in his eyes, "destined to become the British Algeria" (p. 21). Gonard foresees the probability of a long "bush war" (p. 28) for the Rhodesias. Even though he is not far from sharing the opinion of the colonial authorities, according to whom 90 percent of the population has not notion of what the Conventions might be and for whom the spirit of the Conventions lies beyond the level of understanding of Africans (p. 34), he seeks to understand the causes of that situation and notes that the colonial power had done nothing to make the texts known, whether in Rhodesia or in the two Congos.

And in its conclusions, the Gonard report restates the essential lesson which had been drawn from the mission, "the need to make ourselves better known, tirelessly to explain what the ICRC is, its goals, its possibilities, by means of systematic and not only occasional and intermittent propaganda" (p. 89). That analysis of the situation led to a recommendation which the Committee was to follow. And it was perhaps its most important conclusion, as the explosion of violence in Nigeria five years later was to show.

1.4. Conclusion

The extension of activities during the 1970s is generalized throughout the third world, but more marked in Afrika and Latin America. In both cases, the main cause seems to be endogenous: by setting up new structures (the creation of zones directed by a Delegate General at headquarters and the opening of regional delegations), the ICRC has given itself the means for being present simultaneously at the four corners of the earth. This was, for the entire period, the decisive step towards the application of the principle of universality.

The evolution here traced of the worldwide extension of the perspectives and activities of the ICRC is symbolized by the fact that in 1980 there is no longer a single delegation in Europe. They are all in the third world. While they are not (if one includes delegations and sub-delegations) more numerous than in 1945, their responsibilities have evolved so that they now possess significantly greater efficiency and power to intervene.

What remains of the Eurocentrism of 1945? Very little, with the exception of the organization's staff and structures, which we will study later on. So it is that the progressive transfer of the activities of the ICRC from what used to be the center to what is still called the periphery, goes hand in hand with a more general restructuring of the international system.

1.1. Table of the ICRC's Actions of Protection and Assistance

Africa	50	1	2	3	4	5	6	7	8	9	60	1	2	3	4	5	6	7	8	9	70	1	2	3	4	5	6	7	8	9	80
(*)South Africa														/	/			/	O	/	/	/		Ø	Ø	Ø	Ø	Ø	Ø	Ø	Ø
Angola	IIII	IIII	IIII	IIII	IIII	IIII	IIII	IIII	IIII	IIII	IIII	IIII	IIII	IIII	IIII	IIII	IIII /	IIII	IIII	IIII	IIII Ø	IIII O	IIII O	IIII Ø	IIII Ø	Ø	Ø	O	Ø	Ø	Ø
Benin	IIII	IIII	IIII	IIII	IIII	IIII	IIII	IIII	IIII	IIII												O		O		O	O				
Botswana	IIII	IIII	IIII	IIII	IIII	IIII	IIII	IIII	IIII	IIII	IIII	IIII	IIII	IIII	IIII	IIII								O				Ø	Ø	Ø	O
Burundi	IIII	IIII	IIII	IIII	IIII	IIII	IIII	IIII	IIII	IIII	IIII	IIII	/	/	/	/	/				/	/	O	Ø	O	O	Ø	O			
(**)Cape Verde	IIII	IIII	IIII	IIII	IIII	IIII	IIII	IIII	IIII	IIII	IIII	IIII	IIII	IIII	IIII	IIII	IIII	IIII	IIII	IIII /	IIII	IIII /	IIII	IIII	IIII						
Cameroon	IIII	IIII	IIII	IIII	IIII	IIII	IIII	IIII	IIII	IIII	O								O			O	Ø	Ø	Ø		O				
Comoro Islands	IIII	IIII	IIII	IIII	IIII	IIII	IIII	IIII	IIII	IIII	IIII	IIII	IIII	IIII	IIII	IIII	IIII	IIII	IIII	IIII	IIII	IIII	IIII	IIII	IIII				O		
Congo-Brazzaville	IIII	IIII	IIII	IIII	IIII	IIII	IIII	IIII	IIII	IIII											/	/		O	Ø	Ø				/	
(*)Ivory Coast	IIII	IIII	IIII	IIII	IIII	IIII	IIII	IIII	IIII	IIII											O										
Djibouti	IIII	IIII	IIII	IIII	IIII	IIII	IIII	IIII	IIII	IIII	IIII	IIII	IIII	IIII	IIII	IIII	IIII	IIII	IIII	IIII	IIII	IIII	IIII	IIII	IIII	IIII	IIII /	IIII /			Ø
Ethiopia																							O	O	Ø	O		/	Ø	Ø	Ø
Gabon	IIII	IIII	IIII	IIII	IIII	IIII	IIII	IIII	IIII	IIII														O							
Gambia	IIII	IIII	IIII	IIII	IIII	IIII	IIII	IIII	IIII	IIII	IIII	IIII	IIII	IIII	IIII								Ø	Ø	Ø	Ø					
Ghana	IIII	IIII	IIII	IIII	IIII	IIII	IIII																	O	O	O					
Guinea	IIII	IIII	IIII	IIII	IIII	IIII	IIII	IIII																							
Guinea-Bissau	IIII	IIII	IIII	IIII	IIII	IIII	IIII	IIII	IIII	IIII	IIII	IIII	IIII	IIII	IIII	IIII /	IIII	IIII	IIII	IIII /	IIII O	IIII /	IIII O	IIII O	IIII Ø						
Equatorial Guinea	IIII	IIII	IIII	IIII	IIII	IIII	IIII	IIII	IIII	IIII	IIII	IIII	IIII	IIII	IIII	IIII	IIII	IIII				/									
(*)Upper Volta	IIII	IIII	IIII	IIII	IIII	IIII	IIII	IIII	IIII	IIII													O	O	O	Ø	/	O			
Kenya	IIII	IIII	IIII	IIII	IIII	IIII	IIII	IIII /	IIII	IIII /	IIII	IIII	IIII											O	O			O	O		
Lesotho	IIII	IIII	IIII	IIII	IIII	IIII	IIII	IIII	IIII	IIII	IIII	IIII	IIII	IIII	IIII	IIII					/	/	O								
Liberia																							O	Ø	Ø	Ø					
Madagascar	IIII	IIII	IIII	IIII	IIII	IIII	IIII	IIII	IIII	IIII										O			O								
Malawi	IIII	IIII	IIII	IIII	IIII	IIII	IIII	IIII	IIII	IIII /	IIII /	IIII /	IIII /	IIII			/	/		/								O			O
Mali	IIII	IIII	IIII	IIII	IIII	IIII	IIII	IIII	IIII	IIII													O	O	O	Ø					
Mauritius	IIII	IIII	IIII	IIII	IIII	IIII	IIII	IIII	IIII	IIII	IIII	IIII	IIII	IIII	IIII	IIII	IIII	IIII						O	O		O	O	O		
Mozambique	IIII	IIII	IIII	IIII	IIII	IIII	IIII	IIII	IIII	IIII	IIII	IIII	IIII /	IIII	IIII	IIII	IIII /	IIII	IIII /	IIII	IIII O	IIII /	IIII /	IIII Ø	IIII Ø	O		Ø		Ø	O
Niger	IIII	IIII	IIII	IIII	IIII	IIII	IIII	IIII	IIII	IIII													O	O	O						
Nigeria	IIII	IIII	IIII	IIII	IIII	IIII	IIII	IIII	IIII	IIII								Ø	Ø	Ø	Ø	O				O					
(*)Uganda	IIII	IIII	IIII	IIII	IIII	IIII	IIII	IIII	IIII	IIII	IIII	IIII												O	O	O	Ø	O	O	Ø	Ø
(*)Central African Republic	IIII	IIII	IIII	IIII	IIII	IIII	IIII	IIII	IIII	IIII																O				O	
Rwanda	IIII	IIII	IIII	IIII	IIII	IIII	IIII	IIII	IIII	IIII	IIII	IIII			/		/	Ø	/		/	/	Ø	Ø	Ø	Ø	O	O			
Sao Tome and Principe	IIII	IIII	IIII	IIII	IIII	IIII	IIII	IIII	IIII	IIII	IIII	IIII	IIII	IIII	IIII	IIII	IIII	IIII	IIII	IIII	IIII	IIII	IIII	IIII	IIII						
Senegal	IIII	IIII	IIII	IIII	IIII	IIII	IIII	IIII	IIII	IIII													O	O	O						
Seychelles	IIII	IIII	IIII	IIII	IIII	IIII	IIII	IIII	IIII	IIII	IIII	IIII	IIII	IIII	IIII	IIII	IIII	IIII	IIII	IIII	IIII	IIII	IIII	IIII	IIII	IIII					
Sierra Leone	IIII	IIII	IIII	IIII	IIII	IIII	IIII	IIII	IIII	IIII	IIII												Ø	O	O						
Somalia	IIII	IIII	IIII	IIII	IIII	IIII	IIII	IIII	IIII	IIII																	O	Ø	O	/	/
Sudan	IIII	IIII	IIII	IIII	IIII	IIII													O		O	O	O	O			O			Ø	Ø
Swaziland	IIII	IIII	IIII	IIII	IIII	IIII	IIII	IIII	IIII	IIII	IIII	IIII	IIII	IIII	IIII	IIII	IIII	IIII					O	O				O	O		
Tanzania	IIII	IIII	IIII	IIII	IIII	IIII	IIII	IIII	IIII	IIII	IIII				/								O	O					O	Ø	/
(*)Chad	IIII	IIII	IIII	IIII	IIII	IIII	IIII	IIII	IIII	IIII										/	O			O	O				/	Ø	Ø
Togo	IIII	IIII	IIII	IIII	IIII	IIII	IIII	IIII	IIII	IIII		O	O									O	O	Ø	O	Ø	O	O			
Zaire	IIII	IIII	IIII	IIII	IIII	IIII	IIII	IIII	IIII	IIII	Ø	Ø	Ø	Ø	Ø	Ø		/			/	/	/	Ø	Ø	O			Ø	Ø	Ø
Zambia	IIII	IIII	IIII	IIII	IIII	IIII	IIII	IIII	IIII	IIII	IIII	IIII	IIII O	IIII								/	/	/	O	O		O	O	Ø	Ø
Zimbabwe	IIII	IIII	IIII	IIII	IIII	IIII	IIII	IIII	IIII	IIII /	IIII /	IIII /	IIII /	IIII /	IIII /	IIII /	IIII /	IIII /	IIII /	IIII /	IIII	IIII /	IIII /	IIII Ø	IIII Ø	IIII Ø	IIII Ø	IIII Ø	IIII Ø	IIII Ø	O
(*)Namibia	IIII	IIII	IIII	IIII	IIII	IIII	IIII	IIII	IIII	IIII	IIII	IIII	IIII	IIII	IIII	IIII	IIII	IIII	IIII	IIII	IIII	IIII	IIII	IIII	IIII O	IIII	IIII	IIII	IIII	IIII	IIII /

(*)= Cf. Guinea-Bissau (**)The complexity of this table leads us to maintain the original French alphabetical order.

/ =Visits O =Relief IIIIIIII = Dependent Countries White Field Independent Countries

1.2. Table of the ICRC's Actions of Protection and Assistance

Latin America	50	1	2		4	5	6	7	8	9	60	1	2	3	4	5	6	7	8	9	70	1	2	3	4	5	6	7	8	9	80
Argentina														/								/	Ø	Ø	O			Ø	Ø	Ø	Ø
Bahamas	III	III	III	III	III	III	III	III	III	III	III	III	III	III	III	III	III	III	III	III	III	III	III	III				O			
Barbados	III	III	III	III	III	III	III	III	III	III	III	III	III	III	III	III	III														
Bolivia																				/	Ø	Ø	Ø		Ø	Ø	Ø	Ø	O	O	Ø
Brazil										O					Ø	/								Ø		Ø					
Chile											O												Ø	Ø	Ø	Ø	Ø	/	Ø	Ø	Ø
Colombia																				Ø	/	Ø	/	Ø	Ø	Ø	Ø	/	O	Ø	/
Costa Rica						Ø															Ø		Ø								
Cuba										Ø					O														O	O	
Dominica	III	III	III	III	III	III	III	III	III	III	III	III	III	III	III	III	III	III	III	III	III	III	III	III	III	III	III	III	III		
El Salvador		O																		/	/		/	O		Ø	O			Ø	Ø
Ecuador																					Ø	Ø	/	O	Ø	Ø	Ø				
Grenada	III	III	III	III	III	III	III	III	III	III	III	III	III	III	III	III	III	III	III	III	III	III	III	III	III						
Guatemala					Ø	O														Ø	Ø	Ø	Ø	Ø		Ø		Ø	O		
Guyana	III	III	III	III	III	III	III	III	III	III	III	III	III	III	III	III	III					O	O	O	O		Ø		O		
Haiti																		Ø	O	O	O	O	O	O	O	O	Ø	O			
Honduras																				Ø	Ø	O	Ø	O	Ø	Ø	O	O	/	Ø	O
Jamaica	III	III	III	III	III	III	III	III	III	III	III	III	III										Ø			/					
Mexico																				/		/		/		/	Ø	/			
Nicaragua						/				/		/						/			Ø	/	O	/		/		/	Ø	Ø	Ø
Panama																				Ø	Ø	Ø	Ø	O		Ø	O	O	O		
Paraguay																					O		Ø		Ø	Ø	Ø	Ø	Ø	Ø	Ø
Peru																				Ø	Ø	/	/			/	Ø	Ø	O		
(*) Dominican Republic												/				/							Ø			Ø	/				
Saint Lucia	III	III	III	III	III	III	III	III	III	III	III	III	III	III	III	III	III	III	III	III	III	III	III	III	III	III	III	III	III	III	
Saint Vincent and Grenadines	III	III	III	III	III	III	III	III	III	III	III	III	III	III	III	III	III	III	III	III	III	III	III	III	III	III	III	III	III	III	
Surinam	III	III	III	III	III	III	III	III	III	III	III	III	III	III	III	III	III	III	III	III	III	III	III	III	III	III					
Trinidad and Tobago	III	III	III	III	III	III	III	III	III	III	III	III	III									O		O							
Uruguay																							/	Ø	Ø		Ø	O	O	O	Ø
Venezuela					O												/			/	Ø	O	Ø	/		Ø	/	/			

/ = Visits O =Relief IIIIIIIII = Dependent Countries White Field Independent Countries

1.3. Table of the ICRC's Actions of Protection and Assistance

Asia		50	1	2	3	4	5	6	7	8	9	60	1	2	3	4	5	6	7	8	9	70	1	2	3	4	5	6	7	8	9	80
Afghanistan						0																					0	0		/		Ø
Australia				0		0	0																									
Bangladesh	‖	‖	‖	‖	‖	‖	‖	‖	‖	‖	‖	‖	‖	‖	‖	‖	‖	‖	‖	‖	‖	‖	‖	Ø	Ø	0				0		
Bhutan																																
Burma	/	/			0																					0	0	0				
China	0						0																								/	
(*) North Korea		0																														
(*) South Korea		Ø	Ø	Ø	Ø		0	/			0								/													
Fiji	‖	‖	‖	‖	‖	‖	‖	‖	‖	‖	‖	‖	‖	‖	‖	‖	‖	‖	‖	‖	‖	‖					0					
(*) Solomon Islands	‖	‖	‖	‖	‖	‖	‖	‖	‖	‖	‖	‖	‖	‖	‖	‖	‖	‖	‖	‖	‖	‖	‖	‖	‖	‖	‖	‖	‖	‖		
India	/	/		0		0	0		/°		0	0	/	Ø	Ø		Ø	Ø	0				Ø	Ø	Ø	Ø	0	0		0		
Indonesia	Ø	Ø	/	0		0	0		0	0	Ø	0		0				/		0	0	Ø	Ø			Ø			Ø	Ø	Ø	0
Japan		0	0	0	0			/	Ø	Ø	0	0		/		/	0					/									/	
Kampuchea	‖	‖	‖	‖	‖												0	0	0		Ø	Ø	Ø	Ø	Ø	Ø	/				0	Ø
Malaysia	‖	‖	‖	‖	‖	‖	‖	‖/	‖						/	/	/	/					/	/	Ø	Ø		Ø	Ø		/	/
Maldives	‖	‖	‖	‖	‖	‖	‖	‖	‖	‖	‖	‖	‖	‖	‖	‖	‖															
Mongolia																																
Nepal	‖	‖	‖	‖	‖	‖	‖		0			0	0	0	0										0				0			
New Zealand																																
Pakistan	/	0		0		0	0										Ø	Ø					Ø	/	Ø	/		0		0	Ø	Ø
Papua – New Guinea	‖	‖	‖	‖	‖	‖	‖	‖	‖	‖	‖	‖	‖	‖/	‖	‖	‖	‖	‖	‖	‖	‖	‖	‖	‖	‖	‖					
Philippines				0							Ø	/	/	/	/		/		/	/		/		/	Ø	Ø		Ø	Ø	Ø	0	Ø
(*) Laotian PDR	‖	‖	‖	‖	‖	‖					0	0	Ø	Ø	Ø	Ø	0	0	Ø	0	Ø	Ø	Ø	Ø	Ø	Ø		Ø				
Samoa	‖	‖	‖	‖	‖	‖	‖	‖	‖	‖	‖	‖	‖	‖																		
Singapore	‖	‖	‖	‖	‖	‖	‖	‖	‖	‖	‖	‖	‖	‖	‖/	‖	‖									/	/	/				
Sri Lanka										Ø													Ø		Ø	Ø	Ø	Ø	Ø			
Thailand											Ø										/				/	/	/	/	Ø	Ø	Ø	Ø
North Vietnam							0	0									0	0	0	0	0			0	0	0						
South Vietnam	0	Ø	/	Ø	Ø	/	Ø	0	/	Ø				/		Ø	Ø	Ø	Ø	Ø	Ø	Ø	Ø	Ø	Ø	Ø	Ø					
} (North Vietnam and South Vietnam)																												0	0	Ø	Ø	0
Hong Kong	‖	‖0	‖	‖	‖0	‖	‖	‖	‖	‖	‖	‖	‖	‖	‖	‖	‖	‖	‖/	‖/	‖	‖/	‖/	‖	‖	‖0	‖	‖	‖	‖	‖/	‖
East Timor	‖	‖	‖	‖	‖	‖	‖	‖	‖	‖	‖	‖	‖	‖	‖	‖	‖	‖	‖	‖	‖	‖	‖	‖	‖	‖	‖/	‖	‖	‖	‖Ø	‖0

‖‖‖‖‖ = Dependent Countries — White Field = Independent Countries

/ = Visits — 0 = Relief — ° Portuguese Goa

1.4. Table of the ICRC's Actions of Protection and Assistance

Europe		50	1	2	3	4	5	6	7	8	9	60	1	2	3	4	5	6	7	8	9	70	1	2	3	4	5	6	7	8	9	80
Albania		0		0	0	0	0																									
(*) Fed. Rep. of Germany	0	0	0	0	0	0	0	0	ø	ø	ø	ø	ø	ø	/	/	/	/	/	/	/											
Austria	III0	III0	III0	III0	III0	III0	III0	ø	0	0	0	0	0		0																	
Belgium																																
Bulgaria				0	0	0	0		0			0	0			/	/									0		0	0	0			
Canada																																
Cyprus	III	III	III	III	III	III	III/	III0	IIIø	IIIø	III					ø	0									ø	/	/				
Denmark																																
(*) Spain					0	0	ø	/	ø	ø	/	ø	ø											/					/			
(*) United States																																
Finland			0	0	0							0																				
France	0	0	0	0	0	0	0			0	ø	ø	ø	ø	0		0															
Greece	ø	ø	ø	ø	ø	ø	ø	ø	0	ø	ø	ø	ø	0	ø		0		ø	ø	ø	ø	0			0				0		
Hungary			0	0	0	0	0	ø	0	0	0	0	0	0	0	0	0	0	0	0	0	0	0	0	0	0	0	0	0	0°			
Ireland										/																						
Iceland																																
Italy	0	0	0	0	0	0	0		0	0	0	0	0	0																		
Luxemburg																																
Malta	III	III	III	III	III	III	III	III	III	III	III	III	III	III	III																	
Norway	0																															
Netherlands					0																											
Poland	0	0	0	0	0	0	0	0	0	0	0	0	0	0	0	0	0	0	0	0	0	0	0	0	0	0						
Portugal														/												/	ø	ø	ø	ø		
(*) German Dem. Rep.	0	0	0	0	0	0	0		/	/																						
Roumania		0	0	0	0	0	0																0	0	0	0	0	0	0°			
(*) United Kingdom (GB)										/													/	/	/	/	/					
Sweden																																
Switzerland	0	0	0	0	0	0	0														/											
(*) Czechoslovakia	0	0	0		0	0	0		0																							
Turkey				0																						/	0					
USSR	0		0	0	0	0	0	0																								
Vatican																																
Yugoslavia	0	0	0	0	0	0	0			/	ø	ø	/	ø	ø	0											0				0	

° =in 1978 under various

/ =Visits 0 =Relief IIIIIIIII =Dependent Countries White Field = Independent Countries

1.5. Table of the ICRC's Actions of Protection and Assistance

Middle East and North Africa		50	1	2	3	4	5	6	7	8	9	60	1	2	3	4	5	6	7	8	9	70	1	2	3	4	5	6	7	8	9	80
Algeria	‖	‖	‖	‖	‖	‖ o	‖ /	‖ Ø	‖ Ø	‖ Ø	‖ Ø	‖ o	‖ Ø	‖ Ø	Ø	/					o				o	o		o			Ø	
(*) Saudi Arabia															/							/										
Bahrein	‖	‖	‖	‖	‖	‖	‖	‖	‖	‖	‖	‖	‖	‖	‖	‖	‖ /	‖	‖	‖	‖	‖	‖									
Egypt	/						Ø	Ø	Ø	o	Ø	Ø	/		/				Ø		Ø	Ø	/	Ø	Ø	o	o		o	o	o	o
(*) United Arab Emirates	‖	‖	‖	‖	‖	‖	‖	‖	‖	‖	‖	‖	‖	‖	‖	‖	‖	‖	‖	‖	‖	‖	‖									
Iran					o		Ø			o		o																	/	/	/	Ø
Iraq					o	o	Ø								o				o								/					/
Israel and OT	Ø	o	o				/	/	/	/	/	Ø	/	Ø	o	/			Ø	Ø	Ø	Ø	Ø	Ø	Ø	Ø	Ø	Ø	Ø	Ø	Ø	Ø
(*) Libyan Arab Jamahiria	‖	‖	‖			o													/													
Jordan	/	Ø	Ø	o					o								o		Ø			Ø	Ø	Ø	Ø	o	Ø	Ø	Ø	Ø	Ø	Ø
Kuwait	‖	‖	‖	‖	‖	‖	‖	‖	‖	‖	‖	‖	‖																			
Lebanon	/						o	o		o	Ø								/		/	o	Ø	o	Ø	Ø	Ø	Ø	Ø	Ø	Ø	Ø
Morocco	‖	‖	‖	‖	‖	‖	‖ /	‖	o	o	o	o	o	o	Ø	Ø												Ø	/	/	o	
Mauritania	‖	‖	‖	‖	‖	‖	‖	‖	‖	‖	‖	‖													o	Ø		Ø	/	Ø	Ø	/
Oman	‖	‖	‖																									o				
Qatar	‖	‖	‖	‖	‖	‖	‖	‖	‖	‖	‖	‖	‖	‖	‖	‖	‖	‖	‖	‖	‖	‖	‖									
Syria	/																		Ø	o	Ø	/	Ø	Ø	Ø	Ø	o	o	o	o	Ø	Ø
Tunisia	‖	‖	‖	‖	‖	‖	‖ /	‖	o	o				Ø	o						o				o							
Yemen, Republic															Ø	Ø	Ø	o	o	o	o	o	o	o	Ø	Ø	Ø	Ø	Ø	Ø	o	Ø
Yemen, Dem. Rep.	‖	‖	‖	‖	‖	‖	‖	‖	‖	‖	‖	‖	‖	‖	‖	‖ /	‖ /	‖ /	‖ Ø	Ø	Ø	Ø	Ø	Ø	o	o	o	o	o	o	o	o

/ =Visits O =Relief ‖‖‖‖‖‖ =Dependent Countries White Field=Independent Countries

2. ICRC Actions (Visits and Relief) in the World

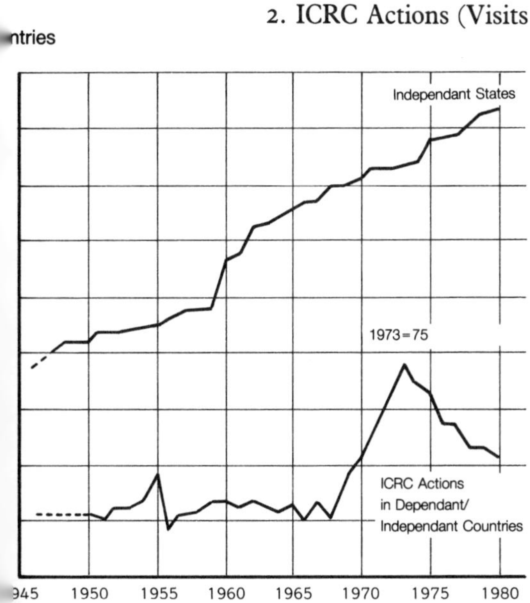

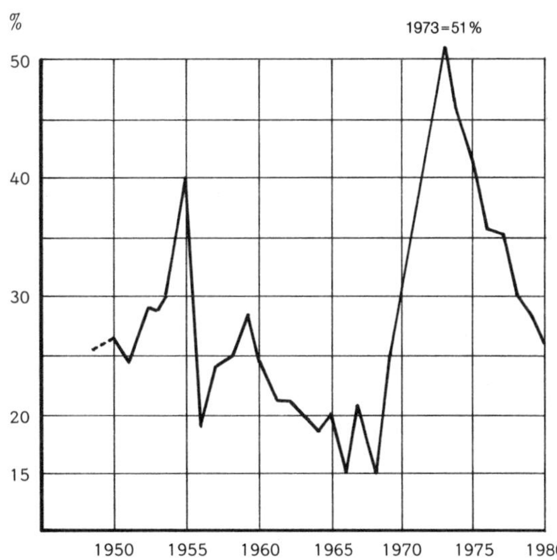

3. Conflicts and ICRC Actions

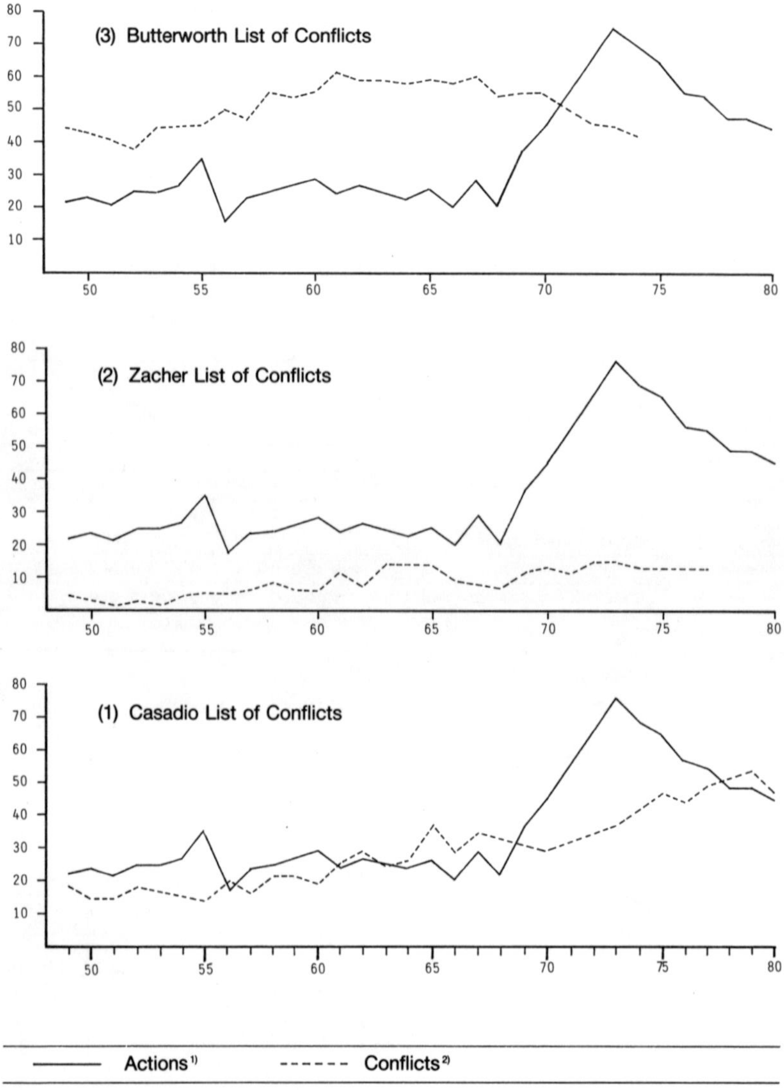

4. ICRC Actions in Europe and the Third World

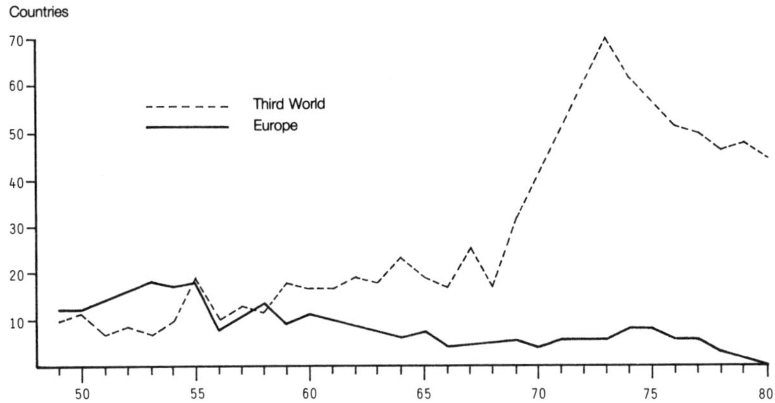

5. ICRC Actions in the World: Ratio of Visits to Relief

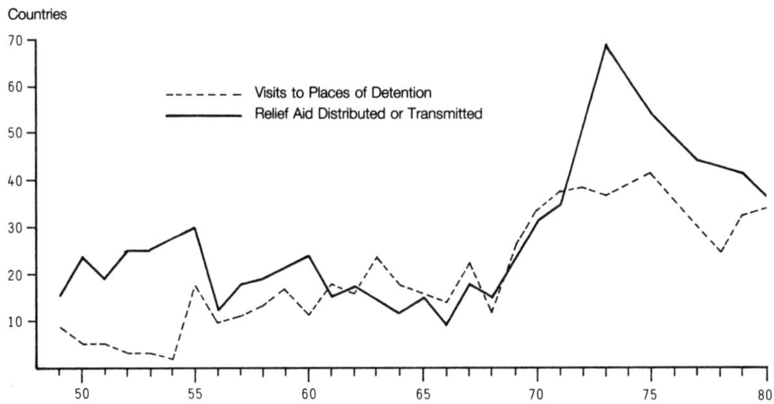

6. ICRC Actions by Geographic Zone

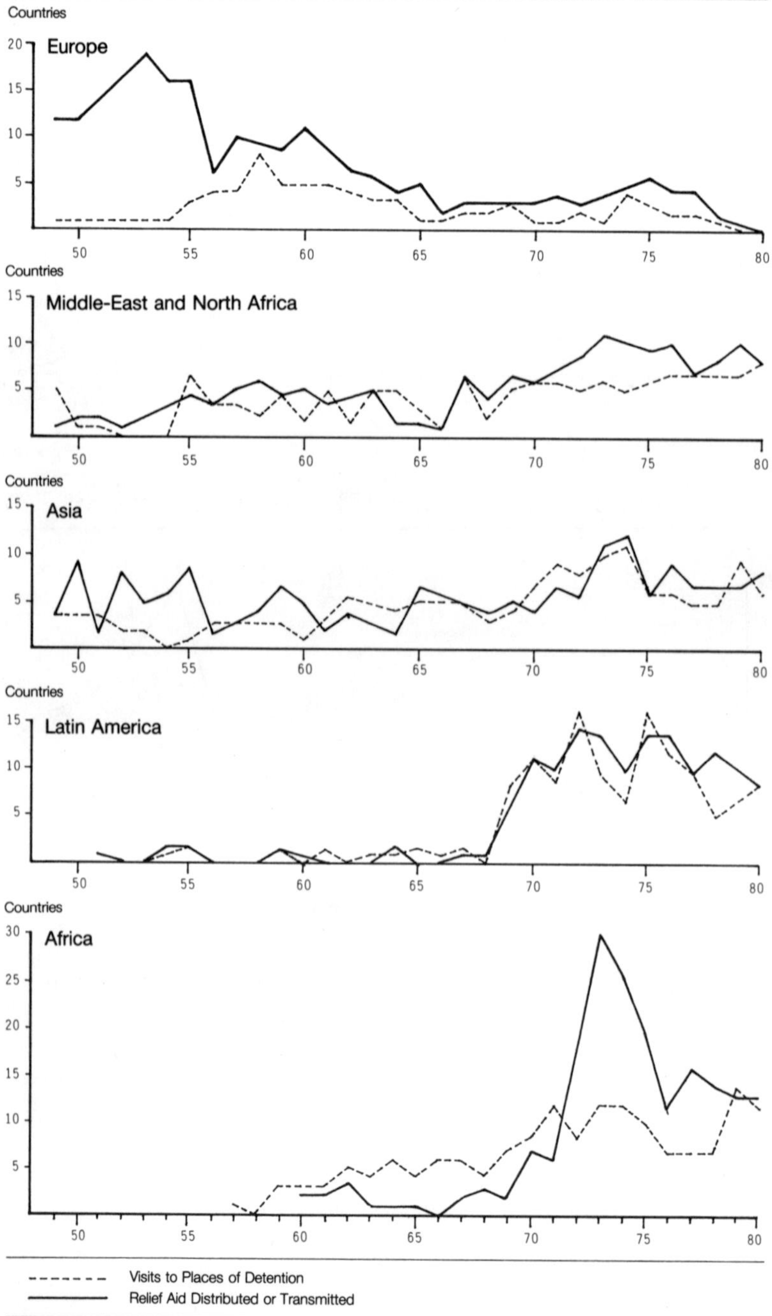

CHAPTER 2

The Increase in Volume of External Activities

In the preceding chapter, we analyzed the geographic extension of the ICRC's action after the Second World war. The evolution in this area led to an increase in the volume of its activities. It is primarily through the analysis of the organization's expenditures during the same period that we will be able to evaluate that increase in volume.

2.1. The ICRC's Expenditures (Tables 7-10)

Expenditures do not reflect the entire volume of the ICRC's activities. One would have to add to them that portion of relief aid which was given to the ICRC in kind and which, logically, is not reflected in the budget. Since the annual volume of gifts in kind is not known,[1] it is impossible to trace the evolution of the total volume of activities.

The evolution of the overall budget (cf. Table 7) is characterized first of all by the 1968-1969 explosion. It clearly subdivides the post-war period into a section which precedes and a section which follows the Nigerian conflict.[2] Up until 1967, the volume of activities (in terms of cost) is relatively modest, whereas, during the 1970s, it is on average four to five times as great in terms of real value.[3]

Wild fluctuations in the volume are the second characteristic. They are more numerous beginning with the Nigerian action, and appear to be more spectacular. One must however in this respect point out that the increase in

[1] With a few exceptions the *AR*s do not give indications on the subject. For the largescale relief actions, one can refer to the reports of Peat, Marwick, Mitchell & Co.

[2] The Nigeria/Biafra action (July 1967-January 1970) is the most important post-war action. In 1968-69, the greater portion of the overall budget is spent on this action.

[3] The real value is obtained by deducting the portion of the increased value corresponding to inflation.

the total budget in 1957 is of the same order as that which is to be noted in 1979-1980 (an increase of 2.3% as compared to 2.5%).

The regular budgetary increase during the 1970s and the acceleration in significant yearly variations indicate that the ICRC has, generally, significantly increased its actions during this period. On this point, therefore, the budget's evolution confirms the geographic extension, even if the two curves are quite different.

As of 1953, a chapter of the Annual Report is devoted to the financial situation.[4] The aspect which is of primary interest to us here, concerns expenses for "operational activities"[5] linked to the increase in activities. Let us note from the outset that a detailed analysis is problematic. For our conclusions on the overall period (1945-1980) we have limited ourselves to generalities. One must keep in mind the fact that our main aim, which is to follow the evolution in the volume of external activities, will be based on approximate figures and will only permit provisional conclusions.

2.1.1. *Breakdown of Annual Accounts*

Table 8 illustrates the elements which enter into the overall volume of external activities. Upon examination, one discovers that the accounting methods of the ICRC have always distinguished between relief actions (which correspond to "special" expenditures) and the "Account for Ordinary Receipts and Expenditures."[6] We are going to respect the separation between the two types of expenditures, by beginning with an examination of ordinary expenditures on external activities.

There are three accounting periods beginning in 1949. An analysis of the evolution of the volume over the entire period is limited by variations in accounting methods. This is especially true for the first period (1949-1963) of "Delegations Abroad" and "Missions from Geneva".[7]

[4] Prior to that, the presentation of finances was listed as a sub-chapter in the chapter entitled "Services". From 1954 to 1973, the chapter is called "Financial Situation" and, thereafter, "Finances".

[5] The designation of these activities changes several times over a period of 30 years. They are, roughly speaking, called "External Affairs" during the 1950s and 1960s, and "Operations" during the 1970s.

[6] As the account is called from 1955 to 1970. The word "ordinary" is therefore added two years after the publication of the first "General Account for Relief Actions" (1953). Even if, from 1949 to 1952, reports on activities do not show accounts for special activities, one can deduce from the existence of the fundraising to drive among the Swiss people ("Collection in Switzerland") whose proceeds went into this account, that there must have been separate accounting.

[7] From the breakdown of receipts and expenditures accounts we have noted not only the item "Delegations Abroad" 1952-1963, (its title was slightly different from 1949 to 1951) but also the item "Missions from Geneva", which is found under "Special Expenses". The missions, logically, are to be counted as external activities. The table of the 1949 Account even lists them under a single title.

This first period displays a more limiting conception than the two which follow, in that it only considers expenses incurred away from headquarters. During the second period (1964-1969) the title "Activities Abroad" already includes expenses incurred by delegations and missions, by the Central Tracing Agency, by "Staff at ICRC Headquarters in Geneva" (working on activities abroad) and by "Equipment and Organization". The 1964 Annual Report is not very explicit as to the reasons which led the ICRC's administration to group expenses according to "Centres of activity". The only reason given is "in order to show the general organization and action of the International Committee of the Red Cross more clearly".[8] It would seem that the reorganization took place for reasons internal to the financial administration.

The third period (1970-1980) includes in activities abroad the expenses of the Operations Department and of the Central Tracing Agency.[9] The beginning of this period coincides with the complete reorganization of the ICRC's finances, which is presented and analyzed in the introductions to the chapter "Financial Position" in 1970 and 1971.

There are three characteristics of that reorganization, which was intended to increase transparency and efficiency:

a) The Statement of Receipts and Expenditures is from now on presented as a double-entry table. On the horizontal line is found the distribution according to centers of activity and on the vertical, a presentation of the tripartite structure including permanent, temporary and occasional activities. This means that expenditures for special activities are listed in the Account of ordinary receipts and expenditures, even though, since they belong to the occasional structure, they continue to be administered outside of the ordinary budget.

b) The notion of a temporary activity is thus introduced, and this type of activity is included in the ordinary budget. Upon the conclusion of the Nigerian action, the ICRC had become aware of a new degree of urgency in certain situations. In the light of a situation such as the Nigerian-Biafran war, relief actions covering several years, like Israel-Palestine or Yemen, for example, can no longer be considered urgent and thus financed outside the budget. On the contrary, such activities are at least partially predictable and can therefore be included in the budget, although with caution. This combination of conclusions and the accounting decision which followed proved judicious, so that the tripartite budget becomes bipartite as of 1975,

---

[8] *AR*, 1964, p. 61.

[9] The CTA becomes a separate item in 1972. It had until then been included in the Operations Department, and had been listed for accounting purposes under "Activities Abroad". Its inclusion in activities abroad appears justified, given the importance of its activities in the field, even though most of the expenses are incurred at headquarters.

the poles being ordinary actions, which include permanent and temporary ones, and special actions, the new definition of "occasional" activity.

c) Principles of management which had allegedly been insufficient during the Nigerian action,[10] are introduced to the institution. The introduction to the chapter "Financial Position" in the 1970 Annual Report stresses the need for the ICRC to manage its activities as though it were a company.[11] The increasing differentiation of "centers of activity" (which go from 3 in 1969 to 12 in 1978) in the expenditure accounts, is one of the consequences of the new practices in the area of management. It illustrates, as do the changes as a whole, the principle that greater transparency ensures a better functioning.

2.1.2. *Evolution of the Volume of Ordinary External Activities* (Table 9)

The present analysis, thanks to the insight we now have into successive accounting methods, will make it possible for us to establish the volume of ordinary expenditures from year to year, and to draw certain conclusions concerning the evolution over the period under study as a whole. The two sections which follow will allow us to do the same thing as concerns extraordinary activities (2.1.4.) and to compare the respective importance accorded over the years to those two types of activities (2.1.5.).

Table 9, which illustrates the overall volume of expenditures per year for ordinary external activities, also traces the curve of the evolution of this volume in relation to total ordinary expenditures.

The study of accounting methods has already made it possible to distinguish three distinct categories for the period as a whole.

a) First period, 1949-1963: "Delegations Abroad" and "Missions from Geneva": it is difficult to compare it to those which follow, since only expenses incurred outside headquarters are considered external activities, whereas in later years, expenses incurred at headquarters for external activities are included.

b) Second period, 1964-1969: the difference of 1.6 million Swiss francs between ordinary expenses for external activities between 1963 and 1964 is enormous and sudden, when one considers that ordinary expenditures for delegations and missions is approximately 0.3 million Swiss francs per year between 1956 and 1963. The question is whether the difference is a real or an accounting one. The three new entries included in the item "Activities Abroad" of the Statement of Receipts and Expenditures for 1964 (Staff at Headquarters", "Agency" and "Equipment") together make up two-thirds of expenditures for ordinary external activities. The remaining third

---

[10] HENTSCH. *Face au blocus,* p. 144, footnote 42.

[11] *AR,* 1970, pp. 121 and 123.

represents expenditures on two other items, "Permanent Delegations in the Field" and "Missions from Geneva".

By concentrating on these two items, we can compare them with expenditures on delegations and missions through 1963. In 1964 there was an increase of 118%, which implies that there was a real increase in external activities which, without being spectacular, should be considered important since the volume of this type of activities doubled from one year to another.[12] The real growth of the ordinary external volume is confirmed by two further factors:

1. The total budget of ordinary expenditures diminishes instead of increasing during this same year, going from 4.7 million Swiss francs in 1963 to 4.5 million in 1964;

2. The "Relief Action" account (special expenses) simultaneously increases by close to a million francs. These two elements combined prove that we are not simply dealing with a listing of special expenditures as ordinary ones.

This increase in volume is linked to the opening of a delegation in Cyprus and to the considerable intensification of the Yemen action, notably through the dispatch of a medical team and a field hospital.

But the rise in ordinary expenditures for delegations and missions is only passing. In 1966, expenses diminish and, in 1968, they drop to their 1956-1963 level. We are justified in assuming that the Nigerian action, launched in 1968, resulted in the freezing of ongoing matters.

c) Third period, 1970-1980: the volume of expenditures for ordinary external activities is trebled. But, once again, we need to determine whether this increase (of 223%) is entirely real. The answer is not simple since the function of activities abroad, under the new label of "Operations Department", is divided into geographic zones. The old and the new divisions are not comparable, but the elements at hand reveal a real increase.

The comparison (impossible prior to 1972) between Operations Department expenditures for the period in question and ordinary expenditures for activities abroad during the second period, indicates an increase of approximately 60% in permanent external activities in 1970. That estimate is based on the fact that the ordinary expenditures of the 1972 Balance Sheet are divided more or less equally between permanent and temporary activities of the Operations Department. The volume remains constant between 1970 and 1972. Given the reasonable assumption that there is a similar distribution of funds in 1970 and in 1972, we derive the figure of 60% for the 1970 increase.

---

[12] The comparative analysis of the 1963 and 1964 accounts would suggest the doubling of the volume of activities as the reason for the change in accounting methods. But this does not take into account the stability of other factors, which implies the primacy of internal reasons.

Contrary to what had happened in 1964, when the reorganization of accounting had itself largely explained the increased volume through the inclusion of other centers of activities in expenditures for external affairs, the reorganization in 1970 is made within the Operations Department by incorporating "temporary" activities in the ordinary budget. What we have here is an important consolidation of the external activities budget itself, that budget being in a sense the basis for activities. The consolidation of the basis gives the ICRC the means with which to increase its operations and to reinforce its external presence, as we have seen (Chapter 1), by lengthening the list of countries where it makes its presence felt, and thanks to the fruits of its policy in the area of visits to places of detention (Chapter 2.2.).

We can see, therefore, that the 1970s were marked by a new and clearly expansionary policy in terms of ordinary external activities. The policy was put into practice at the outset thanks to subsidies by the Swiss and American governments: the ICRC's available funds suddenly increased in 1971 by 4.015 million Swiss francs, or 55%.

2.1.3. Proportion of Ordinary Expenditures Devoted to External Activities in Relation to Total Ordinary Expenditures (Table 9).

In order properly to understand the evolution we have just traced, we must now establish the proportion of the volume of ordinary external activities in relation to total ordinary expenditures (table 9).

a) First period, 1949-1963: once again, this period is not really comparable to the two which follow. But one should note that, during the years which followed the Second World war (1949-1952), the ICRC was present in the Greek, Korean, Indo-Pakistani (over Kashmir and Bengal), Indochinese and Indonesian conflicts. That presence absorbed approximately one third of its overall ordinary expenditures. If one were to take as a base the second period accounting system, the percentage would probably be higher. One must also note that, during the period 1949-1952, the ICRC does not present an overall account for extraordinary expenditures, which leads one to believe that the greater part of its external activities, except the 1949 Palestine action, is covered by ordinary expenditures. This indicates that the means employed were modest or rather, that a relatively large presence was ensured through modest means.

As of 1952 the volume (and therefore the curve) declines and does not rise again, since extraordinary expenditures are presented separately, and one notes, for example, that in 1956-1957, despite the important Hungarian action, the curve remains constant. It is not until 1960-1961 that the single case presents itself where a special action (Congo-Leopoldville) is included in the ordinary accounts.

b) Second period, 1964-1969: one is struck by the proportional decrease of ordinary external activities in 1968 and 1969, whereas they had slightly increased in comparison to 1967. It would seem that the institution as a whole was taken up in the Nigerian action, and was obliged to respond by an increase in staff and capacities, which is reflected in the increase in the total ordinary budget beginning in 1969.

c) Third period, 1970-1980: in 1970, one observes a 223% increase in external activities expenditures and a 123% increase in total expenditures, from which one may conclude that the institution as a whole, while increasing its capacities by more than 100%, devotes nearly three-quarters (72%) of that expansion to external activities. This is, as we have already shown, a real increase in the external activities base, which signifies a significant reinforcement of the ICRC's presence in the international community beginning in 1970.

2.1.4. Volume of Extraordinary Operational Activities (Table 10)

The expenditures for extraordinary operational activities are separately presented in the "General Account for Relief Actions" (1953-1964) which, from 1965, is entitled "Special Fund for Relief Actions" (from 1973 on "Special Fund for Current Operations") without varying as to its functions.[13]

For a long time, the Fund thus financed was the only instrument through which the ICRC managed its operational activities (relief actions). Even a largescale one like Hungary could be integrated into this structure (in part because the ICRC received more than 90% of its grants *in kind*). In 1969, the Fund to be managed is twenty times the average for preceding years, nine-tenths of which are spent on the Nigerian action! Faced with this situation, the ICRC decides, on the one hand, to handle the financing and accounts of that action separately from the others and, on the other hand, to put into place a new "special financing" structure.

Ad hoc financing, which is more flexible, permits important fundraising appeals, almost from one month to the next. Accounts concerning the management of those funds are presented in the Tables designated as "Occasional Operations".[14] From 1969, then, one can get an idea of the financial importance of different extraordinary actions, whereas before (with a few rare exceptions, such as the Hungarian action) the ICRC only gave overall figures for expenses incurred for operational activities. The Nigerian

[13] "This Fund is quite distinct from the Ordinary Expenditure and Receipts Account. It is financed separately by an annual nation-wide fund-raising campaign in Switzerland, and by donations for the International Committee's Relief Actions." *AR*, 1965, p. 68.

[14] This concerns the period from 1970 to 1974. In 1969, a Table indicates the "Special Fund for Relief Actions". Beginning in 1975, two Tables entitled "Movement of Funds for Special Operations in 1975" present receipts and expenditures devoted to activities.

action therefore leads to a heightened awareness in the institution and to a change in attitude. The ICRC becomes aware of the fact that it might be implicated in relief actions whose dimensions surpass the framework and the means of the institution. The events which followed were to show that this reasoning had been correct. Given the size of grants, mere confidence is no longer sufficient, it becomes necessary to demonstrate the ability correctly to manage the funds so entrusted, by striving for the transparency of accounts.

The volume of extraordinary activities for the years 1970-1971 seems quite unimportant (cf. Table 10), which is due to the institution's reorganization. One should not forget that the total volume of external activities is significantly superior to that of the 1960s, even if the volume of extraordinary activities in 1970-1971 is of a level comparable to that of the 1960s. From 1972 on, the volume once again increases with the Bangladesh action.

There is one other highly significant change in the use of the extraordinary operations budget beginning in 1973: it is spent on several simultaneous largescale actions, usually three or four, whereas the previous high-water marks reflected the involvement in one single largescale action at one time (Hungary, Nigeria, Bangladesh).

2.1.5. *Proportion of the Volume of Ordinary Operational Activities in Relation to that of Extraordinary Operational Activities*

For the period as a whole, the volume of extraordinary activities is almost always much greater than that of ordinary activities. The years 1965-1966 and 1970-1971 are exceptions. The budgetary underpinnings of ordinary activities is constantly surpassed by extraordinary activities. The management of such a volume of extraordinary activities requires on the part of the institution a great degree of flexibility. This is illustrated by the irregularity of the expenditures curve (cf. Table 7).

During the years when the imbalance is strongest, namely 1957 (Hungary) and 1968-1969 (Nigeria), the volume of ordinary activities covered by the foreseeable budget is so weak that it is not exaggerated to say that the part of the institution dealing with operational activities is in a situation of total improvisation. The Hungarian and Nigerian actions practically monopolize the capacities of the ICRC.

One should also note that the proportion of ordinary activities in 1957 would be greater if the basis for calculating it had been the second-period accounting; the entire first-period curve would have been raised by a few degrees.

The ICRC emerges from the Hungarian action – a gigantic one in terms of the means it disposed of at that time – without altering its financial structure: the volume of ordinary activities as well as the proportion of total volume they represent remain constant, and, as soon as the action is concluded, the volume of extraordinary activities falls back to its previous level.

As we have seen, the volume of ordinary activities increased in 1970 and maintained its new level, and we concluded that part of the activities previously labeled extraordinary had been integrated into the volume of ordinary activities, through the distinction, introduced in 1970, between "permanent" and "temporary" external activities.

This leap reveals, first of all, the political decision made by the ICRC to modify its structure through the consolidation of its infrastructure. This idea is confirmed by the evolution of financing which, from 1971, is also at a higher level, thanks to constant arrivals of funds.

It must be noted that the decision is taken under great external pressure (the Nigerian events), which proves that the institution expands by reacting to external needs and not due to the Parkinsonian principle of bureaucratic mutation. It can even be stated with certainty that the level of bureaucratization of the institution remains very low.

In 1972, the curve drops sharply beneath the parity level, which indicates a new surge in extraordinary activities, the ordinary activities remaining constant. During the period 1972-1978, however, the institution is no longer pushed to the limits of its capacities. This is a period which allows it enough leeway to engage itself on several fronts. The ICRC therefore owes to international events and to the restructuring which it undertakes from the beginning of the 1970s a significant strengthening which allows it to assume a greater presence in the international community.

7. Overall (Ordinary and Extraordinary) ICRC Budget

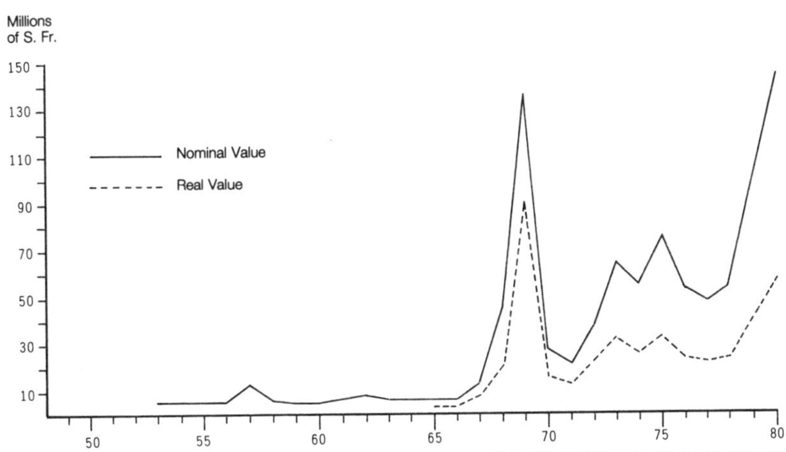

8. Synoptic Table of Annual Presentations of Accounts

<table>
<tr><td>Title of Tables</td><td colspan="3">General Account of Receipts and expenditures as of Dec. 31, 19 . .</td><td colspan="2">Account of Ordinary receipts and Expenditures for the year 19 . .</td><td>Annual Account of the Results for 19 . . by Activity Center and Structure</td></tr>
<tr><td>Distribution</td><td>Del. + Miss.</td><td>Del. + Costs</td><td>Del.</td><td>1953
1. Delegations Abroad</td><td>1964
1. External Activities</td><td>1970
1. Operations Department
2. (+ CTA as of 1972)</td></tr>
<tr><td rowspan="2">ORDINARY BUDGET

Items Under Operational Activities</td><td colspan="3"></td><td>2. General Costs in Geneva
3. Special Costs (Including an Item: “Missions Sent from Geneva”)</td><td>2. Humanitarian Law and Information
3. Administration</td><td>3. Assembly and Executive Council Secretariat
4. Dept. of Principles and Law
5. Personnel Dept.
6. Del. Training Dept.
7. Finance and Admin. Dept.
8. Press and Info. Dept.
9. Public Relations
10. Del. to I.Os.
11. Internat. Tracing Service</td></tr>
<tr><td colspan="4">1. in 1960:
a) Pay, Expenses and Insurance of Delegates
b) Travel Costs and Delegates’ Living Expenses and Delegations’ General Costs</td><td>1. in 1964:
a) Employees at Geneva Headquarters
b) Perm. External Dels.
c) Missions Sent from Geneva
d) Central Tracing Agency
e) Equipment and Organization</td><td>1. in 1980:
a) Dir. and Support Services
b) Relief Division
c) Medical Division
d) European + N. American Zone
e) African Zone
f) Asian-Oceanian Zone
g) Middle Eastern Zone
h) Latin American Zone</td></tr>
<tr><td>EXTRAORDINARY BUDGET</td><td colspan="3">1953 General Account of Relief Actions</td><td>1965 Special Fund for Relief Actions</td><td>1973 Special Fund for Current Actions</td><td>1969 Occasional Structure/Special Financing</td></tr>
</table>

9. Ordinary Budget of the ICRC

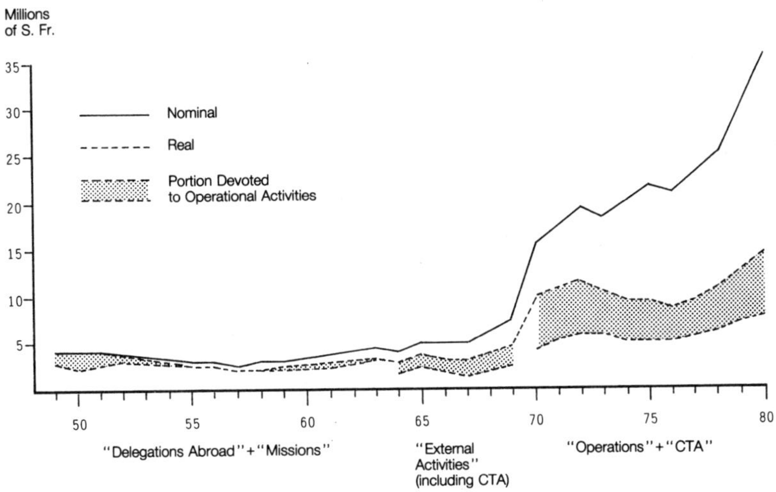

10. Extraordinary Budget

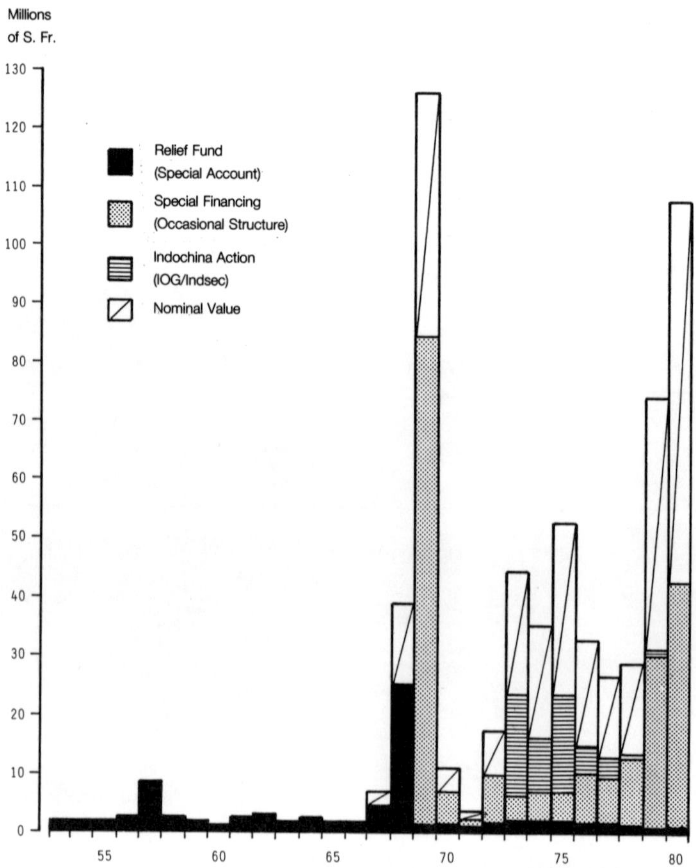

2.2. Protection (Tables 11,12)

The ICRC, as co-guarantor, with the signatory powers, of the four Geneva Conventions of 1949, is involved in a whole range of activities aimed at ensuring the protection of military and civilian victims of conflicts.

The activities in question take place, on the one hand, at the Geneva headquarters and, on the other hand, in the field.

1. At Geneva headquarters, the main concern, in critical situations where the violation of international humanitarian law is flagrant, is to appeal to the conscience of decision makers in the international community in the hopes of reducing and eliminating those violations. The procedure employed is the issuing of solemn appeals, of which, however, the Committee only makes moderate use. The main effort develops through continuous diplomatic action, which takes up a large portion of the ICRC President's time, as well as that of his close colleagues and main collaborators. If the ICRC President is more and more often led to travel throughout the world, if the number of missions of members of the Committee is constantly on the rise, if the Director of Operations and the chiefs of geographic sectors are often in the field, it is because headquarter's priority is given over to personal contacts and discrete diplomacy. Tasks of assistance and major relief actions can take place in the glare of publicity. But the accomplishment of missions of protection requires not only ability but, above all, discretion. One must set up relations of confidence with the government involved, with parties to very diverse types of conflicts whose reality, no matter how much suffering they may cause, one often doesn't dare to acknowledge.

Such diplomatic action, which is taken within many different contexts, official and private, and whose effectiveness largely depends on a network of personal relations slowly developed throughout the entire world, cannot be understood by the use of statistics. The success of an undertaking often depends on personal qualities of Committee members, on personal relations they have established and maintain in the framework of their profession, and on their moral and intellectual authority. One can therefore not begin to give an annual account of trips made by members of the Committee or colleagues at Geneva headquarters in order to evaluate the importance of diplomatic action aimed at ensuring the realization of tasks of protection.[15]

One must also include in headquarters' protection activities, the work, which is considerable and decisive to the development of a long-term humanitarian policy, carried out by the group of collaborators of what is known nowadays as the Department of Principles and Law, whose action is quite clearly exercised in favor of the fundamental mission assumed by the

[15] Let us point out that it is precisely the need to tailor short-term behavior to a humanitarian strategy based on the respect of the Conventions which distinguished the ICRC's action in Nigeria from that of the Churches and which forbade certain circumstantial initiatives.

ICRC. That is the Department which prepares international Red Cross Conferences and which in particular did the work and conducted the negotiations which led to the convening of the major Diplomatic Conference for the Reaffirmation and Development of Humanitarian Law. It carries out the delicate task of adjusting actions as a function of principles and law, on behalf of the Committee, it sees to the permanent subordination of tactical movements imposed by circumstances to humanitarian strategy. It inspires and is responsible for tasks of education through the diffusion of Red Cross principles.

Solemn appeals are therefore only the tip of the iceberg. They are only issued in case of extreme necessity and usually out of despair.

2. In the field, activities are more concrete: the ICRC, by its presence, bears witness, and reminds the authorities of their responsibilities in the matter of the protection of victims. It undertakes three types of specific actions which mean that protection is at the origin of the entire panoply of the organization's activities:

a) medical activities, when they are made necessary, to replace or supplement those of the belligerents and in particular of an occupying power;

b) family reunions or, at least, the transmission of messages within a family separated by conflict. This is the role of the Central Tracing Agency;

c) visits. This is, as far as the political and legal aspect of things is concerned, the quintessential protective function, and we will therefore elaborate on it in this chapter.

In the analysis which follows, we refer (as illustrated by Tables 11 and 12) to all the visits mentioned in the Annual Reports. People visited include: prisoners of war, combatants captured arms in hand, civilians of foreign nationality interned as the result of conflict or simple tension between the detaining power and their country of origin, and political detainees. One must therefore remember the fact that, in our totals, we do not include "partial" visits, limited to a certain category of detainees, or to an arbitrarily chosen group or one encountered by chance.

2.2.1. Evolution in the Area of Visits

Let us note at the outset that it is impossible to establish statistics for the number of visits on the basis of the Annual Reports.[16] There are too many gaps in the reports prior to 1972. But one can draw some interesting conclusions based on the manner in which the question is treated.

One can, in the presentation made by the reports of visits to places of detention, distinguish several successive states:

[16] Table 11 is based on figures provided by the Detention Service of the ICRC.

1. 1949-1952: there is no systematic information. Visits to prisoners are sometimes mentioned, as are the number of visits per country. But there are in general no data concerning the number or the quality of detainees. It is mainly in Europe, in Greece which continues to experience the sequels to the civil war, that one can note a regular practice of visits during this period.

2. 1953-1957: this is the first phase during which one finds expressed the ICRC's concern for detainees not belonging to the category of prisoners of war. This emerges from the revealing sub-titles in the Annual Reports, such as "Protection of Political Detainees" (1954), "Political Internees and Detainees" (1955), "Political Detainees" (1956).

These section titles also display the ICRC's will to integrate the question into its traditional field of activity. "Traditional Activities" (1953) thus become "Assistance Tasks" (1955), to emerge as the synthesis of these two ideas, "Traditional Assistance to Victims of Conflicts and their Consequences" (1956). There is therefore the desire that the visit to "places of detention" be considered as a simple extension of the visits to prisoner of war "camps" such as had been carried out in the past. The fact that assistance is considered traditional does not rule out the possibility that the place of exercise of the activities should be new. The title of the chapter for the year 1957, "Assistance to Victims of Internal Disturbances", leaves no doubt on this score. An introduction of nearly two pages underlines the high degree of attention now accorded by the ICRC to this question.

The ICRC had always been concerned with victims of internal disturbances and non-international conflicts, and that is one of the reasons why it viewed as progress the inclusion, in 1949, of Article 3 common to the four Conventions. This article, however, covers non-international armed conflicts and therefore, civil wars, but not internal disturbances. Nonetheless its interpretation and therefore its application were always the object of debates due to the increasing internationalization of so-called national problems. The ICRC was thus constantly brought to engage itself in the name of its right of initiative without referring–and even avoiding reference–to the Conventions. It may be said that the ICRC understands the full extent of the problem of political detainees during this period, more precisely around 1955. Visits to that type of prisoners are at first concentrated in the European zone. This is a first level in the evolution of visits. Concerning the other zones, it can be noted that a few individual visits begin to be made in Latin America.

3. 1957-1961: the dynamics of the previous period are broken by the will of the ICRC itself, which does not seem to want to follow to its conclusion the logic of its initiatives. One continues to pay attention to visits to political detainees, but especially to those in Europe. This happens in Greece, the Federal Republic of Germany, the German Democratic Republic, Bulgaria

and Yugoslavia which, although not subject to serious internal disturbances, open their prisons to the ICRC.

Latin America is also subject to a few individual actions during the second half of the 1950s, and these raise great hopes concerning the application of Article 3 bearing on non-international conflicts and, even more, concerning the positive reaction of certain governments to ICRC initiatives.

The dominant action of this period is the important series of visits which the ICRC carries out during the Algerian conflict, from 1955 to 1963. This was probably the first time that Article 3 was invoked in a major conflict.

4. 1962-1968: this period is characterized by the resurgence in two major conflicts, in the Indochinese peninsula and the Middle East. The tasks of protection of the ICRC become more onerous. In the wake of the Six-Day war between Israel on the one hand, Egypt, Syria and Jordan on the other, in particular, the Committee undertakes its whole range of protection activities.

During this period, efforts previously carried out in the framework of the Algerian war, even though its nature was that of an internal conflict, make it possible, upon the reestablishment of peace, to obtain the recognition on the part of the Algerian authorities of the ICRC's protective role in favor of the emprisoned harkis.

5. 1969-1971: this is the period of a great and durable change, with the indeniable increase in the number of visits in Latin America, Africa and Asia. This increase would seem even more spectacular if one were to base oneself on the number of visits and not only on the countries in which visits were effected. For Asia, it is mainly prisoners of war in South Vietnam who are visited, but there are also visits to political detainees in that country, as well as, to a lesser degree, in Laos. Vietnam takes a large place in the activity of the ICRC, even though the steps undertaken to gain access to American and Vietnamese detainees in North Vietnam failed one after the other. Visits also continue on a larger scale in Israel and the occupied territories, as well as the two Yemens.

The year 1969 is therefore a second important level in the area of visits.

6. 1972-1977: the tendency observed in 1969 is amplified and systematized as can be seen in the Annual Reports, where there is now an item "Visits to Places of Detention", whereas the part devoted to "Operations" is now subdivided into "Theaters of Conflict", for example "Cyprus", "Chile", etc. and into "Regional Delegations". It is in the latter section that can be found the list of countries (by zone) with the number of places and of detainees visited.

In Latin America, the ICRC's presence is ensured almost permanently through systematic visits. This coincides with the agitated socio-political phase the continent is undergoing. As for Europe, Cyprus, Northern Ireland and Portugal now join the list of countries where there are numerous and regular visits.

7. 1978-1980: a new significant level is reached, which confirms the evolution of the two preceding periods. Annual Reports contain an important and detailed item (contrasting with those of the years 1957-1968) entitled "Activities in Favor of Political Detainees".

The involvement of the ICRC in the question of the protection of prisoners and all types of political detainees is sufficiently firm and constant to be considered an element of its humanitarian policy which should be perfected by the end of this century. At the same time, a growing number of largescale actions lead the ICRC to regularize its presence, so as to be able to visit prisons regularly, whether or not conflict exists.

Supported by headquarters and encouraged by the practical results of the Diplomatic Conference, the delegate now sees visits to detainees as belonging to his routine, and tends to convince governments of the correctness of this idea.

The last three decades have thus witnessed a notable progression in the number of visits to different types of detainees, prisoners of war, individuals coming under Article 3, and detainees covered by the ICRC's right of initiative, often called "detainees by reason of circumstances" so as to respect the susceptibilities of governments, which almost unanimously deny that they have any political detainees.

This increase applies to all regions of the world except Europe, where the number of visits and persons visited is declining. And it can clearly be seen that the great majority of detainees visited are political detainees (2/3 to 3/4, or even more, of the total number of visits made since 1952). One must conclude from this that the ICRC, along with the increase in its activities in other areas, is determined to reinforce activities deriving from its duty of protection, and even, in order to do so, is going beyond the existing degree of codification.

11. Visits to Detainees*

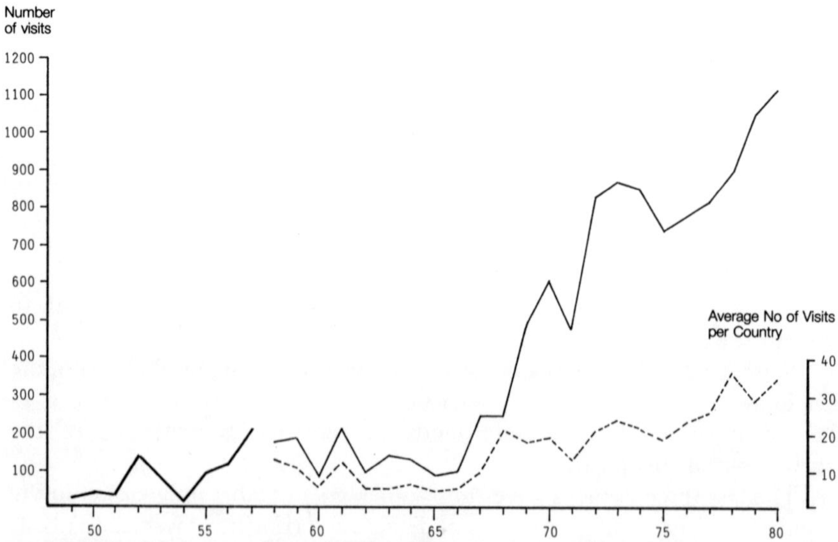

* One must add in { 1978 = 1350, 1979 = 2770, 1980 = 2600 } Visits to Detainees in Israel and the occupied territories. The increase is explained by the introduction of individual visits to detainees under interrogation.

12.1. Visits to Detainees by Geographic Zone and by Category

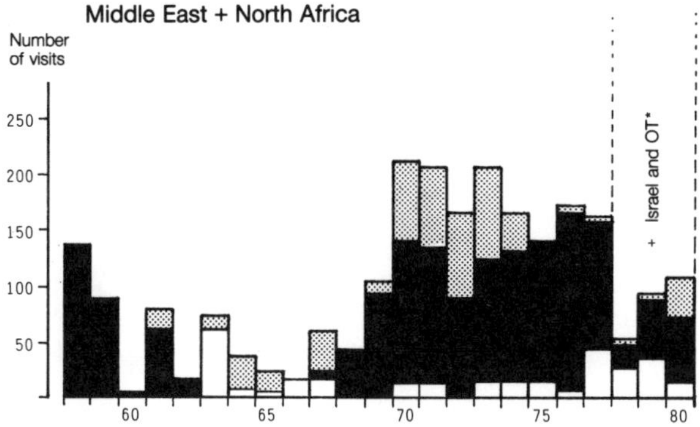

* See explanations to the graph "Visit to Detainees".

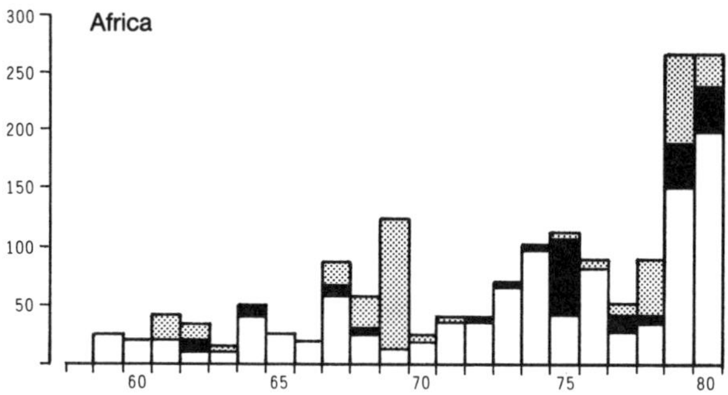

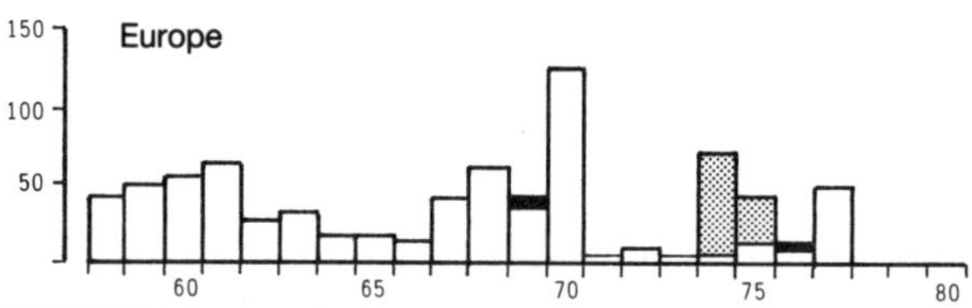

- Visits based on the 3rd Convention (Prisoners of War)
- Visits based on the 4th Convention or on Article 3 of the four Conventions (Foreign Civilian Internees, Combatants not recognized as POWs)
- Visits based on the ICRC's right of initiative (Political Detainees)

12.2. Visits to Detainees by Geographic Zone and by Category

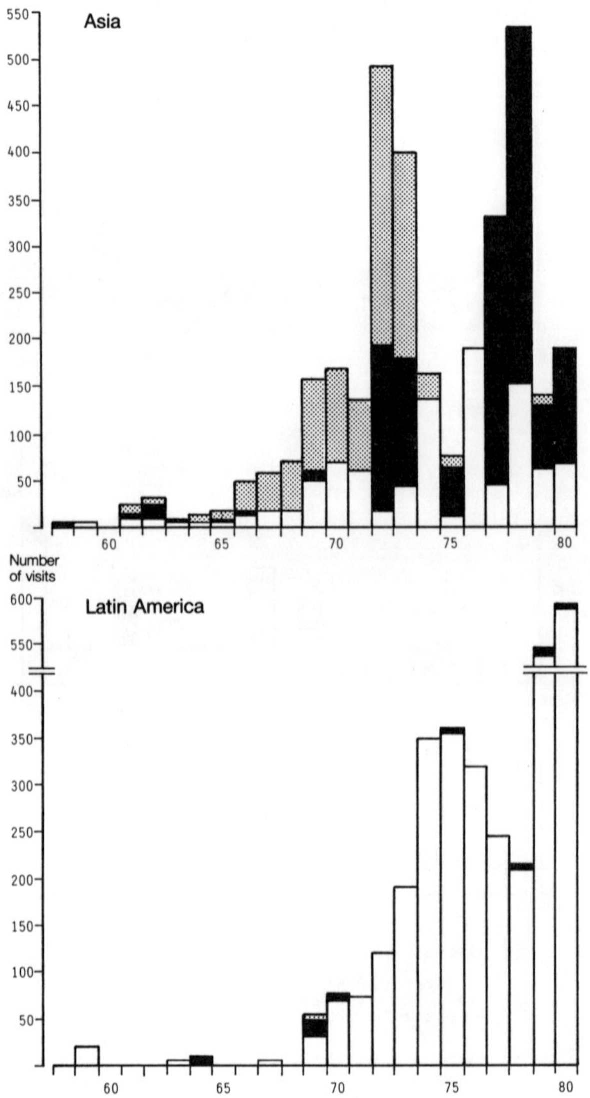

2.3. Assistance (Tables 13-17)

2.3.1. Definition

Assistance and protection are the two areas of action of the ICRC. The notion of assistance essentially involves material aid in food, medicines, and medical equipment and services. Assistance can be, either directly delivered to the victims, or transferred by the ICRC to a National Society which takes charge of its distribution. The activities are together commonly called "relief actions", a notion which includes material and medical aid, but not medical services or the services if the Central Tracing Agency or the services offered detainees, namely visits by delegates.

While this logical distinction is practiced even in the Annual Reports and internal reports, in practice, assistance and protection are tightly intertwined. It is therefore just as logical that all ICRC activities in favor of victims should be directed by a single Director of External Affairs until 1969 and the Director of the Operations Department since then.[17]

2.3.2. The ICRC's Policy in the Area of Assistance

Since the assistance activities of the ICRC are often considered to be a recent and sometimes negative development on the part of the institution, it may be useful briefly to recall the origin and evolution of these activities.

As of the Franco-Prussian war (1870-1871), the Committee organized relief actions in favor of certain categories of victims. But needs became more pressing after the First World war which had ruined the economies of several European countries. Between 1919 and 1939, the ICRC several times created "relief services" within its structure. Assistance granted during the Second World war was from every point of view the most important in the history of the institution.

There were, then, from the very origins of the Committee, numerous relief actions organized by it and their volume often sustains comparison with the post-war period.[18]

In terms of beneficiaries of relief actions, one observes a profound evolution. In 1870-1871, only sick and wounded personnel in the hands of the enemy received assistance. During the Second World war, the ICRC's assistance mainly went to POWs and foreign civilian detainees.[19] Between the two, there were some cases of assistance to the civilian population (the

[17] From 1974 to 1981, the Central Tracing Agency is not included in Operations.

[18] The value of relief distributed in 1870-1871, for example, was 3 million Swiss francs of that time.

[19] There were, however, important assistance activities in favor of civilian populations. The action in Greece during the occupation (1941-1944), for example, was essential to the survival of the population.

case of the Spanish Civil war is the most important). The post-war period is however undeniably characterized by assistance to civilian populations affected by conflicts. It has become the main category of beneficiaries, by far. The main reason for this evolution surely lies in the transformation of conflicts, which have made the civilian population the first victim.

But one can detect more specific lines of action which contributed to marking the evolution of ICRC assistance.

Speeding relief to the war wounded was the initial undertaking from which the Red Cross Movement was born. Assistance came before the elaboration of legal instruments which legitimated it. It will become the criterion by which the Committee is guided in the choice of its actions.

But the Committee has always strived to limit its relief actions to the categories of persons protected by the Conventions, whereas, in the area of protection, it has always tended to interpret the Conventions in a broad sense, so as by basing itself on the principle of analogy, to help out categories of persons not explicitly protected.

Insofar as victims not protected by the Conventions are concerned, the Committee generally sought out other means to help them. Prior to the First World war, it several times founded ad hoc organizations. There was, in 1870, the "International Committee for Aid to Prisoners of War" (which adopted the green cross on a white field as an emblem) and the "Central Agency for Aid to Military Personnel Interned in Switzerland".[20]

After the First World war, the international community became concerned over the fate of civilian populations affected by the consequences of the conflict. Organizations were created in which the ICRC actively participated (notably the International Union for the Protection of Children of which the ICRC was a co-founder, and the International Relief Union). But it was with the young League of Red Cross Societies (1919) that the ICRC mainly organized relief actions in favor of civilian populations (cf. 5.1.3.). All of those assistance activities show that the ICRC, on many occasions, was ready to bring relief to victims not protected by the Conventions, while being careful not to overstep its mandate.

From this brief historical sketch, two principles for action can be perceived in the area of assistance:

– the will to limit oneself, if possible, to categories of victims protected by the Conventions;

– a concern with seeking other channels for victims not explicitly protected.

---

[20] Since the organizations were placed under the responsibility of members of the International Committee of the Red Cross, they were to a certain extent legal fictions. But they were born precisely out of the legal concern not to drag the young Red Cross into assistance actions outside the framework of the Convention.

Post-war material assistance, as we have just observed, mainly went to civilian populations who were victims of conflicts or of post-conflictual situations. With assistance to this category of victims, which forms a part of the ICRC's mandate since the adoption of the fourth Convention (1949), the task has become more complex. And the ICRC, whose first reflex is prudence, was to take a certain amount of time before establishing criteria for its intervention.

It was not, however, the volume of relief to be managed that needed to cause it worry. The ICRC had acquired a solid experience during the Second World war. It had created its own foundation for the organization of Red Cross Transports. The value of relief distributed had reached 3.4 billion Swiss francs.[21]

In this respect, one must also note that two major actions (Palestine, 1949-1950 and Hungary, 1956-1957) were carried out efficiently without modifying the position of principle of the ICRC in relation to assistance. The fisrt signs of «bolder» involvement by the ICRC are to be observed as of 1960, but it was the Nigeria/Biafra action (June 1967-January 1970) which transformed the post-war assistance policy.

2.3.3. *The Post-War Volume of Assistance*

The value of aid distributed over the entire period (1948-1980) amounts to approximately one billion Swiss francs (cf. Table 16). If one compares this figure to expenses incurred for relief actions between 1940 and 1947, one cannot claim that the inclusion of the protection of the civilian population in the Conventions transformed the institution into a relief agency.

The examination of the movenemt of relief aid distributed[22] between 1948 and 1980 leads us to distinguish two phases:

1. 1948-1966: these years are marked by a contrast; two major relief actions stand out against a background of very modest actions. Palestine and Hungary apart, the yearly average of relief aid distributed is approximately two million Swiss francs.

2. 1967-1980: with the operations engaged in the Middle East and Nigeria, the volume of assistance increases spectacularly, and does not drop again. The volume for the 1970s is situated at a level twenty times greater

[21] This figure *excludes* relief distributed by the Joint Committee (League/ICRC).

[22] The main source for the calculation of the volume of assistance is the series of *Annual Reports*. The results obtained were corroborated by a comparison with ICRC Summary Reports presented at the Red Cross International Conferences of 1952, 1957, 1965, 1969, and 1973. For major emergency actions (cf. Table 14) we also had to refer to ICRC Action Reports (Palestine and Hungary) or to reports drawn up by the London firm of Peat, Marwick, Mitchell and Co. (Nigeria, Bangladesh, Indochina and Kampuchea).

than that for the period 1950-1966,[23] an average level of 41 million Swiss francs in yearly expenses.[24]

Those years also witnessed several major actions: Middle East, Nigeria, Bangladesh, Indochina, Lebanon and Thailand/Kampuchea. The Nigeria action was on a far greater scale than any of the others.

The small and medium actions,[25] on the other hand, were more numerous and, especially, more voluminous than in the past. The volume of such actions for the years 1977-1980 is significantly greater.[26] It is, for example, nearly 20 times greater than that for 1960-1964 and nearly four times that for 1969-1972. Furthermore, the proportion of the volume of those actions, beginning in 1976, is clearly on the rise in relation to that of major actions.

In other words, until 1974, the place occupied by major actions is such that a large part of the capacities and means of the institution is engaged in them. But the other actions are not interrupted. They suffer from the place taken up by the major action. This remains true, though to a lesser extent, for recent major actions (Lebanon and Thailand/Kampuchea). One can therefore conclude that, in the present period, beginning approximately in 1974 and contrary to past practice, the ICRC is better able to conduct several simultaneous relief actions.

2.3.4. The Resources of the ICRC in the Area of Assistance

The increase in volume is not only due to the fact that the ICRC is better equipped to manage relief actions. It can also be explained by progress achieved in the techniques of mobilization of funds.

The organization does not possess great autonomy in the dispatching of material aid. It does not dispose of sufficient ordinary funds to buy or even transport significant quantities of aid; the ICRC, every time it wishes to respond to a major emergency, must issue appeals to donors. The aid distributed mainly comes from gifts in kind or in cash earmarked by donors for specific actions. Those donors must become interested and motivated. The ICRC undertakes this more systematically and, one might say, even professionally, with varying degrees of success.

Clearly, the reaction of donors is different during the two phases we have distinguished:

---

[23] If, once again, one excepts the Hungarian action, which represented 90% of aid dispatched in 1956.

[24] The comparison is based on nominal value. But even taking inflation into account (cf. Table 13), the two periods are clearly distinguishable.

[25] *Cf.* Table 15.

[26] *Cf.* Table 17.

1. 1948-1966: this period is marked by the softness of responses by donors to appeals, except for the two appeals in favor of the victims of the Palestinian conflict (joint ICRC and League appeal, July 1948), and in favor of the Hungarian population (appeal of October 28th 1956). Given the worldwide impact and capital political effects of the two crises, it is not surprising that the response of donors should have been positive. It is rather the softness of responses during the rest of this phase which commands our attention, notably during the years 1951-1955 and 1958-1960. During those lean years, the ICRC itself must furnish more relief than it gets from donors. Expenses incurred for relief actions[27] are, during those years, superior (by an average of 50%) to the overall value of relief distributed. Since those expenses are partially devoted to the purchase of relief aid, the comparison obviously has only indicative value.

The observation is confirmed by the evolution of receipts of the General Account for Relief Actions.[28] It shows that "Earmarked Funds" which represent the donors' response to the Committee's appeals, during the period 1958-1964, only covered one-half of the expenses incurred for relief actions.[29] This is a percentage significantly inferior to the average for the post-1967 period.

While there is, beginning in 1961, a noticeable increase in earmarked contributions (except in 1963), one must note that the response to appeals remains relatively weak. Both the Nepal action (June 1960 to May 1963) and the first important medical action in Yemen (Uqd hospital, November 1963-November 1965) yielded deficits,[30] grants for the lattter action only covering 52% of costs incurred.

The ICRC, at any rate, encountered such difficulties in financing its permanent activities (those pertaining to the ordinary budget) that it had, after 1948, to reduce its general expenses by a third. The assistance policy suffered from this at the time, and one can suppose that there was, during those years, too parsimonious a management, one inspired by the probably imaginary fear as of financial disaster, and that these factors hampered the Committee in its actions.[31] It did of course launch relief actions, but how

[27] As they are stated in the "General Account for Relief Actions" beginning in 1953. Reference to this Account is made in the Balance Sheet of the 1951 *Annual Report,* but without a specific accounting of expenses.

[28] From 1955, there is a distinction between non-earmarked grants and those for specific actions. The latter are comparable to the "Special Fund for Relief Actions" listed as of 1967 in the *Annual Reports.*

[29] 8 million Swiss francs in cash contributions as compared to expenses of 16.5 million for relief actions.

[30] Deficits are "temporarily" covered by advances on the part of the Swiss government.

[31] The unspent balance of 4.5 million Swiss francs left over a Swiss government credit accorded in 1946 remained intact until 1962!

insistently? One is obliged to note that habitual donors were far more generous towards the League during the same period (see below). Whether this is the reason or not, the ICRC's assistance policy had to undergo the effects of the low level of grants during this entire first period.

2. 1967-1980: beginning with the Nigerian action, the ICRC elicited far more generous reactions from donors than before.

The international economic situation was surely one cause.[32] It must also be noted that, in its assistance policy, the ICRC, doubtless motivated by the heightened awareness created by the Nigerian-Biafran war, pursued a far more dynamic policy. As of 1970, it is rewarded by successive accords with the EEC and the Swiss government, foreseeing the regular delivery of considerable amounts of grants in kind. With those accords, the ICRC achieves a greater degree of independence of action since it can to a great extent itself determine their use.[33] More recently, the ICRC attempted further to increase its freedom (and therefore its availability in case of an emergency, by launching general appeals to donors (in particular for Africa).

2.3.5. *The Donors*

Traditional donors to the ICRC are National Red Cross Societies and governments.[34] Certain specialized agencies bring their support to a few actions. In the case of the Palestine action, in 1949-1950, the UN even covered almost all costs.

Since the Second World war, the main donors have been governments.

The proportion of government donations in relation to those by National Societies varies depending on the period. Between 1948 and 1967, the portion coming from National Societies is proportionately more important.[35] Let us here recall that contributions in services (essentially medical teams furnished by National Societies) are not numerically evaluated and must be added to grants in cash or in kind.

---

[32] The ICRC simultaneously registers an increase in its volume of relief aid.

[33] From 1971 to 1974, the ICRC underwent the apprenticeship of its new freedom. This was the period where third world countries were "peppered" (cf. Table 5 showing the number of beneficiary countries).

[34] *Cf.* also Chapter 6.2., "Extraordinary Budget".

[35] The Tables in the *Annual Reports* do not distinguish between governments and National Societies until 1972. Indications may be found, however, concerning the actions in Hungary, the Congo (1960), Nepal (1961-1962), Yemen (1963 and 1965) and the Middle East (1967).

2.3.6. *Comparison Between the Relief Actions of the League and the ICRC.*

National Societies are the main contributors to the League's relief actions. The latter differ in various respects from those of the ICRC, so that a direct comparison is not possible.

– Three quarters of the relief aid accorded by the League are destined to victims of natural cartastrophes.

– The organization of relief actions on the part of the League is generally limited to the delivery of aid to National Societies, which are requested to provide a report on distribution. The ICRC, on the other hand, organizes and controls the majority of distributions itself. The League's Relief Office thus functions as a sort of import and export agency,[36] the importers and exporters being the National Societies.

Despite this fact it is possible, to an extent, to compare volumes of relief and draw certain conclusions concerning the response of donating National Societies.

The first comparison concerns the 1952-1964 period.[37] The value of material assistance delivered during those years is, for the ICRC, 102 million Swiss francs, for the League, 515 million Swiss francs.

After deduction of the Hungary action (ICRC) and the "Hungarian Refugees" action (League), the contrast becomes even more marked. The ICRC receives 17.5 million Swiss francs, the League, more than 434 million.

The volume of the League's relief actions is therefore twenty-five times that of the ICRC for this period. True, relief actions in cases of catastrophes represented the major portion of the League's actions. But even when one limits the comparison to relief actions in favor of the victims of conflicts, grants of funds to the League are greater:[38]

ICRC: 17.5 million Swiss francs;

League: more than 50 million Swiss francs.

This proves that the ICRC of the immediate post-war era did not want or was unable to mobilize donors the way the League Secretariat did.[39]

In the wake of efforts undertaken by the ICRC beginning with the Nigerian action, in order to bring greater relief to victims of conflicts, the ratio of volumes of relief delivered by each institution to that category of

---

[36] According to the League itself. *Cf. Rapport général de la Ligue*, 1957, p. 69, and that for 1952, p. 63.

[37] The idea being to analyze the reactions of National Societies during the period when they were relatively important donors to the ICRC.

[38] Always after deduction of the two actions in favor of the Hungarians.

[39] The League's relief actions, it is true, often take the shape of bi- or multilateral aid between National Societies. This nonetheless reveals the fact that the means of the donating National Societies can be important.

victims was inversed in favor of the ICRC. This is illustrated in a striking manner by the following little Table:

Relief to Victims of Conflicts[40]

	League In millions of Swiss francs	ICRC
1948-51	60.0	73.5
1952-55	5.7 (+?)	4.7
1956-57	80.8 (+?)	87.3
1958-64	43.3	9.7
1965-68	27.4	49.0
1969-72[41]	195.4	195.2
1973-76	35.9	78.8
1977-80	33.7	More than 220.0

[40] Major joint League/ICRC actions are not included, namely the Middle East (more than 20 million in 1967), Bangladesh (21 million in 1972), AICR Indochina (150 million, 1973-1977). Parallel actions, on the other hand, like those in Palestine, Hungary, Algeria, etc., are included. Source for the League's figures: General Reports and Annual/Biannual Reports.

[41] Actions in Indochina for the League, in Nigeria for the ICRC.

13. Relief Distributed or Transmitted

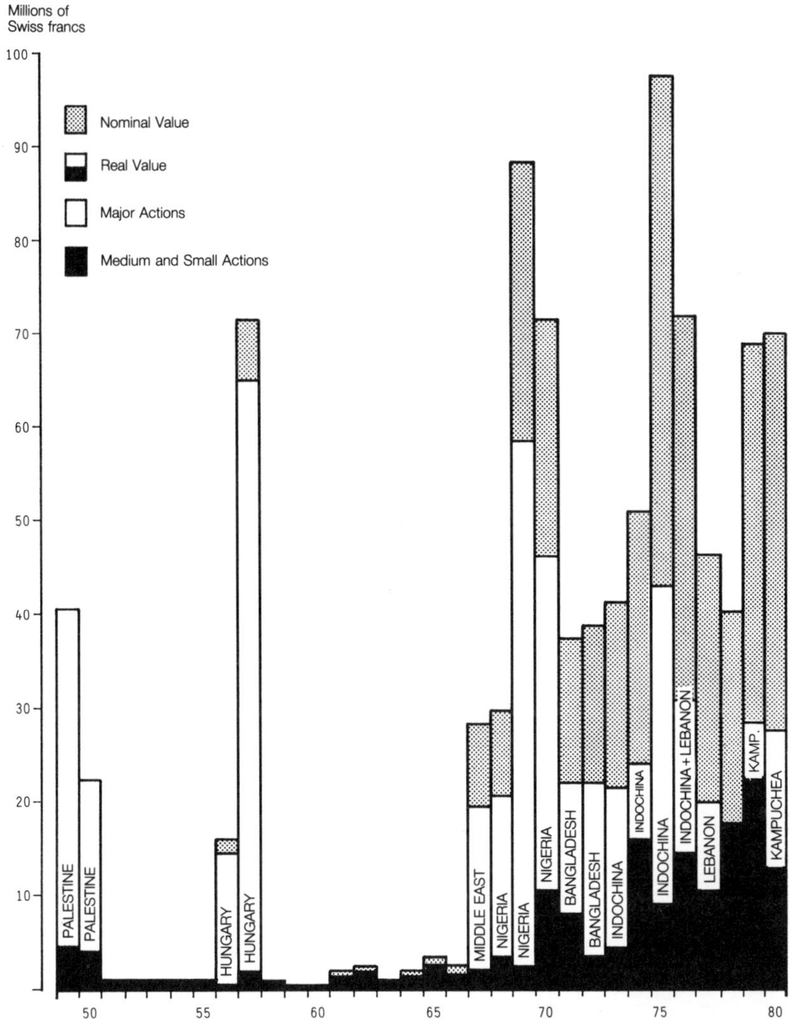

14. Major[1] Relief Actions in Chronological Order

Actions	Dates	Duration	Total Volume in Millions	Yearly Average	Real Value in Millions of Sw.Fr.
1) Palestine	January 1949*-April 1950	16 months	56.6	42.5	3.578
2) Hungary	October 1956-December 1957*	15 months	84.2	67.4	5.133
3) Middle East	June 1967-January 1968	8 months	25.4	38.1	2.210
4) Nigeria	January 1968*-January 1970	25 months	165.7	79.5	4.358
5) Bangladesh	December 1971-December 1972*	13 months	56.4	52.1	2.512
6) AICR Indochina	1973-1976*	48 months	142.7	35.7	1.374
7) Lebanon	1976*-1977*	24 months	46.1	23.1	0.829
8) Kampuchea	October 1979-December 1980*	15 months	50.2	40.2	1.333

[1] Volume of relief of at least 15 million Swiss Francs per year (nominal value).

* The date given does not correspond to the beginning/end of the action, but marks the limit of the "intense" period.
Criterion of intensity: the real value per month.

15. Medium-Size Relief Actions in Chronological Order

Actions	Dates	Duration	Total Volume in Millions	Yearly Average	Real Value in Millions of Sw.Fr.
1) Jordan	Sept. 1970-Dec. 1970	4 months	11.6	34.8	1.855
2) Chile	Sept. 1973-1976*	40 months	15.0	4.5	0.166
3) Israel + O.T.	1974*-1980*	84 months	31.3	4.5	0.159
4) Cyprus	July 1974-March 1975*	9 months	10.5	14.0	0.530
5) Angola	June 1975-June 1976	13 months	9.7	9.0	0.327
6) Philippines	1976*-1980*	48 months	14.6	3.7	0.125
7) Rhodesian Conflict	July 1977*-May 1980	35 months	15.1	5.0	0.178
8) Erythrean Conflict	Feb. 1978*-1980*	35 months	13.8	4.7	0.162
9) Nicaragua	Sept. 1978-Aug. 1980*	24 months	12.5	6.3	0.213
10) Sino-Vietnamese Conflict	June 1978-1980*	31 months	14.8	5.7	0.196

* The date given does not correspond to the beginning/end of the action, but marks the limit of the "intense" period.
Criterion of intensity: the real value per month.

16. Relief Distributed by the ICRC 1948-1980

(in Millions of Swiss Francs)

	48-51	52-55	56-59	60-64	65-68	69-72	73-76	77-80
a) *Nominal Value*								
Africa	–	–	–	445	25 483	143 751	14 570	51 433
Latin America	5	19	18	18	35	2 383	24 630	23 366
Asia-Oceania	710	1 488	286	2 195	6 248	58 380	154 057	94 058
Europe-North America	14 963	3 144	86 397	1 089	791	425	11 919	175
Middle East-North Africa	57 784	55	2 210	4 216	30 342	30 704	55 676	56 887
Total	73 462	4 706	88 911	7 963	62 899	235 643	260 852	225 919
								Total for 33 years 960 355
b) *Real Value*								
Africa	–	–	–	372	18 174	88 277	6 765	21 271
Latin America	5	18	16	15	25	1 463	11 436	9 663
Asia	711	1 416	260	1 834	4 456	35 851	71 528	38 899
Europe-North America	14 988	2 992	78 571	910	564	261	5 534	72
Middle East-North Africa	57 882	52	2 010	3 523	21 639	18 855	25 850	23 526
Total	73 586	4 478	80 857	6 654	44 858	144 707	121 113	93 431

Approximately 570 Million Fr. in 1948

17. Relief Distributed by the ICRC During Small and Medium Actions Exclusively

(in Millions of Swiss Francs)

	48-51	52-55	56-59	60-64	65-68	69-72	73-76	77-80
a) *Nominal Value*								
Africa	–	–	–	445	–	3 343	14 570	51 433
Latin America	5	19	18	18	35	2 383	24 630	23 366
Asia-Oceania	710	1 488	286	2 195	6 248	1 959	11 366	43 872
Europe-North America	14 963	3 144	2 232	1 089	791	425	11 919	175
Middle East	1 236	55	2 210	4 216	4 946	30 704	31 724	34 722
Total	16 914	4 706	4 746	7 963	12 020	38 814	94 209	153 568
b) *Percentage*								
Africa	–	–	–	5.6	–	8.6	15.5	33.5
Latin America	0.0	0.4	0.4	0.2	0.3	6.1	26.1	15.2
Asia-Oceania	4.2	31.6	6.0	27.6	52.0	5.0	12.1	28.6
Europe-North America	88.5	66.8	47.0	13.7	6.6	1.1	12.7	0.1
Middle East	7.3	1.2	46.6	52.9	41.1	79.1	33.7	22.6
Total	100%	100%	100%	100%	100%	100%	100%	100%

CHAPTER 3

Qualitative Enlargement of Activities

3.1. The Central Tracing Agency (Tables 18-19)

During the period in which we are interested, the Agency changed its name once. The Central Prisoners of war Agency (1939-1960) became the Central Tracing Agency (CTA, 1960-).[1]

3.1.1. Objectives

The complexity of the Agency's activities is such that a preliminary presentation of its objectives and mechanisms appears essential. The initial idea which led the Red Cross from its inception, to create Agencies in cases of conflict, is simple. For its illustration let us quote from a letter of the International Committee to various French and German relief Committees two weeks after the outbreak of the Franco-Prussian war:

"...But in addition to physical injuries, there are moral injuries which are not less painful, and to the relief of which it seems to us that we could effectively contribute. We refer mainly to the correspondence between the wounded who have fallen into the hands of the enemy and their families, as well as that of healthy prisoners."[2] Prisoners of war had not been protected by the 1864 Convention.

Upon the invitation of the International Committee, the Basel Agency[3] also came to centralize and transmit "nominative information"[4] to families

[1] Quoted in DJUROVIČ. *L'Agence Centrale de Recherches,* which should be consulted for the history of the CTA.

[2] *Ibid.*, p. 10.

[3] The Basel Agency (1870-1871) thus created the first correspondence and information office. The following ones were the Belgrade Agency (1912-1913), the International Prisoners of War Agency (in Geneva, 1914-1918), the Tracing and Individual Cases Services (1919-1953), the Spanish Service (1936-1939), the CPWA (1939-1960), etc.

[4] The term used by G. Moynier, quoted by DJUROVIČ, *op. cit.*, p. 14.

of wounded military personnel. The lists of "healthy prisoners and the dead" which the Committee had requested were not, however, obtained.

These activities, for all successive Agencies, remained the main objective: "to find persons separated by war, and reestablish communication between them".[5]

These activities engendered a legal precedent, which successive Conventions recognized for a growing number of categories of persons: in 1909 for sick and wounded military personnel, the 3rd Convention of 1929 for prisoners of war, and the 4th of 1949 for the entire civilian population of the zone of conflict or in an occupied territory on condition that there be a family tie.

In practice, the ICRC has always attempted to bring the benefits of the Agency's services to the greatest number of persons possible. In addition to the prisoners of war of the Franco-Prussian war, one can cite the "civil section" which the International Agency of Prisoners of War had organized from the beginning of the First World war.

The realization of the main objective, the centralization and transmission of information, led to the creation of an "Information Service".[6] Thanks to it, the Agency was able to render certain other services which were, in turn, included in the provisions of the 1949 Conventions.

All categories of military personnel protected by the Conventions are beneficiaries of these services, whereas, among the civilian population, only the civilian internees are expressly declared to be beneficiaries.[7] These services are described in the next chapter.

The enlarged objective, as it presents itself in 1979, can thus be summed up in five so-called "conventional"[8] tasks:

– registering all information concerning victims of conflicts civilian and military, living or dead;

– organizing the exchange of information ("family messages" and others) between persons separated when normal means of communication no longer work;

– if necessary, undertaking searches (or "conducting investigations") for persons concerning whom the family has requested news;

– writing up documents, on the request of the person concerned (various papers, travel documents, etc.);

– organizing family reunions or "regroupments", repatriations and transfers.

---

[5] DURAND 2, *Histoire du Comité*, p. 26.

[6] *AR*, 1978, p. 56.

[7] Defitition of persons protected: Fourth Convention, Art. 140: "A Central Information Agency for protected persons, in particular for internees, shall be created in a neutral country".

[8] Paraphrase of the 1979 *Annual Report*, p. 66.

Conventional tasks have remained unchanged since 1949.[9] In the 1949 Annual Report,[10] however, they are presented with less logical rigor, since the enumeration mixes classification of beneficiaries with the tasks themselves.

One notes that two of the tasks listed in 1949 are no longer present in 1979:

"d) Inventories, and personal property of combatants or prisoners",

"e) Attempts to identify military personnel buried without proper identification..."

These tasks are, however, still occasionally carried out. In Shaba,[11] for example, the ICRC "participated in operations... to exhume and rebury some 800 corpses buried after the fighting... to make a further attempt at identification". They are proportionately much less important than they had been during and after the Second World war, because the nature of conflicts has changed.

There are no new categories of beneficiaries since 1949. Refugees and political detainees, for example, already benefited from the Agency's services in 1949–the latter ever since the First World war.

On the other hand, the proportion of civilians has continued to increase. This is probably the reason why the ICRC adopted the new designation, "Central Tracing Agency". The Annual Report, however, does not give this reason, but concentrates on legal arguments: the ICRC has been entrusted with the creation of "an information agency for civilian persons. When these provisions were put into effect, the ICRC decided to adopt the new designation as from July 1, 1960.[12]

In conclusion the objectives of the Agency have remained constant since 1945. In practice, the Agency has continued to be flexible, especially in the definition of beneficiaries.

---

[9] DJURIVIČ, *op. cit.*, (chapter 9, Art. 3) speaks of the "present tasks of the Agency, resulting from recent armed conflicts, etc.". The tasks evoked–family reunions and travel documents–result more from the Second World war. Points 3 and 4, on the other hand, deal with new categories of beneficiaries, and point 1 with the internal reorganization of the Agency. There have not, on the other hand, been any new tasks since 1945, at least not according to our definition.

[10] Pp. 64-65.

[11] *AR*, 1978, p. 24.

[12] *AR*, 1960, p. 27. The argument reflects the will to fortify the legal base, but it is unclear why it took 11 years to put the provisions into effect, whereas the practice of providing civilians with the Agency's services had preceded the Conventions by 45 years.

3.1.2. *Functioning*

So as to be able to carry out its Conventional tasks properly, the Agency has had to develop complex structures. We will simplify them here so as to bring out the principles involved.[13]

a) Concordance

The Agency centralizes and manages information and requests bearing on the victims of conflicts.[14] Both are registered. An index card is drawn up[15] for each name and placed in the files. The (colored) information cards refer to sources of information and the (white) request cards to personal files which are classed separately. The meeting, in a file, of an information card and a request card under the same name, "establishes the current".

This so-called "tallying"[16] method makes it possible to respond to a request, in cases where the CTA has some information, but also when information arrives even years after the request.

The files are the core of the Agency. In times of conflict, the Agency opens one or several files.

b) Information

The Agency systematically regroups and treats all official information on persons protected by the Conventions: sick or wounded military personnel, the dead, prisoners of war and civilian internees. It does the same, by analogy, for other categories of civilians: political detainees, "dispersed family members", deportees, displaced persons and, sometimes, refugees.

Official sources of information are organs whose creation in case of conflict is called for by the Conventions: national information offices. In their absence, official information may also come by order from the belligerent powers, governmental (legal, etc.) authorities, National Red Cross Societies and ICRC delegates (for example when visiting places of detention).

Information provided by individuals, families, etc., is also often indexed, but not systematically. Its sorting out is done according to common sense criteria.

As to the nature of information, the key element is the complete name of the person. Additional corollary information comes from elements narrow-

[13] For more details, *cf. L'Agence Centrale de Recherches,* Geneva. ICRC. 5th Edition. 1971. 33 pp.

[14] "The place where two currents meet", *AR*, 1978, p. 53.

[15] Where information has not already been indexed, for example by means of capture cards.

[16] *AR*, 1955, p. 8.

ing down the person's identity and making it possible to locate him or her in space and time.

Information concerning protected persons naturally tends to be more complete given the formal procedures involved. For categories of civilians preserving a relative freedom of movement in case of conflict (displaced persons, refugees), the obtaining of information is more difficult. The volume of civilian population movement in case of conflict can be such that it goes beyond the Agency's capacity for action and forces it to limit itself. It is not possible to define the categories of civilians for which the services of the Agency might be turned down.

In practice, the Agency operates according to a "negative" definition: it integrates civilians not protected by the Conventions to the extent to which international organizations created after 1945 for the precise purpose of responding to the needs of displaced persons and refugees (UNHCR, International Organizations for Refugees) cannot do so for some people. Here are two examples:

– In 1949, the Agency searched for displaced persons whom the IOR would not handle (coming from Central and Eastern Europe).[17]

– In 1979, since "newly arrived persons", "illegal immigrants" according to the designation of the Thai government, did not qualify for refugee status, the CTA initially had to take on identification tasks.[18]

In addition to collection and filing, the Conventions stipulate that the Agency may also be charged with the transmission of information concerning persons protected to the Powers of origin. According to the Conventions, the transmission is required for information on military personnel; concerning protected categories of civilians, it does not take place when it might cause harm to the persons involved or their family (4th Convention, Art. 137).

c) Requests

The Agency responds to any request falling in the category of "services". Requests may come directly from family members or via national information offices, National Red Cross Societies, etc. The services rendered by the Agency can therefore be summed up as follows:

c.1. Transmission of news and other information:

Upon the request of the sender, the Agency may transmit (written) news, packages, funds, personal effects and/or private documents (birth certificates, for example).

[17] *AR*, 1949.

[18] *AR*, 1979.

The transmission of packages, funds and objects is in principle reserved to protected persons (and political detainees).

As we have said, the transmission of family news (4th Convention, Art. 25) lies at the very origin of the Agency. It has remained from every point of view one of the most important services which the Agency renders victims of conflicts. In order to facilitate the transmission of news,[19] the Agency, at the time of the First World war,[20] created a "message formula", a sort of form letter. But "open" letters continued to be transmitted and sometimes are nowadays.

Message formulas are not always transmitted automatically by the Agency. In certain cases, particularly when the belligerent powers limit the activities of the Agency to the transmission of news, message formulae are treated like an item of information and/or a request: through registration and the opening of a file.

c.2. Checking and Investigation:

The Agency responds to requests for news (or "requests for information"). The response is immediate when the files already contain elements of information.[21]

If such is not the case, the request for news requires the launching of an investigation. Once the means of investigation have been exhausted, the result is communicated to the person making the request.

Results of an investigation are divided into two categories. The result is positive when the fate of the person sought after has been determined. It is negative when the investigation has not found any trace. When elements of a response to an investigation allow one to presume that a person is deceased, but the Agency has no proof, the person is listed as "missing". Cases of missing persons[22] are not communicated before the end of a conflict.

c.3. Issuance of Documents:

The official news which the Agency centralizes during conflicts often makes for more complete archives than those which governmental administ-

[19] Family messages may be subject to censure. The formula was also created in order to accelerate their passage through censorship.

[20] Djurovič. *L'Agence Centrale de Recherches.* Message formulas became important during the Spanish Civil war.

[21] The *Annual Reports* of the 1950s designate this file consultation procedure as "checking" (e.g., *AR*, 1955, p. 8).

[22] It must be noted that cases of missing persons include disappearances, on which no light can be shed.

rations possess. In such cases, the latter rely on capture, illness or death documents which the Agency establishes for persons protected in order that they or their families can receive government compensation.

The Agency has also, ever since 1946, issued *travel documents* which replace a passport in case of repatriation. This travel document is recognized by a number of States. It makes it possible, in particular, for stateless persons having become personae non gratae[23] to go to a new country, but also serves for displaced persons and refugees.

c.4. Repatriations, Transfers and Family Reunions:

"This work... was started after the Second World war."[24] Although it figured on the list of "5 tasks" of the Agency in 1979, it was long presented separately from those of the Agency.[25] It always, of course, required the Agency's participation, if only for the registering of beneficiaries. The ICRC, therefore, also attempts, in cases of family reunions, to limit its collaboration to the search for persons.

"This action is being continued in co-operation with the National Red Cross Societies concerned. In certain cases the Societies carry out the actual work and keep the ICRC informed of the results which have been achieved. In other countries a part of the task is undertaken by the International Committee."[26]

d) Structure of the Agency. Decentralization

We did not intend to present the structure of the Agency in detail, especially since the Annual Reports are exhaustive on the subject. Our only interest is in the recent trends, those of the 1970s.

The CPWA during the Second World war included: a Commission, a Directorate, "General" (Technical) Services, National Services and Specialized Services.[27] This structure was preserved during the 1950s. Beginning in 1961, the organization of national services was modified. Four

---

[23] A recent example: Asians who had to leave Uganda in 1972.

[24] *AR*, 1959, p. 34.

[25] *Cf.*, for example, *Annual Reports* from 1949 to 1969 on the question of family regroupments in Europe.

[26] *AR*, 1960, p. 26.

[27] For more details, *cf.* DJUROVIC, *op. cit.*, chap. 6 and the ICRC Report on its activities during the Second World war, Vol. 2, Geneva, 1948.

"Grouped Services A-B-C-D-" were created.[28] The reason for this modification which, let us recall, takes place at the time of the Agency's change in name, was that the Agency's activities more and more frequently bear on extra-European countries: "World events bring unceasingly new preoccupations to the Central Agency."[29]

Later on, activities bearing on anglophone countries brought the Agency to adopt a division into zones, such as it is practiced by Operations. This modification is not indicated in the Annual Reports, but it took place in 1978.[30] The "structural realignment" based on the other sectors of activity of the ICRC is reflected in the Reports which, from 1972, relate the activities of the Agency in the field by zones of operations.[31]

The integration of the Agency into the operational activities of the ICRC resulted from the first engagement in the field. The first Tracing Agency in the field seems to have been opened in 1956. If that engagement in the field is still experienced as an exceptional situation by the Agency in 1963,[32] the operation has become standard by 1976-1977, to the point where one might be surprised that it hadn't happened earlier. The main reason for this delay was the fact that the Agency was concerned longer than other sectors by the follow-up to a conflict. The Agency thus continued to preoccupy itself with the sequels to the Second World war–and still does so today. During the 1949-1952 period, the two most important national services, the German and the Italian services, furnished on average two-thirds of the Agency's work. And today, "even 35 years after the end of the Second World war, one-third of the CTA's activities are still connected with the sequels of that conflict."[33]

---

[28] *AR*, 1961:

A. Western and Southern Europe, French-speaking countries of Africa and Latin America;

B. Central and Southeast Europe;

C. East and Northeast Europe, North Asia;

D. North West Europe, North America, English.

[29] *AR*, 1962, p. 45.

[30] Interview with Mr. N. Vecsey, Deputy Director of the CTA.

[31] The *International Review of the Red Cross* likewise suspends its account of the CTA's activities and, from 1974 on, describes Agency's activities along with others (DJUROVIC, *op. cit.*, p. 274).

[32] "For the third time the Agency was temporarily divided into two parts with the setting up of a regional tracing service. After having established a similar service in Cairo in 1956, then in Leopoldville in 1960, it was to set up a provisional bureau in Algiers in September 1963", *AR*, 1963, p. 36.

[33] This proportion appears enormous if one considers that the Agency manages a dozen offices in the field in the same year. One must understand this to mean one-third of the Agency's activities at headquarters. *AR*, 1979, p. 65.

Why create Tracing Agencies in the field?

1. During internal conflicts, the (divided) country would be hard put to create a neutral and impartial office.[34]

2. Another reason is "the inadequacy and sometimes the absence of national information and tracing agencies, in situations not covered or not explicitly covered by the Geneva Conventions, but also in the framework of armed international conflicts."[35]

The chronological list of the establishment of Agencies in the field shows that the CTA is approximately seven years late in engaging itself in the field as compared with "Operations". The geographic extension of the Agency begins in 1976, whereas that of Operations takes place as of 1968-1969. This is also illustrated by the growth of the Agency's budget which was stable from 1964 to 1971, doubled between 1972 and 1976 and doubled once again by 1979.[36]

3.1.3. Volume of the CTA's Activities (Table 18)

The nature of the Agency's activities and the complexity of its functioning make the quantitative approach more difficult than for other sectors of activity of the ICRC. The significant unit is the individual case, the name. On the basis of files in the archives, it would be technically possible to define the total number of names stored there. In the same way, it would be possible to compare the number of names concerning which the files have information to that of names which are the object of one or several requests. Thirdly it would be possible to specify the number of names for which a "concordance" has been established. The CTA has, however, never kept such statistics and tens of millions of entries which the CTA possesses would require too great an effort. It is also certain that, given the considerable differences of time which may be spent on the treatment of cases (from a few minutes to years of searching), figures concerning the number of names would only give a very relative idea as to the volume of work of the activities.

One could envisage a different quantitative approach: according to service, as found in the figures provided by the Annual Reports. But a glance at the comparative Table (Table 18) is enough to observe gaps so important as to exclude the method of extrapolation.

Before analyzing the volume of the various services, let us briefly study:

---

[34] But one should also take account of the danger that may be represented by the search for personal information in the context of a conflict. The CTA's personnel might be suspected of espionage, with all the grave consequences which result from that.

[35] Djurovič, *op. cit.*, p. 202.

[36] *Cf.* Table 19.

a) The volume of mail (Table 18).

The number of letters received and sent is the only more or less regular information which may be gleaned from the Annual Reports.[37] The tendency over the period as a whole is marginally decreasing. This is to be explained by:

– the very slow reduction of activities devoted to the sequels of World War two, from three-quarters or more in 1949 to a third in 1980;

– the increase of the Agency's activities in the field during the 1970s.[38]

Since the overall figures are not broken down, it is difficult to explain them. The 1956-1958 peak surely reflects the increase due to the Hungarian conflict, although one must not forget the activities in favor of stateless persons living in Cairo and Alexandria in the wake of the Suez crisis.

The main problem with statistics on the volume of mail resides in the fact that a letter may contain one or several names and that the proportion can of course not be determined. Only the 1956 Annual Report (p. 32) relates the number of letters received to the number of cases (75 103 letters representing approximately 90 000 cases or 120%). The Reports for 1972-1974 make it possible to relate the number of names listed on cards to the number of cases, successively 322%, 344%, and 273%.

One cannot draw any major conclusions from these quotients (which vary from 1.2 to 3.4), except possibly the fact that, during periods of classical conflicts, lists of names are longer.

b) The volume of files.

As we said in the previous chapter, every name and every request is reported on a card. Indications on the number of new cards going into the files would therefore be more revealing than statistics concerning mail. But here too, the proportion of name-cards is impossible to determine. There may under a single name be one or several cards.

A glance at the comparative Table (Table 18) shows that information provided by the Annual Reports is too sporadic to permit any conclusions concerning the linear evolution of the volume of cards.

The Reports, however, give figures concerning the total number of cards and a few remarks are permitted.

How many cards were classed in Second World war files? 40 million, according to the 1955 Report, 36 according to the 164 Report, 38 according to the 1974 Report. Would 10% of the cards have been destroyed between 1955 and 1964? This goes counter the customs of the Agency which occasionally destroys old files to which the cards refer, but never the cards, which contain concentrated information. Would 2 million new cards have

[37] With the exception of the years 1953, 1960, 1961.

[38] Concerning which there are no systematic statistics in the *AR*s.

been filed between 1964 and 1974, without any reference to them in the Annual Reports?

What is the total number of cards contained in the files? 40 million in 1949, 47 million in 1956, 45 million in 1957 (sic!), 49 million in 1975.

Does this mean an increase of 9 million between 1949 and 1975? This isn't certain. The 1949 Report does not specify whether the 40 million cards relate only to the CPWA (opened in 1939) or if they include the approximately 5 million cards of the IPWA (1914-1918).[39]

How many cases are represented by those cards? 15 million cases! This figure would seem to be correct, since, according to the 1956, 1957 and 1964 Reports, the 47 and 45 million total number of cards as well as the 36 million of the Second World war together represent 15 million individual cases.

Despite these considerable variations, an important conclusion may be drawn from these observations: in thirty years, the cards have increased by a percentage which varies from 12% to 25%)[40]. In other words, the files from the Second World war are 4 to 5 times more important than the combined files of recent conflicts!

c) The volume of "Investigations".

Two-thirds of the Annual Reports give figures as to the number of investigations undertaken. More than a third give the percentage of successfully concluded investigations, that is to say those having resulted in the identification of the person sought for, whether living or dead. Percentages of positive results go from 30% to 52%, the average being 40%. In the other 60% of cases, either the investigations did not–or did not yet–result in finding the person, or they resulted in strong presumptions as to the death of the person, without absolute certainty. The Reports never give figures, neither overall, nor relative to a conflict, on percentages of negative results or of missing people.

Overall figures of investigations undertaken are, furthermore, not very revealing, the less so since the investigations undertaken by Tracing Agencies in the field are not included. An analysis of this question according to type of conflict would alone reveal the barriers which the Agency encounters in carrying out its searches.

d) The volume of family messages.

The Agency only gives an accounting of messages having passed through headquarters, in its overall figures. And yet, these figures are insignificant in

---

[39] "4 895 000 cards", DURAND 2, p. 35. According to the Deputy Director of the Agency, the overall figures include the previous CPWA cards. Interview of December 3, 1980.

[40] The total number of cards in 1949 was between 40 and 45 million. In 1980, it is, according to the Deputy Director of the Agency, approximately 50 million (Interview of March 13, 1980).

relation to the number of messages exchanged via the delegations (or Tracing Agencies) in the field.

One example: in 1972, 32 106 messages pass through headquarters; 1.15 million messages are exchanged between the three Tracing Offices located in Pakistan, India and Bangladesh. Another example: from 1948 to 1970, more than 4 million family messages[41] are exchanged thanks to ICRC delegations between Israel and the Arab countries.

In conclusion, these summary observations as to the volume of activities have shown the impossibility of making a quantitative analysis of the evolution of the Agency, for the following reasons:

- there has been no regular policy in the choice of criteria, which makes for great discrepancies;
- the figures given are not placed in relation to the main objective of the Agency. They should illustrate the extent and degree of success of activities (how many communications established, how many cases treated), illustrate the volume of work furnished by such and such a sector of the Agency. How, then, does one explain the fact that the activities of Agencies in the field are not included in the overall figures? How does one explain the fact that the cards which have been sent back to headquarters are not counted in the total number of cards filed?
- the weight of activities devoted to the Second World war has been too great.

These observations should not be seen as a critique of the Agency. The main mission of an institution which is a jewel in the crown of the ICRC is not to establish statistics but to search for people, soldiers or civilians who have fallen victim to conflicts.

To the extent to which conflicts have "transnationalized" themselves, disorder in one place results in unrest elsewhere, the proportion of civilians victims of violence rises and, with it, that of the missing. The Agency is brought to deal with these cases. It is a duty which derives from respect for the principle of humanity, a task for which it is prepared by experience acquired in the search for the persons left missing by international conflicts. It has therefore engaged itself–with its traditional discretion, which makes the reconstitution of its activity difficult–in countries where the elimination of adversaries through "disappearance" has been erected into a system of government, and, in even more cases, in which disappearances are the result of the collapse of the structures of the State. It has therefore not published reports comparable to those which were presented by the Organization of

[41] *AR*, 1970. This figure is to be taken for what it is, namely approximation. An internal report from 1980 gives the figure of 3 million messages exchanged between 1948 and 1980!

18. Volume of Work of the Agency (CPWA-CTA) at Headquarters (excluding the field)

	Letters	Registration	Cases treated	Investigations opened	closed	of which % positive	Messages via HQs.
1949	252 000	–	–	15 172	–	–	–
1950	143 579	–	–	16 355	–	–	–
1951	180 564	–	–	–	–	–	–
1952	162 000	–	–	–	–	–	–
1953	–	–	–	(10 435)	–	–	–
1954	152 161	–	–	15 094	–	–	–
1955	125 000	–	–	14 330	–	–	–
1956	163 199	174 632 cards	90 000	19 432	–	–	–
1957	309 324	–	187 429	33 112	–	–	–
1958	197 430	–	113 928	35 482	–	–	–
1959	172 000	–	87 000	18 000	–	–	–
1960	–	–	–	25 000	–	31	–
1961	–	–	66 348	20 525	–	33	–
1962	79 000	–	60 500	15 700	–	42	10 500
1963	97 800	23 000 cards	–	–	12 000	40	4 000
1964	122 436	–	–	–	–	–	–
1965	113 819	–	–	15 907	–	31	–
1966	124 390	–	–	14 846	–	30	–
1967	151 077	–	–	15 445	–	–	16 954
1968	109 010	–	–	13 072	–	40	11 390
1969	109 779	–	–	10 715	11 301	44	15 010
1970	88 826	–	–	10 091	10 661	46	–
1971	97 977	–	–	10 270	10 454	45	–
1972	161 883	265 538 names	–	12 951	14 810	52	32 106
1973	122 800	207 156 ,,	–	17 000	13 068	–	–
1974	192 692	297 857 ,,	–	32 625*	19 878*	–	–
1975	210 000	–	–	13 936*	13 164*	–	–
1976	203 918	153 536 information	–	13 066	14 106	43	–
1977	124 290	110 000 ,,	50 000	8 368*	9 836*	–	–
1978	82 054	90 000 ,,	–	6 400*	5 700*	–	–
1979	88 000	125 000 ,,	–	5 200*	6 900*	–	–
1980	92 000	589 400 names	65 000	–	–	–	8 500

* Figures obtained by the CTA

19. Ordinary Budget of the CTA (including ITS since 1974)

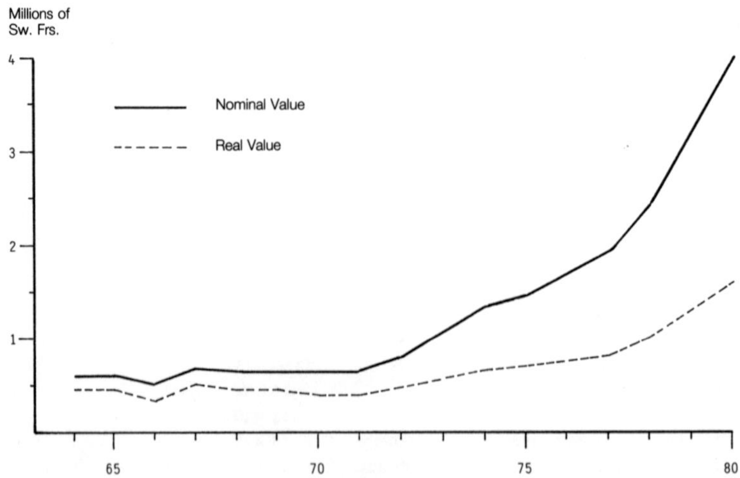

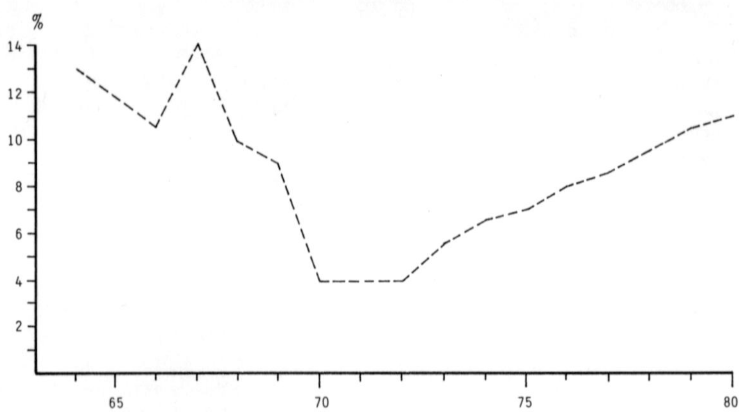

American States[41] or by the working group created within the Human Rights Commission.[42]

But internal studies do furnish proof of the particular attention which is devoted to this problem located at the intersection of humanitarian law and human rights. Moreover and most importantly, the ICRC has, in the field, despite the obstacles it has met, proven its efficiency and a competence which the General Assembly of the United Nations has underlined in various resolutions.

3.2. Medical Activities

Medical activities like relief and the protection of detainees, are an integral part of "External Activities", or of "Operations". In the Reports, "External Activities" are presented as a whole, without any subdivision, until the reforms which began in 1969-1970. One has to wait until 1977, the year of the (re-)creation of the Medical Division, before one can grasp the relative importance of the medical sector. Information on medical activities, which had been contained in Annual Reports, is presented separately from that, concerning sanitary personnel, assistance to war invalids, and a third category requiring the participation of doctors: compensation for victims of pseudo-medical experiments.

3.2.1. Structure

The Annual Reports say little on the subject. There is some information concerning the restructurings of 1949, 1950 and 1977.

Is it possible to infer that the structure remained the same from 1954 to 1977? We doubt it.

1949: the Medical Affairs Service, along with 6 other Services,[43] belongs to the Medical Division and the Relief Division. The latter's Director belongs to a Commission on Medical Affairs and for the Study of Sanitary Equipment, made up also of five members of the ICRC. The commissions are charged by the ICRC with inspiring and controlling the work of the various Services.[44]

1950: the Executive Director is responsible for the Administrative Division and the Executive Division including eight Services, four of which

[41] "Report on the Situation of Human Rights in Argentina", OAS Inter-American Commission on Human Rights, 1980.

[42] "Question of Human Rights of All Persons Subjected to Any Form of Detention or Imprisonment, in Particular: Question of Missing and Disappeared Persons", 1981.

[43] Prisoners – CPWA – Delegations – Treasury – Administration & Personnel – Relief.

[44] *AR*, 1949, p. 10.

pertain to medical affairs: Medical Service, Pharmaceutical Service, Invalids' Service, Nurses' Service.[45] The Commission on Medical Affairs, etc. remains in place.

How does one explain this surprising division of the Medical Affairs Division into four Services? The Reports of the 1950s and succeeding years give no information on this subject. A few factors make it possible to propose a hypothesis. Proportionately, the medical actions in Bengal (India-Pakistan, 1950), and Palestine (1948-1949) were very important. It would seem, at any rate, that the size of those actions resulted in the preparatory training courses[46] which the ICRC organized in 1951.

Did needs become less pressing in succeeding years? Were the three doctors and thirteen nurses who participated in one of the two courses enough to ensure "readiness to face any eventuality"? Whatever the case may be, the Reports do not speak of similar experiences before 1977.

In 1954, the Medical Commission presented the studies it had undertaken for the purpose of facilitating and coordinating the work of National Red Cross Societies and armed forces health services at the international level.[47] This is the last reference to be found in the Reports concerning the existence of the Medical Commission and the structure of medical affairs, until 1977.

The activities of the Invalids' and the Nurses' Services (which become "Sanitary personnel" in 1952) were carefully accounted for until their end in 1971. The disappearance of the War Invalids' Service and that of Sanitary Personnel at the end of 1971, as well as the absence of any reference to a Chief Medical Officer in 1976, imply that there had in the meantime been a restructuring.

1977: Who evaluates medical and paramedical needs in times of conflicts? Who organizes actions in response to them? Who decides to send doctor-delegates and who prepares them for their activity? To none of these questions do the Annual Reports provide clear answers from 1954 to 1976. Of course, there had been medical activities during this period–and perhaps proportionately as many as before and after–but it would seem that the management of these activities was not in the hands of a strong and competent direction.

This is at least the impression gleaned from a reading of the explanations when a Medical Division was created:

---

45 Plus CPWA – Prisoners, Internees and Civilians – Delegations – Relief.

46 "So as to be prepared for any eventuality, the ICRC had decided... to organize for doctors and nurses wishing to participate in its missions, a 3 to 4 week training course in Geneva, so as to inform them of the traditional activities and the principles of the Red Cross" (*AR*, 1951, p. 51).

47 *Cf. AR*, 1954, p. 8.

"A Medical Division was created within the Operations Department in 1977, to enable the ICRC to carry out and coordinate the medical aspects of its activities in the field."[48]

The sentence makes no reference to the past. The accent is placed on the determination to act in future on clearly defined and solid structural bases.

The Division "recruits, appoints and prepares" doctors and auxiliary medical personnel. It "is also responsible for the planning of each action before it is set in train". Finally, the "Pharmaceutical Section", which is probably the successor to the "Pharmaceutical Service" set up in 1950, is attached to the Medical Division.

In order to train doctors, the Medical Division organizes training courses. The first took place in 1977, and is qualified as "the first experience of its type", which implies that the similar experience[49] of 1951 was not renewed and had been forgotten.

If the Medical Division (correctly, in terms of organization) presents itself as innovative, the definition given by the Report[50] of the "medical function" harks back to tradition: it falls under the competence of the Physician-in-Chief or Chief Medical Officer who, as a member of the Directorate, answers directly to the Executive Board. Among his tasks, let us mention those already listed in the Reports of the 1950s:

"– to follow and encourage the development and dissemination of humanitarian law in the field of medical and health services...

– to remain in touch continuously with other international humanitarian bodies, with those in charge of medical activities in National Red Cross Societies, with army medical services, with national medical associations, universities, etc."[51]

We will, under paragraph b), speak of the ICRC activities which relate to these two objectives. Let us here simply point to something which characterizes the evolution which *seems* to have taken place in relations between National Red Cross Societies and armed forces health services. In 1954, the ICRC Medical Commission sees itself as a centralizing organism (cf. its mandate which is to favor and *coordinate* the work of National Societies and health services *at the international level).* In 1977, there is no longer any question of "maintaining permanent contact" in view of the rational organization of the medical activities of the ICRC.

---

[48] *Cf. AR,* 1977, p. 34.

[49] The 1951 training programme is not mentioned in the Reports. A distinction nonetheless emerges between the two experiences. That of 1951 had as its sole aim to familiarize doctors and nurses with the ICRC, the one which began in 1977 includes in addition, a reflection on "preventive and tropical medicine». This new element reflects the effort to adapt medicine to needs in the field.

[50] *AR,* 1977, *loc. cit.*

[51] JB.

3.2.2. Aspects of Medical Activities

a) In Case of Conflict

Rare are the ICRC's major actions in which it has not been morally obligated to carry out medical activities.[52] In its interventions, the ICRC attempts to adapt to the needs of victims. The nature of battle and the conditions of the terrain, however, often make a large number of victims inaccessible. The different types of actions are:

- medical support teams,
- mobile clinics,
- mobile medical teams,
- field hospitals,
- emergency sanitary actions,
- medical assistance to displaced persons,
- medical assistance to orphanages,
- distribution of medicaments,
- emergency nutritional aid,
- treatment abroad.

Let us note that this is a recapitulative list. In other words, not everything is done at every moment. The recent evolution places the accent on the mobility and emergency character which ICRC medical interventions must possess. This also implies a distribution of medical and paramedical relief according to more severe criteria and under stricter ICRC control.

b) Visits to Places of Detention

Ever since the beginning of the 1970s, the ICRC, in principle, always carries out its visits with a doctor-delegate. This practice had also been frequent in previous years, but it is not possible on the basis of the Reports to assert that there had always been doctor-delegates.[53]

The tasks of the doctor-delegate are the observation of questions of hygiene and nutrition and of the state of health of the detainees, and visiting sick detainees. In serious cases, he may propose transfer or freeing of the detainee.

A particular disposition was foreseen by the Conventions (Art. 112 and 113 of the 3rd Convention) for the question of sick or wounded prisoners of war: mixed medical commissions made up of two doctors appointed by the ICRC (in accord with the protecting power) and a doctor of the detaining power were to examine their state of health with a view to repatriating them.[54]

---

[52] One of the exceptions is the Korea action (1950-1954), in which the Parties to the conflict had limited the ICRC's action to the protection of prisoners.

[53] The 1966 and 1967 *Reports*, for example, imply that delegates in Africa had visited places of detention alone.

Finally, the doctor-delegate physically examines injuries and observes whether they are due to torture.

c) Post-War Situations

The ICRC in general limits itself to emergency action during conflicts. In the medical field, however, the situation of the mutilated (amputees, paraplegics, and those traumatized by fear) reveals a character of urgency.

So it is that, throughout the entire period of interest to us, mention is made of aid to war invalids. From 1950 to 1971, the ICRC has a service for relief to the invalids of war and aid has since then not ceased. Assistance may be provided in "collective actions" or upon individual request (especially for Second World war invalids).[55]

Collective and individual assistance: equipment distributed to invalids by the ICRC:

- medicaments, fortifiers;
- crutches, various prostheses, including ocular ones;
- Braille watches, typewriters for the blind, knitting equipment for the blind;
- wheelchairs for the handicapped, tray-tables, radios.

Collective assistance:

- equipment and machines for the fabrication of prostheses;
- equipment for re-education rooms;
- dispatching of specialists (orthopedists, physiotherapists, etc.);
- films, pamphlets.

Evolution of the volume of assistance: between 1949 and 1955, assistance fluctuates between 75.000 and 150.000 Swiss francs per year, the average being approximately 110,000 Swiss francs per year. Between 1961 and 1963, it may be estimated at an average level of 16,000 Swiss francs per year.

Since 1968, it must have been significantly higher, since the ICRC installed workshops for fabricating aids in the field by sending specialists whose task is to train local personnel:[56] in Nigeria in 1968, in Yemen in 1970, etc.

In addition to aid to invalids, the ICRC, at the end of the Second World war, pursued an information campaign on the "Reintegration of War Invalids" (pamphlet title). The ICRC also had several films which it lent to National Societies.[57]

---

[54] One example (the only one?): in 1949 in Palestine.

[55] In 1963 and 1967, for example, there were no collective actions.

[56] The only precedent for this policy: a workshop in Vietnam (Saigon) in 1955.

[57] In 1950, at the Polish Red Cross, for example.

In conclusion, we can note that assistance to war invalids on the part of the ICRC was regular, but that its policy was strongly modified. The action was broad and diversified at the outset, whereas it has increasingly been concentrated on clearly delimited projects. The transition information on invalids to the training of specialists capable of assisting them denotes the same desire to work on concrete projects.

d) The Sanitary Personnel Service

Several tasks concerning nurses (and auxiliary medical personnel in case of war) are carried out by this service, of which one finds no trace in the Reports since 1972 (contrary to the Invalid Relief Service).

These tasks are:

- aid (clothing) to needy nurses in the post-war period;
- information office on the availability of professional training programs, as well as questions of international equivalency and exchanges;
- dissemination of the Geneva Conventions and, more specifically, the rights and duties of sanitary personnel in case of conflict;
- contacts with National Red Cross Societies and with military health services.[58] In addition to the dissemination of the Conventions, their aim is mainly to contribute to the preparation of sanitary personnel in case of conflict (preparing them for their humanitarian role);[59]
- beginning in 1968 (Nigerian action), to prepare ICRC delegates leaving for tropical countries:[60] uniform rules of hygiene to be respected, vaccination plans, delivery of a medical kit.

e) Compensation for Victims of Pseudo-Medical Experiences (1961-1972)

The ICRC has served as an intermediary in distributing financial assistance offered by the Bonn government to victims of pseudo-medical experiences practiced in German concentration camps under the National Socialist regime.[61] This assistance concerned former detainees residing in countries with which Bonn had no diplomatic relations, namely Poland, Czechoslovakia and Hungary.

The ICRC carried out several missions (in general composed of a doctor-delegate and a delegate) in those countries, in order to complete the files of

---

[58] These are taken over by the Chief Medical Officer in 1977.

[59] *Cf.* for example the Report presented by the ICRC to the 19th International Red Cross Conference, 1957.

[60] *AR*, 1969, p. 64.

[61] *AR*, 1961.

persons concerned. Those files were then transmitted to a neutral commission made of three (Swiss) experts appointed by the ICRC.

In 1969, the government of the FRG, and the Czechoslovak organizations concluded an accord for the payment of a given sum to the cases which remained. In 1970, the same was done with the Hungarian government and, in 1972, with the Polish government.

3.2.3. *The Volume of Medical Activities*

It is not possible to define the importance of medical activities simply on the basis of Annual Reports. The amount of medical and paramedical equipment used and/or distributed by the ICRC is not indicated, nor its proportion in relation to other types of relief aid.[62]

Another precious indication would be the proportion of medical equipment in relation to the total number of delegates in the field.

	Medical Personnel	%
1972	26	23
1973	26	23
1974	38	30
1975	68	38
1976[63]	115	33
1977	43	17
1978	80	25
1979[64]	511	?

The only basis of comparison which we have for the preceding years is information in the 1951 Annual Report: four medical delegates, or 29% of total personnel (after deduction of numerous benevolent delegates and correspondents abroad). These data do not, for the present, make it possible to draw any conclusions as to the evolution of the medical presence in ICRC delegations. Detailed studies of major actions might some day fill this gap.

Conclusions concerning the volume of medical activities are inevitably meagre. One can nonetheless observe a constant activity and a variable but regular presence in almost every major action. As for the intensity of the presence, it seems greater at the end of the Second World war and during the 1970s. Negative proof for this can be drawn from the fact that the Annual

---

[62] Only the 1977 and 1978 *ARs* give figures making it possible to calculate the proportion: 6% in 1977 and 18% in 1978.

[63, 64] The Lebanese action (1976) and Thailand/Kampuchea (1979) are responsible for these strong variations.

Reports of the end of the 1950s and the 1960s place more emphasis on contacts with National Red Cross Societies, armed forces health services and nurses.

3.3. The Area of Political Detainees

The problem of victims not belonging to armed forces is posed early on in the history of the ICRC, even if interventions in their favor, before the Second World war, were rare and almost fortuitous. From the Franco-Prussian war to the 1939-1945 war, through the First World war and the Hungarian Soviet Republic of 1919, prisoners of war, civilian internees and even, sometimes, political detainees, were the objects of attempts at their protection on the part of the ICRC. Between the two World wars, delegates were even able to visit political detainees in at least ten countries suffering from domestic unrest or even "simple internal tensions".[65]

It is not surprising that a beginning of an attempt at systematization in the area should have coincided with the Bolshevik revolutionary upheaval of 1917. The fact that the ICRC had no delegate in Russia at the time of the 1917 revolutions and until October 1918[66] explains that no intervention on behalf of political detainees was undertaken at the beginning of the process. The main effort was to intervene on behalf of members of the Russian Red Cross, but it was also possible, for a short period of time, to visit foreign imprisoned or wounded civilians.

This was in itself not new since the broadening of the functions of the ICRC beyond military victims had, as we have noted, taken place as of 1870; but the first conscious action with respect to national purely political detainees dates from the spring of 1919, upon the establishment of the Hungarian Republic of Councils.[67]

It is logical that it should have been the delegate in the field and not the Committee who dealt with this specific problem, given the relations he entertained with leaders who now, in their own words, are "perfectly conscious of the fact that the Geneva Red Cross is not an alliance of governments but one of peoples."[68] At any rate, during this short experience in Budapest, the Committee became aware of the fact that a new step forward had been made[69] by the delegate in Budapest by visiting political detainees, and the qualitative nature of that step could not but have consequences.

---

[65] MOREILLON, Jacques. *Le Comité international de la Croix-Rouge et la protection des détenus politiques*. Geneva, Henry-Dunant Institute, 1973, p. 44.

[66] *Ibid.*, p. 47.

[67] *Ibid.*

[68] MOREILLON, *Ibid.*, p. 49, footnote 1.

[69] *Ibid.*, p. 51.

The interwar period witnessed the political triumph of ideologies, and the notion of "horizontal" conflicts among monolythic nation-States found itself rivalled and even overtaken by the "vertical" struggle among classes belonging to the same people. Revolutions and counter-revolutions dominated the stormy skies of European internal and external affairs. They created victims that the ICRC could not ignore.

But a problem remains, which becomes an open crisis with the establishment of the National Socialist regime. What should be done to protect political detainees thrown into concentration camps? How should one intervene? The ICRC bears the brunt of the opposition on the part of governments to what they consider intrusion in their internal affairs. It cannot base itself on any legal text, or any commitment which might have been made by a German government. As to invoking the principle of humanity in order to justify an initiative, it is not possible to envisage it with such a regime. The attempt made by Carl J. Burkhardt, which resulted in a brief visit to a camp, was not to set a precedent. A resolution voted by the sixth Red Cross Conference in London, in 1938, according to which political detainees should in no case be subjected to a less favorable treatment than prisoners of war, was to remain without effect. The war which broke out in the fall of 1939 at any rate absorbed all of the energies of the ICRC. But the existence of concentration camps whose population was to swell until the massive extermination of their inmates was to preoccupy it all the more since it had no means for intervening and the criticisms leveled against it underline even more the limits of its influence.

These limits are those which result from the existence of an international system made up of sovereign States. They continued to exist after the disappearance of the National Socialist regime, long after the so-called post-war years. The increasing interpenetration of societies and the ever-clearer influence of their internal conflicts on inter-State relations contribute to stimulating a search for the extension of the field of application of the Conventions. The first tangible result of that search was, as we know, Article 3 common to the four 1949 Conventions, imposing respect for "minimal humanitarian standards"[70] in case of conflicts not presenting an international character.[71]

That article, it is true, does not include the category of political detainees. It refers to armed conflicts of a non-international character. It can be interpreted as applying only to "civil wars", but not to what are called cases of internal disturbances. But its inclusion in the Conventions is nonetheless encouraging for those who would see the area of application of the Conventions extended to the protection of human rights. For some of

[70] *Ibid.*, p. 97.

[71] *Cf.* Article 3 for the precise wording.

them, Article 3 might possible serve as a means of penetration in the reserved area of sovereign States.

The ICRC, however, was only to make use of Article 3 with extreme prudence and only rarely referred to it, for example in offering its services to the parties to the Vietnamese conflict. It is in fact its right of initiative which it invokes without invoking it, as we mentioned, when it engages itself in an area which it knows to be full of political barriers. A right which it more often mentions within the organization, but rarely on the outside, and of which one speaks in order to encourage or legitimate the actions of those who, in the field, undertake initiatives. The Committee is convinced by experience that there is no point in publicly challenging States, when the primary task is to convince governments. It has been accused of excessive prudence. It was, in particular, criticized for not having fought as it should have before and during the Diplomatic Conference of 1974-1977 for the inclusion of internal disturbances in the field of application of the Additional Protocols. It was also blamed for the apparent slowness with which it offered its services in certain crises considered internal by those in power and international by their opponents, those who had launched a liberation movement.

But the number of initiatives undertaken in the field continues to increase, and the ICRC progressively manages to extend its protection to a greater proportion of political detainees.

It is possible, in the post-war period, to distinguish four distinct periods in the treatment of the problem on the part of the ICRC.

1. 1946 to 1958.

This is the period when reflection and a certain practice pick up again. Beginning with the case of a European country, Greece during its civil war, from 1946 to 1949, the ICRC rapidly came, at the beginning of the following decade, to preoccupy itself with political prisoners on other continents, in anti-colonial conflicts, like Tunisia from 1952 to 1955, and Vietnam in 1954 and 1955. If during this period, its intervention was hesitant on the occasion of minor internal unrest in the third world, like Venezuela in 1952 or Syria in 1955, it intervened more actively in the Guatemalan civil war in 1954. In 1955, it became involved in Algeria at a time when the nationalist dissidence was considered by France to be an internal affair. It also undertook significant activities, in Cyprus from 1955 to 1958, in Eire and Northern Ireland in 1957 and 1958. As for Europe, it intervenes even when political detentions result from minor tensions, notably in the Federal Republic of Germany and the German Democratic Republic in 1957 and 1958. This first period witnessed to extension of the definition on the part of the ICRC of its area of responsibility, to include the protection of political detainees.

2. 1959 to 1970.

This is a period where visits are multiplied. 54 countries in all regions of the world authorize at least one visit to political detainees, for a total of 992 visits to 400 prisons, which permits the ICRC to visit more than 100,000 persons.[72] It is interesting to note that the range of reasons given to convince States to accept its intervention is now very large, going from general humanitarian considerations to the stating of precedents, to its recognized right of initiative. The ICRC now also invokes Article 3, even in situations which cannot be designated even as non-international armed conflicts.[73] The impressive number of initiatives which were successful demonstrates the sensitizing of public opinions to the protection of human rights and the resulting obligation for governments to be attentive to them.

There continue to be important limits to this type of intervention. They are often created despite the increasing pressure, by the opposition of the authorities, by the insufficiency of financial means. In certain cases and notably in conflicts which break out within the colonial system, when the dissidence is still barely manifest, the ICRC prefers to abstain. But its reserve tends to diminish through the years.

As for the results obtained by this evolution in the ICRC's practice, they remain modest as concerns the tangible and permanent improvement of the fate of political detainees.[74] The ICRC nonetheless attempts to create the conditions necessary to the improvement of results, by avoiding single visits, and, if possible, by forcing the detaining powers to give their consent to the systematic re-visiting of places already seen by delegates.

As in other areas, the end of the decade of the 1960s witnesses the spectacular increase of the organization's activities. The number of visits goes from 140 in 1969 to 440 in 1970, only for internal unrest and tensions, to the exclusion of civil wars (and therefore of the Nigeria/Biafra conflict).

The end of this period poses as many questions for the ICRC as it resolves, in terms of how to proceed. One thing is certain. So as to be able to progress in its practice, it expects a great deal from the Geneva Diplomatic Conference for the Reaffirmation and the Development of Humanitarian Law, which it actively prepares and which begins in 1973. This is because of the organization's consciousness of the fragility of its legal base,[75] which causes it, as stated above, not to seek to include internal disturbances in the area of application of the Additional Protocols.

---

[72] MOREILLON, *op. cit.*, pp. 189-190. These figures apply only to internal unrest and tension and do not even include civil wars.

[73] *Ibid.*, p. 192.

[74] *Ibid.*, p. 198.

[75] *Ibid.*, p. 232.

3. 1971 to 1976.

This period is dominated by the preparation of the Diplomatic Conference and by its unfolding, at least in the theoretical field. In practice, the ICRC's action with respect to political detainees continues along the lines established during the preceding period.

The Conference represents the attempt to codify a reality which is marked by the "two threats which weigh on our contemporary societies and on the work of the humanitarian organizations: nuclear war and the fragmentation of wars among non-identifiable adversaries..."[76]

As such it goes beyond the framework of this study, but one must retain the fact that the hopes of certain agents of humanitarian law, first and foremorst the ICRC, are somewhat betrayed, to a certain extent through their own doing, for the question of political detainees was not placed on the agenda of the Conference. It must even be recognized that concessions had to be made to the reticence of States,[77] concessions likely to "slow down the development of the autonomous action of the ICRC in favor of political detainees."[78]

In its defense of the right to visit and protect political detainees as elsewhere, the ICRC perhaps showed itself to be excessively timid, on the occasion of the Diplomatic Conference,[79] but at a time when the latter was not even over, an observer was already in a position to ignore that relative failing on the part of international law as compared with new practices:

"It would appear... indispensable that the ICRC should inform members of the Conference, during the third session, of its will to pursue its activities (in the area of political detainees) and that it undertakes new initiatives..."[80]

While the Additional Protocols issued from the Conference reflect the wish of the governments to reserve their sovereignty, the practice of the ICRC in the second half of the 1970s in fact go considerably beyond codified law, and there results an undeniable combination of a quantitative mutation and a qualitative increase of activities, in a context where the lack of codification leaves the organization in an ambiguous posture.

---

[76] FREYMOND, *Guerres, Révolutions, Croix-Rouge,* p. 115.

[77] *Ibid.,* p. 122.

[78] *Ibid.,* p. 123.

[79] *Ibid.,* pp. 127-129.

[80] *Ibid.,* p. 123. This point of view is not of course uncontested. *Cf.* for example Jacques Moreillon, who reckons that "in wanting to go too fast and too far, the Committee risks compromising its credit with governments and, by an excess of zeal, seeing the closure not only of the doors of prisons, but also of the possibilities of action heretofore permitted." (*Le Comité international,* p. 232).

4. 1976 to 1980.

The ICRC continues to refine the distinction between types of conflicts (wars, civil wars, internal disturbances, internal unrest), and categories of detainees.

There are, in addition to prisoners of war (who continue during the entire contemporary period to be protected by the ICRC, whether in Vietnam or on the occasion of successive Arab-Israeli conflicts), common law detainees (a flexible status by which the detaining powers would generally like to designate all of their prisoners except classical prisoners of war), administrative detainees, detainees "due to circumstances", that is to say, and governments sometimes recognize this fact, political prisoners.

In going through the Annual Reports for the years 1976 to 1980, one notes that the ICRC accorded more and more attention to political prisoners. In 1979, for the first time, it goes so far as to give them a separate chapter in which the names of countries concerned by visits to political prisoners are given, with the total by country and the overall total of persons visited.

This practice is not pursued the next year, but, by going through the list of activities according to country, it is possible to know which governments authorize visits to political detainees and the number of visits made.

There is an ever greater activity on behalf of this category of detainees, and concrete examples accentuate this evolution. Let us first note that of Palestinian detainees in Israel. That State only recognizes the existence of common law prisoners, but has let it be known that it is not in general opposed to the ICRC's visiting *all* those who belong to that category of prisoners. Israel does not recognize the applicability of the 4th Convention, but grants the Committee the *de facto* status of being an organism with "authority" in the matter, without recognizing its status as the "substitute" of the protecting power. Thanks to that accord, the ICRC was progressively able to pay visits, not only to Palestinian prisoners, but also, in regular fashion–and with certain limitations–to those who are still under interrogation. There are now therefore individual (and no longer general) visits to police stations and other places of interrogation, which in itself, should the practice be pursued and generalized, promises a better protection of political prisoners who have often not been condemned, while being kept under detention and interrogation for many years.[81] There was for this evolution a short-lived precedent, in Greece (1968-1969), and it would seem that the Committee is resolved to proceed along this path by attempting to obtain the accord of more and more governments.

---

[81] It was necessary, in order to arrive at a positive result, for the ICRC to exercise constant pressure on the Israeli government ever since 1969. Note that our period does not include the situation resulting from the invasion of Lebanon in 1982.

The other concrete example of the ICRC's action in favor of political detainees during the last period is that of Iran. For once, the Committee has decided to publish the reports concerning successive visits made to detainees in 1977-1978, because the Iranian government itself had published part of them. The relative effectiveness of visits, especially when they are repeated, is demonstrated by these successive reports which present great interest because of the information they bring concerning the working methods of the ICRC.

The evolution is slow, but it continues to take place in the sense of an intensification of the practice of visits and protection to political prisoners, and we are therefore in the presence, there is no doubt about it, of a further diversification of the activities of the ICRC.

There is also a diversification in the dramatic struggle being waged against torture. Nobody ignores the role played in this area by Amnesty International and by numerous intergovernmental and non-governmental organizations. The effort undertaken to mobilize public opinion must not lead one to underestimate the effective part played by the ICRC in this long and difficult battle. Here again, the discretion which is essential to carrying out these activities does not make it possible to evaluate the results obtained. But it is clear that visits to detainees are one of the most effective means for putting an end to bad treatments, as demonstrated, to give only one example, by the three reports of visits in Iranian prisons.[82]

[82] The three visits were undertaken in April-May 1977, October 1977 and April-May 1978. The government of the Islamic Republic of Iran rapidly published the first, which demonstrates the extent of torture under the regime of the Shah. The ICRC felt justified in publishing the two following which show, on the one hand, the pressures which it had exercised with insistence in favor of an improvement of the treatment of prisoners and, on the other hand, the relative efficiency of these pressures which resulted, in particular, in a strong decrease in physical excesses. *Cf. Reports* of June 21, 1977, February 22, 1978, and October 17, 1978.

PART TWO

Impact on the Institution

CHAPTER 4

Changes in Structure

We will analyze the structure of the institution from two points of view, that of the internal organization and that of personnel. The analysis does not claim to be exhaustive, and concentrates on changes which have taken place in the area of activities. When and why were there changes?

4.1. Internal Organization (Table 20)

The main problem posed to the Committee is that of the conduct of affairs. According to the Statutes, it is the collective responsibility of the Committee. But if decisions of general policy belong to the Committee convened in plenary meetings, the execution of decisions was delegated to an administration whose services were placed under the direct responsibility of one or the other of the members of the Committee. The broadening of the areas of activity, the increasing complexity of problems which are intertwined, were to bring about the abandonment of this formula.

a) When Max Huber, in 1946, resumes the presidency, he implements a reform.[1] The Huber reform had as its principal aim clearly to delimit areas of competence. The conduct of affairs was henceforth in the hands of the President, assisted by two Vice-Presidents who support him and ensure continuity.

But the Presidency associates itself with the Committee for the conduct of affairs. On the request of president Huber, the Committee created, within its organization, a leadership group. "He also requests that a clear distinction be made between the role of the Committee which would control and establish the major lines of action on the one hand, and that of the Directorate on the other hand, which would assume executive functions and the management of daily activities."[2]

[1] He made this a condition for his return. DURAND 2, *Histoire du Comité,* p. 571.

[2] Committee Session of January 3, 1946/int. Huber, quoted by DURAND 2, *op. cit.*, p. 571.

This Directorate, composed of the President, one Vice-President and three, then four members of the Committee, was initially known as the "Bureau", the "Presidency Council" from 1949 to 1973 and "Executive Council" since 1974.

The Huber reform which reinforced the authority of the President while maintaining a group system, created the conditions for a more direct and expeditious management of the affairs of the International Committee. It resisted the test of time despite inevitable tensions within the Committee and also between the Committee and the administration.

The role of the Committee has resulted in numerous discussions within the institution and outside of it.[3] Some have suggested its abolition; others were content to envisage its transformation into a Senate which would "conceive" humanitarian action. In fact, the formula adopted in 1974 and which, while confirming the principles of the Huber reform, creates a clear hierarchy of responsibilities between the Committee and the Executive Council, seems to give satisfaction.

It gives the President and the Executive Committee the freedom of action which is indispensable to the conduct of operations in a troubled period, while offering them the possibility of relying on the advice of colleagues less directly involved and who can give them the benefit of the various relations which they have established in Switzerland and abroad in the framework of their professional activities.

In this way the Committee, which embodies the institution and which, by its very existence, stresses its originality in relation to other international organizations, through its individualized outside contacts, also offers an opening on a changing world. It is thanks to the information which comes to it, on the one hand, from delegates often sent out in the field very young and, who are therefore very sensitive to the new currents and movements of the "front", and on the other hand from Committee members, whose relations are situated at the national decision-making level, that the central administration perceives changes which occur in the international system and in the political and moral climate. It is thanks to this dialogue between the man in the field and the man at the rear, a dialogue which takes place through the administration and the Executive Council, that the "professionals" of the organization are protected from the risk caused by administrative routine and that the entire administration is forced daily to evaluate the relations between strategy and tactics, between the principle of humanity and humanitarian policy. A difficult task, which requires, from all those who assume it, whatever their place and their role in the decision-making process, a personal commitment which goes beyond the mere distinction between amateurs and professionals.

---

[3] *Cf.* in particular the pamphlet devoted to the ICRC of the Tansley Commission.

As far as the administration itself is concerned, it was subject to a series of reorganizations, essentially dictated by a concern for adapting the instrument to changes taking place in its activities. The reduction of those activities, characteristic of the years 1946-1950, was to lead the Committee to reduce the Central Administration from three to two Directors (Table 20). The latter by 1950 had concentrated their services in three Divisions: Executive Division and Administrative Division under the responsibility of the "Executive Director", Roger Gallopin; the Division for General Affairs, under the responsibility of Director Jean Pictet, assumed all permanent tasks, with the exception of assistance to victims of conflicts.[4] This separation of tasks was respected until 1974.

The General Secretariat answers to the Presidency Council. In practice, it is more of a bureau for the Council. For a brief period, from 1970 to 1973, its mission was to make the link between the Presidency Council and the Departments and Divisions. The new name which is given to it in 1974, "Secretariat to the Presidency", better expresses its true function. Contrary to other international organizations, the ICRC has thus never had a strong Secretary General. The management of current affairs has always remained in the hands of the Directors, whose number could vary.

As for services, they were modified according to the needs of the moment.

Successive reorganizations took place in 1955 and probably in the period 1960-1962, but were not mentioned in the Annual Reports.[5] In our opinion it is in 1960-1962 that the restructuring of services occurs which we find in the 1969 Chart (Table 20).

A comparison with the 1949-1950 Chart reveals several important changes.

In the Division of External Affairs, the most important change is surely the creation of geographic sectors divided into two groups. Whereas in 1949, the Service of Prisoners, Internees and Civilians and the Service of Delegations Abroad were by themselves able to carry out all external activities, the increase in such activities beginning in 1960 required the setting up of at least six regional services. The Delegations Service was maintained, but its functions were reduced to logistic support for actions (hiring of delegates, transport and radiocommunications). The Medical Services, on the other hand, which numbered four in 1950 (Medical, Pharmaceutical, Invalids and Nurses), were regrouped in a single one (Nurses and Invalids), which indicates the decrease in activities in this sector, so that the Medical and the Pharmaceutical services were probably

[4] *AR*, 1950, p. 8. The Chart shows how the Services are divided among the Divisions.

[5] The only element of the 1955 reorganization mentioned is the incorporation of the International Tracing Service (Arolsen ITS).

managed by non-specialists, responsible for geographic sectors. But what should above all to be emphasized is the disappearance of the Prisoners Service. This indicates that the ICRC, while increasing its activities oustide Europe, during this period reduced its protection activities both proportionately and in absolute terms.

One surprising detail stands out: the International Tracing Service was not integrated into the Central Tracing Agency, whereas their parallel activities would surely have required frequent collaboration. This, in addition to the fact that the Agency is not led by a Deputy Director like the other services, indicates an unfortunate downgrading of its role, due in part to the fact that it lagged behind external activities.[6]

The comparison between the two Charts thus reveals a very clear evolution towards the engagement of the ICRC in the field outside Europe. On the other hand, the most important activities during the Second World war, like the protection of prisoners and medical assistance, diminished, so that their administration was broken up. The Central Tracing Agency, which continued to be absorbed by the sequels to the world conflict, had as yet been poorly integrated into the new activities.

Let us note, finally, that the Personnel Management Service and the Treasury Service were fused.

The second period of profound transformation took place as a result of the reevaluation of the organization subsequent to the Nigerian action, from 1970 to 1974.

The most important decision of 1970 was to regroup the support services which participated in external activities in an Operations Department. In addition to geographic sectors, now called "zones of intervention", the Delegations and Relief Services as well as the CTA and the Medical Service were integrated into it.[7]

The Division of External Affairs is dissolved. The Administration and Finance Service as well as the Personnel Service become independent Divisions. A Press and Information Division is created, which answers directly to the President.

But these reforms of 1969-1970 only made up one stage in a succession of attempts at reorganization. The rapid increase in the activities of the ICRC which, beginning in 1967, is present on all the continents and even strongly involved in major conflicts in Vietnam, the Middle East, Nigeria, Bangla-

---

[6] Whereas the geographic sectors were divided into one "European" sector and five distributed over the other continents, the CTA included three European sectors and one for "current conflicts".

[7] The Delegations Service is entrusted with new tasks. The Relief Service is named Logistics Division. The Nurses' and Invalids' Service disappears. The Medical Service is directed by a "Medical Advisor", who assists the Director of Operations.

desh, poses problems of conduct and coordination of operations at all levels of the administration.

Beginning in 1974, the "executive branch" of the institution was divided among five Directors who together make up the Directorate and three Sector Chiefs (the Chief Medical Officer, the Delegate to International Organizations and the Chief of the Press and Information Division). These eight persons constitute the enlarged management group.

This new structure confirms the evolution begun in 1970. The increase in activities entails an increase in responsibilities for each activity sector and, therefore, a diversification of its functions.[8] This tendency continues to develop itself within the Operations Department and the CTA. Within Operations a Medical Division (1977) and a Detainees Service (1978) are created, the Logistics Division once again becomes the Relief Division (1975) and the Telecommunications Service, made a part of the Logistics Division in 1970, is directly responsible to the Director of Operations. The CTA has since 1978 been in the process of restructuring. In 1982, the system of the enlarged management group was abandoned in favor of a system of only three Directors (Operational Affairs, General Affairs, Administrative Affairs).

In the analysis of structural modifications, we have placed the accent on operational services; for they are the ones which are most immediately influenced by the development of activities in the field. It is clear, nonetheless, that the support system which must follow had to make a considerable effort at adaptation.

The Department of Principles and Law also underwent important transformations in the 1970s.

The analysis of expenses shows that, during the year 1970, their volume for the Legal Department and for the Delegation to International Organizations doubled, and quadrupled for the Press and Information Division.[9] It is nonetheless interesting to note, reading the Table, that the activities of the Legal Department represent a greater percentage of the ordinary budget during the years 1964-1969 than in following years, even though beginning in 1971, the Department's budget increased considerably. The phenomenon may be explained by the overall increase of the ordinary budget most of which was spent on operations.

The Legal Affairs Division was very important from 1945 to 1950 (preparation of the voluminous reports on the activities of the ICRC during the Second World war and preparation of the Diplomatic Conference).

---

[8] In organizational Charts prior to 1974, staff members could have several activities. The most striking example: in the 1970 Chart, Miss P. Tombet was simultaneously chief of the CTA and Secretary to the President! The Chart which covered the period up to 1969 shows several similar cases.

[9] *Cf.* MODOUX, Alain, "Les problèmes du Comité international de la Croix-Rouge en matière de relations publiques", *IRRC*, Vol. 60, 1983, pp. 307-317.

20. Expenditures of the Department of Principles and Law 1964-1980

(Nominal Value, Thousands of Sw. Frs.)

Dept of Law	Press & Info.		Dels. to I.O.s	*ICRC* Review	Total[20]	% of Ord. Budget
1964	937				937	21
1965	1 447				1 447	28
1966	1 371				1 371	29
1967	1 026				1 026	20
1968	1 165				1 165	19
1969	1 562				1 562	22
1970	1 584	505			2 089	13
1971	2 144	608			2 752	16
1972	2 278	914			3 192	17
1973	2 360	938			3 298	17
1974	2 020	631	204		2 855	14
1975	2 097	753	242		3 092	15
1976	2 468	987	259		3 714	18
1977	2 229	1 001	261	377	3 868	17
1978	2 535	1 191	202	268	4 196	17
1979	3 320	1 487	236	225	5 268	17
1980	3 545	1 971	408	248	6 172	17

[20] The total includes expenses for activities which, from Jan. 1 1982, depends on the Director of General Affairs.

21.1. ICRC Chart – 1949

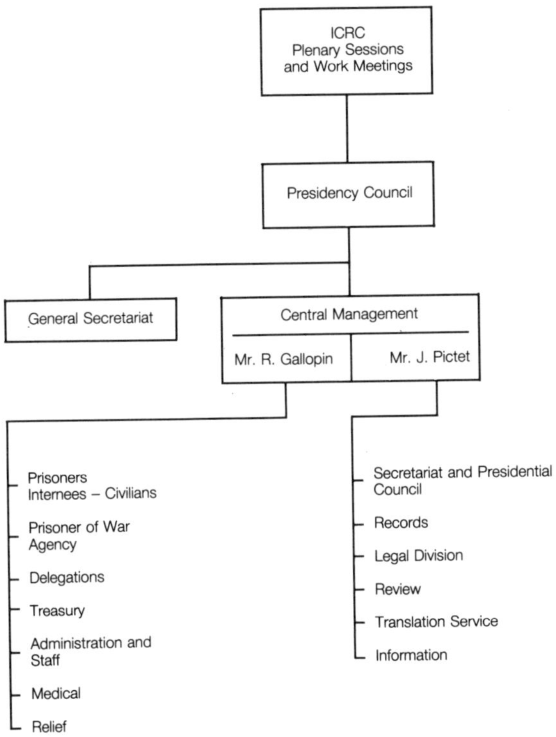

21.2. ICRC Chart – 1969

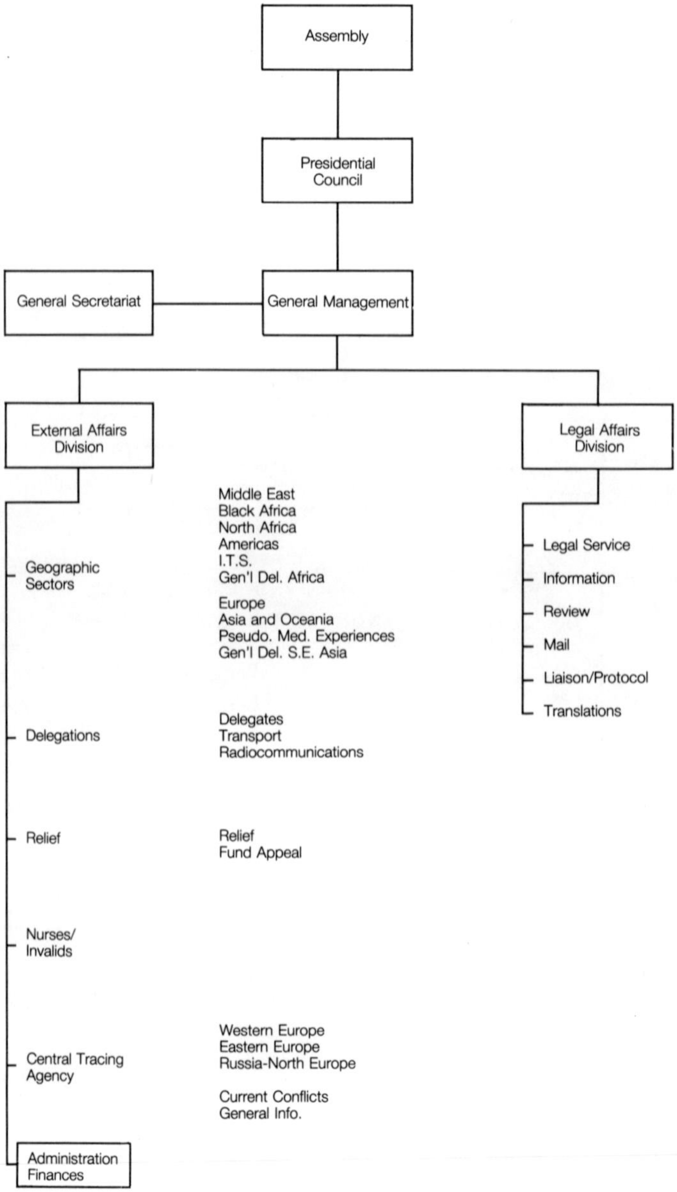

21.3. ICRC Chart – 1970

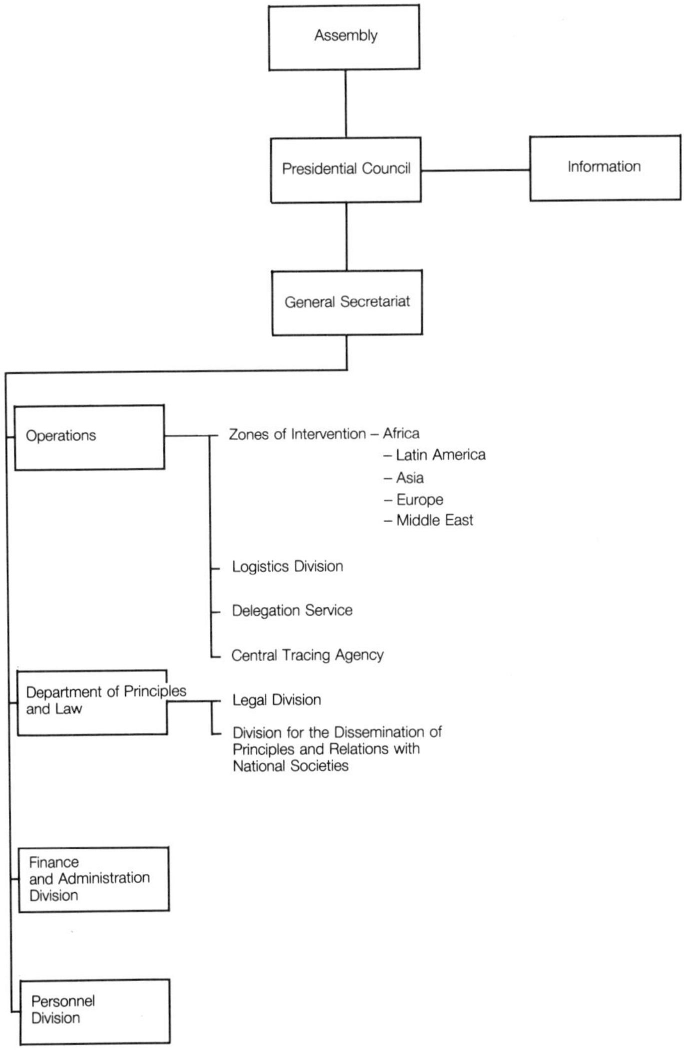

21.4. ICRC Chart – 1980

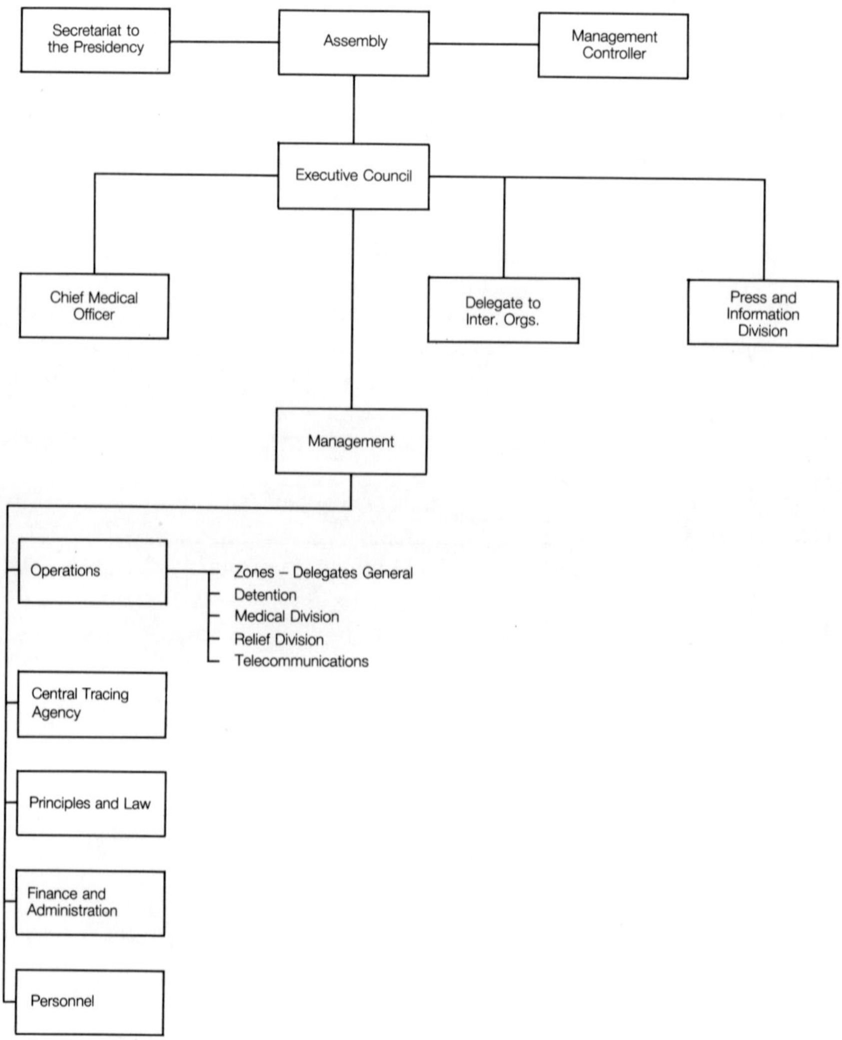

4.2. The Question of Personnel (Tables 22, 23)

4.2.1. Evolution of Personnel

a) Overall Evolution

At the close of the Second World war, the institution had about 3700 employees: 1 900 were remunerated and 1 800 volunteers (March 1945). In December 1950, after the reorganization, there were only 360 left, among whom 50 or so were paid. The decrease in the number of unpaid persons in the post-war period is greater, but paid personnel are also strongly reduced, five out of six paid personnel leave the institution.

The reduction in staff is mainly due to the decrease in activities felt after July 1947.

As of that date, the resources of the International Committee, which had, from the end of hostilities, expressed its desire to cut back on its activities, are trimmed. This is the beginning of a period of serious financial difficulties for the ICRC (see Chapter 6). It is the main reason, in our opinion, for the second phase of staff reduction which took place after reorganization. Between 1949 and 1960, remunerated staff decreases by 50%.

The Six Day war and especially the Nigerian conflict forced the institution to undertake new commitments beginning in 1967.

During the 1970s, the level is 50% higher than during the 1960s. As from 1978–development of services to respond to the development of activities–numbers increase by a relatively significant proportion. But it is not until 1979 that the ICRC has as many employees at headquarters as in 1949! At the present time, the tendency is for a continued rise.

b) Volunteer Collaborators

During the Second World war, as during the First, the ICRC asked for the aid of unpaid collaborators. Throughout the period, the number of unpaid collaborators exceeds that of paid employees, but it diminishes, in absolute as well as relative terms, beginning in 1941, which indicates that, for technical as well as personnel reasons, the ICRC progressively moved in the direction of professionalization. In terms of work hours furnished, the paid employees outclassed unpaid ones since the latter worked an average of 12 hours per week.[10] Up until 1945, almost all the volunteer collaborators worked either in Geneva, or in one of the 24 "auxiliary sections" which had been created in other Swiss towns. After the war and during the 1950s, most volunteers were abroad, their number remaining constant in absolute terms.

[10] Nobs, Marguerite. *Les collaborateurs bénévoles du CICR*. Geneva, ICRC, 1954, p. 4.

But in relation to paid personnel abroad, their number was two to three times higher. Their job, nonetheless, was usually honorific and limited to that of an "ICRC correspondent abroad".[11] Since the ICRC had delegates everywhere in the world[12] and very few operations, one may deduce that the majority of benevolent delegates did not participate directly in them. Since the 1960s, the ICRC, with rare exceptions in the field, no longer calls upon volunteer personnel.

c) Proportion of Collaborators at Headquarters and in the Field.

During the Second World war, the ICRC "covered" the field from headquarters. It had only a few permanent delegations, with very few delegates (a few dozen, or 1% of the total).

During the 1950s, the proportion of remunerated delegates in the field in relation to collaborators at headquarters was between 5% and 10%. It was only 12% in 1956, the year of the (simultaneous!) actions related to Hungary and Suez.

It rises beginning in the 1960s, as a result of the increase in operations. In Africa, the Congolese intervention represents the first major medical action of the post-war period. Throughout the Mediterranean basin, the ICRC is called upon to intervene: in Algeria during and after the war and in Yemen where, excepting protection missions, it has to take charge of a field hospital, in Greece and in Cyprus. It also had to send people to Vietnam and Laos, which represent a heavy load for a number of years. The increasing number of delegates in the field for the period 1960-1966 is still low in relation to headquarters staff.

This suddenly changes in 1967 upon the resurgence of the war between Israel and the Arab countries. The protection of persons in territories occupied by Israel requires a permanent presence. It is likewise in this period that the war in Nigeria takes place, which will force the ICRC to mobilize its new forces,[13] if only to provide direction for temporary collaborators who strengthened the staff of the Geneva central administration and worked in the field.

In 1972, finally, the Bangladesh crisis erupts.[14]

It is therefore not surprising to find that the proportion of people permanently employed in the field progressively rises to more than a third of

[11] *AR*, 1949, pp. 13 ff. The Table does not differentiate between unpaid and paid delegates.

[12] In 1949, the ICRC had a "network of representation" including delegates in 35 countries.

[13] 433 expatriate collaborators at the highpoint of the action (October 1968). This figure includes medical personnel and technicians.

[14] 128 expatriate collaborators in April 1972.

the total number of permanent collaborators of the ICRC. This is just an estimation, given the intensity of movement between Geneva and the various operational theaters. It is clear that headquarters had to follow with sustained attention the operations which were taking place in the field. It can be imagined that in a period of crisis, written reports, telegrams and radio are no longer enough, all the more so since, given the legal and political obstacles raised to communicating in code, it was almost impossible to preserve the secrecy of operations. This is why the missions from headquarters increased considerably. The difficulty in communicating likewise posed a delicate problem: that of the place of residence of the Delegate General for a given zone. Should he install his offices at the center of his zone and go to Geneva to report at regular intervals? Or should he reside in Geneva, from where he will tour his zone? Opinions are divided within the Committee and Management. If the final decision was to regroup the Delegates General in Geneva, it is probably because that city offered the best basis for the "manœuvre of the neutral party" who overcomes political obstacles to his freedom of movement and reaches whomever he wants by various means. So many capitals, even those prossessing good aerial communications, become guarded camps the minute a crisis erupts.

4.2.2. Recruitment

In a world which oscillates between war and peace, in a state of tension which degenerates into acts of violence, the ICRC is permanently mobilized. The very mission which it must assume, and with which the international community has progressively charged it, oblige it to maintain its capability so as rapidly to undertake an action which may suddenly be required.

But its financial means in the 1950s and 1960s did not permit it permanently to hire a significant number of delegates. It therefore moved to build up a reserve of delegates mobilizable at short notice.

After the post-war demobilization, the resurgence of tensions posed the problem with a new urgency. The question was then asked whether it was possible to create that reserve of persons. The Red Cross Movement could of course furnish contingents, but certain activities could only be carried out by Swiss collaborators, because the nature of a conflict, and the attitude of the parties obliged the ICRC to act in this way.

The 1962 Cuban crisis caused the Committee to go from reflection to action. The eventuality had to be faced once again of creating a high level action group, since what was involved was a particularly delicate control mission.

The Committee was finally not called upon to intervene, but the warning was heard. And at the initiative of the ICRC's President, the GIM (Group for International Missions) was created in 1963 in Bern.[15]

The GIM was to know rapid success. Two years after its creation, 110 members were ready to leave at any moment. The ICRC thus had permanent non-financed personnel at its disposal.

History shows, however, that the ICRC only hired on average 20% of available persons.[16] There was therefore a gap between the GIM's offer and the ICRC's demand, at a very time when, particularly after 1967, it felt an urgent need for delegates. This can be explained by the reticence of certain ICRC leaders to use what was a good working instrument, costing practically nothing. Among the people in question, some of whom were highly qualified experts and sometimes younger delegates, relations were not always easy. The brevity of the engagement and insufficient training[17] in humanitarian action of GIM members also played a role. Carrying out activities with persons available for only two months resulted in too many inconveniences.[18] That was surely one of the difficulties which the ICRC faced in its Nigerian action. To the very extent to which a crisis was prolonged and political pressures on the ICRC increased, the rotation of support teams complicated the conduct of operations. But the Nigerian conflict not only challenged the GIM formula, it often cruelly underlined the insufficiency of moral and intellectual training of the many delegates who had to be engaged in the field for humanitarian tasks, without its even having been possible to give them the most elementary training. This is one of the reasons why the Committee decided to entrust the Delegations Service with the new task of training future delegates.

Since 1970, the "Cartigny courses" (lasting 3, then 5 days) are organized two to five times a year, according to need, for the delegate-candidates who have first been selected on the basis of their record and several interviews.[19] The courses provide information on the ICRC's activities and are a final selection process for candidates.

---

[15] The group was to recruit persons (in the universities, the army, industry and administration) who would commit themselves to be "available on alert" (*Historique succinct des GMI*, Bern, GIM, 1980, p. 1.), that is to say vaccinated and ready to leave from one day to the next. The duration of missions would not exceed eight weeks. Persons thus recruited were committed for a period of two years.

[16] *Cf.* Table 23.

[17] "Instruction courses" took place from 1964 to 1966 and from 1969 to 1971 for GIM members. Those courses, lasting from one to two-and-a-half days, generally given at headquarters, mainly dealt with technical aspects (medical, transmission) of missions.

[18] Short missions are appropriate mainly for medical and technical personnel, because they are immediately operational. It is therefore not by chance that most GIM members having gone on mission for the ICRC belonged to the medical corps.

[19] Beginning in 1972, the GIM members were included.

Successful candidates, within a fairly brief but undetermined period, were offered missions whose average was six months. Mission contracts were renewable, but no basic contract tied the institution and the delegate beyond that period. It was therefore, as for the GIM, a "seasonal" system, where the employee-delegate was totally free and bore all the economic risk. For the latter reason, a number of delegates did not remain after a few missions. The financial advantages of the "seasonal" system to the ICRC therefore had the drawback of a constant loss of experienced persons.

With the development of activities–experienced delegates were cruelly missing–the ICRC decided in 1974 to employ the services of approximately thirty for a period of five years. That number quickly proved insufficient. In 1978, the institution resolutely decided to brush aside its "fear of peace". Since that year, candidates selected at the end of the Cartigny course are immediately offered one-year work contracts. At the end of this period, a five-year contract is offered in case of "mutual satisfaction".

Complementary training courses for staff (three times one week) which the ICRC has organized since 1980 are to make it possible to respond to the urgent need for medium- and upper-level employees caused by the expansion of activities.

Preliminary Remarks to Table 22

1) Definitions/Notions

OPERATIONS (O): includes everything involving operations proper, from executive management and Secretariat through geographic sectors, logistics and relief.

SUPPORT (S): includes everything involving administrative and financial affairs, questions of personnel and maintenance, the legal sector , support for operations proper as well as ICRC advisers and their Secretariat.

AGENCY (A): includes everything involving agency and tracing activities. It does *not* include Swiss auxiliary section personnel.

22. Evolution of ICRC Staff Remunerated Personnel Unpaid

Date		Headquarters			Field		Total	(of which,
		O	S	A	Total	Total		in the field)
1949	1.1.	–	–	–	315	35	60	–
1950	–	–	–	–	–	–	45	(38)
1951	1.1.	40	163	40	243	47	52	(38)
1952	1.1.	42	160	39	241	10	58	(34)
1953	1.1.	42	148	36	226	11	47	(30)
1954	1.6.	37	130	30	197	–	53	(37)
1955	1.11.	34	115	26	175	10	51	(?)
1956	1.1.	30	120	23	173	18	45	(30)
1957	–	–	–	–	–	–	50	(30)
1958	1.1.	19	104	47	170	–	43	(31)
1959	1.1.	21	102	42	165	37	?	(?)
1960	1.5.	17	100	41	158	–	etc.	
1961	1.6.	18	113	39	170	–		
1962	15.5.	23	121	36	180	49		
1963	–	–	–	–	–	–		
1964	1.5.	22	128	40	190	–		
1965	1.3.	21	134	38	193	–		
1966	31.1.	18	127	33	178	–		
1967	31.1.	18	105	23	146	78		
1968	4.3.	39	133	25	197	–[1]		
1969	1.12.	42	128	26	196	–		
1970	31.12.	58	136	28	222	46		
1971	31.12.	68	141	26	235	65		
1972	(average)	73	140	26	239	87[2]		
1973	”	62	142	35	239	111		
1974	”	44	144	40	228	125		
1975	”	54	149	35	238	85		
1976	”	56	151	34	241	77		
1977	”	61	153	38	252	89		
1978	”	70	146	41	257	97		
1979	”	99	153	61	313	150		
1980	”	114	189	81	384	262[3]		
1981	”	98	218	93	409	270		

Sources: Internal Documents of the ICRC
O: cf. p. 196
S: cf. p. 196
A: cf. p. 196

[1] Nigeria Action Total, cf. p. 190
[2] Bangladesh Action Total, cf. p. 190, note
[3] Medical Personnel *Not* Included (442 in Jan., 209 in Dec.)

23. Group for International Missions (GIM)

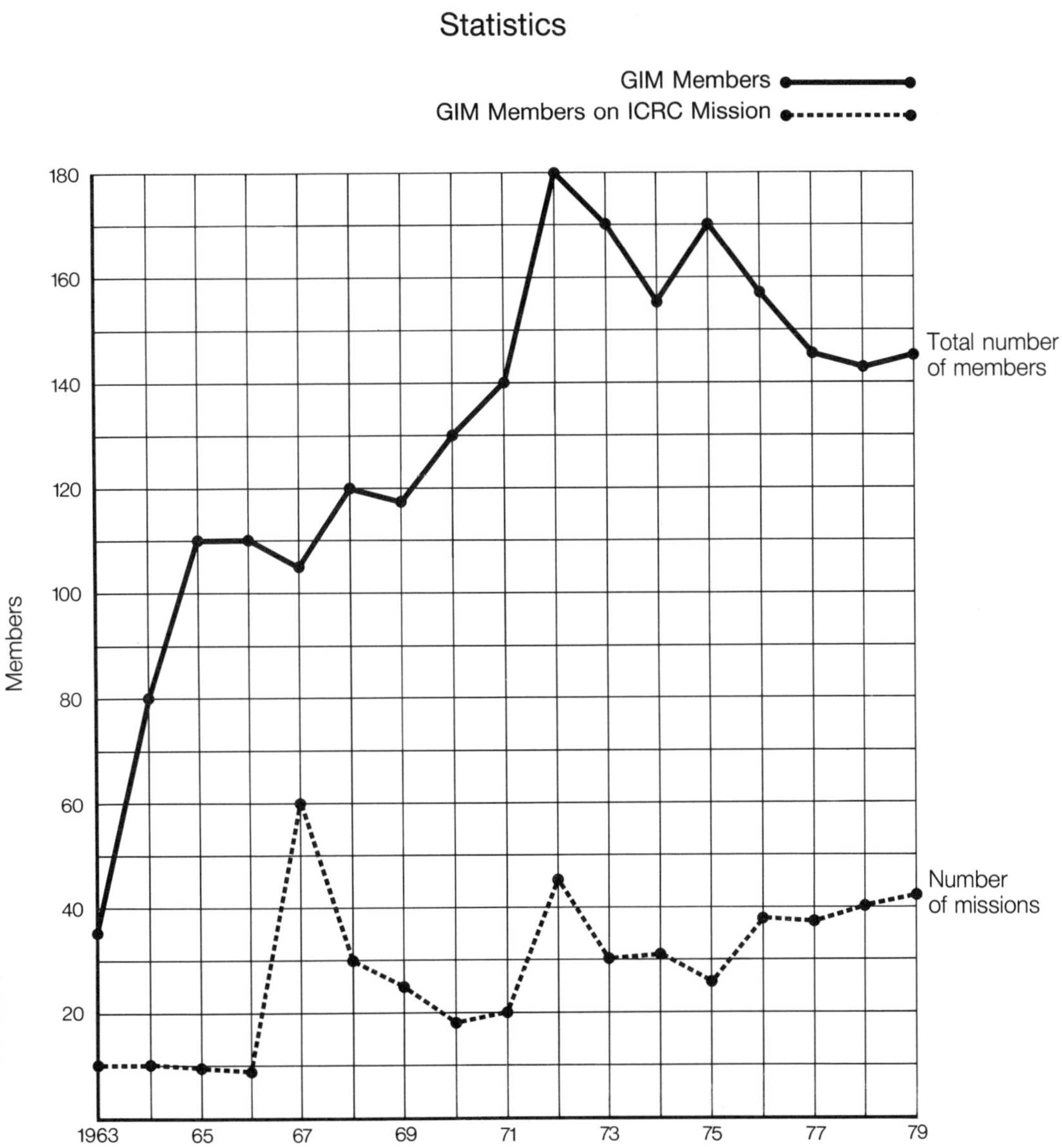

Source: GIM, internal document

CHAPTER 5

Relations with the League

5.1. 1919-1952

5.1.1. *Creation of the League*

Before going into the question of joint actions and the distribution of tasks foreseen for such occasions, we must briefly describe how the two organisms fit into the International Red Cross Movement (IRC). Through the creation of the League (May 5, 1919), the IRC Movement suddenly found itself endowed with two centralizing organs. This automatically led to a problem of responsibilities which only found a first solution after ten years, for the founders of the League had not clearly delimited its aims. Perhaps they thought it should be substituted for the Committee through the latter's integration into a sort of "Society of National Red Cross Societies"[1]

Despite frequent contacts[2] between the ICRC and the founding members of the League, the latter was created at a time when a disagreement with the ICRC subsisted over certain fundamental points. The Committee did not oppose the idea of an association of National Societies. The ICRC could not, however, accept that the League refuses to admit certain National Societies of the defeated nations of the First World war, at a time when they had already been recognized.[3] It was not until the decision of the second session of the League General Council (March 28, 1922) to admit any National Society recognized by the ICRC that the universality of the IRC Movement was reestablished.

But the question of the IRC's organization remained entirely open. At the outset, the League wanted nothing less than *fusion* with the ICRC. The 11th International Conference (Geneva, 1923) appointed a Commission charged with studying the "international organization of the Red Cross".[4] In

[1] It is not by chance that the League of Nations and the League of Red Cross Societies were founded the same year, and both on American initiative.

[2] DURAND 2, *Histoire du Comité*, pp. 119-129.

[3] *Ibid.*, p. 143.

[4] DUNNING, H.W. *Eléments pour l'histoire de la Ligue des Sociétés de la Croix-Rouge*. Geneva, League, 1969, p. 39. *Cf.* also DURAND 2, *op. cit.*, p. 150 ff.

the Commission, the League's conception found itself in a minority (it was defended by representatives of the League and by American and British Red Cross Societies). Despite that negative vote the League's Council of Governors did not follow the Commission and maintained its position[5] at its Paris meeting of June 22, 1925.

After numerous "diplomatic" turns, the ICRC and the League were able to settle the capital question of the organization of the IRC. Together they drafted[6] Statutes which were adopted by the 13th International Red Cross Conference at The Hague in 1928.

5.1.2. The Statutes of the International Red Cross, 1928 and 1952.

The 1928 Statutes maintain existing IRC organs: the International Conference and the Council of Delegates, and somewhat specify their areas of competence. They institute a third organ, the Permanent Commission, made up of nine members.[7] In its initial conception, the Commission was to act as an arbiter. It was to decide in cases of disagreements concerning the interpretation and the application of the IRC Statutes, as well as disagreements between the ICRC and the League. In practice, arbitration was never exercised.

By decision of the 17th International Conference in Stockholm in 1948 (Resolution 13),[8] the Permanent Commission was charged with ensuring the coordination and harmonization of the efforts of the ICRC and the League. In its quality as coordinator, it was to press the ICRC and the League to conclude an accord. Finally, the Commission was charged with the organization of International Red Cross Conferences.

The IRC Statutes also defined the areas of competence of the ICRC and the League. A comparative reading of relevant articles[9] demonstrates that the definition of the ICRC and its responsibilities has hardly changed. But the definition of the Leagne has been changed fundamentaly[10] and its objectives have been formulated more explicitly, whereas the 1928 Statutes only make indirect reference to them.

---

[5] *Ibid.*, p. 44 ff.

[6] Notably Max Huber, President of the ICRC since 1928 (whose nomination had a positive effect) and Col. von Draudt of the German Red Cross, Vice President of the League.

[7] Five members appointed by the International Conference, two representatives of the ICRC and two of the League.

[8] The wording of this resolution was included in the IRC Statutes at the 1952 revision; *cf.* PERRUCHOUD, *Les résolutions des Conférences*, p. 65.

[9] ICRC: Art. VII (1928), VI (1952); League: Art. VIII (1928), VII(1952), in *Handbook of the IRC*, 1971.

[10] Defined in 1928 as *an* Association of several National Societies, the League has become in 1952 *the* International Federation of *the* National Societies.

There is a strong nuance, however, in the formulation of articles concerning the ICRC. The 1928 formulation demonstrates the concern of the ICRC with asserting itself in the face of any challenge and with defending the traditional tasks pertaining to its responsibilities.[11] The 1952 revision removes from the previous formulation its defensive accent and replaces it with a much stronger formula: affirmation pure and simple.[12] In the meantime, the two Red Cross institutions had time to assert themselves, to get to know one another and to collaborate.

As concerns collaboration between the ICRC and the League, whose bases are defined in Article 9 (1928), an important point deserves to be raised. This Article specifies that the institutions collaborate particularly in assistance efforts in cases of national or international calamities.

Here, as in Article 7, the ICRC insists on its will to act also in peacetime (Art. 7)[13].

There was a single revision in more than fifty years: the IRC Statutes form legal framework both firm enough to guarantee the stability of the IRC organization and flexible enough so that the two organizations can adapt to change.

5.1.3. Successive Accords Between the ICRC and the League

The 1928 and 1952 Statutes call for "collaboration" and then "coordination" of activities among the two organisms, but they were careful not to delimit expressely the area of collaboration or to issue directives. They thus left it up to the ICRC and the League to reach agreement concerning their "humanitarian activities" there where the division of responsibilities was not established by the Statutes, and particularly in the area of assistance.

Before even having settled the controversial problem of the organization of the IRC, the ICRC and the League had, in a spirit of pragmatism, concluded a preliminary "working agreement" (February 4, 1921) instituting a Mixed Commission (composed of three members from each institution) whose main task was the "coordination of relief in *times of peace*").[14]

"As for times of war, the ICRC preserved its traditional responsibilities, whereas responsibility for relief in case of catastrophe in such circumstances belonged, either to the Mixed Commission, or, provided that it should agree, to the ICRC alone".[15]

---

[11] It is thus repeated that the ICRC "remains" what it is and "continues" to act. Once, reference is even made to the ICRC's "exclusive domain".

[12] The ICRC "remains", "maintains", "assumes", etc...

[13] Ever since the creation of the League, the ICRC has asserted that will. *Cf.* DURAND 2, *op. cit.*, p. 137.

[14] DURAND 2, *op. cit.*, p. 138; *cf.* also DUNNING, *Eléments pour l'histoire de la Ligue,* p. 33.

[15] DURAND 2, *op. cit.*, p. 138.

The agreement provided for a division of responsibilities which entrusted the ICRC with negociations with governments and with the League of Nations and the League with the coordination of the efforts of National Societies. Actions in cases of catastrophes would be undertaken, either by the ICRC, or by the League under the direction and control of the Mixed Commission. The Mixed Commission initiated two major actions. In 1921, it appointed an "International Commission for Relief to Russia".[16]

The second action was undertaken directly by the Mixed Commission itself, following the earthquakes in Japan which, on September 1, 1923, caused 200 000 deaths and millions of homeless. The Mixed Commission was able to assemble donations totalling 277.3 million Swiss francs.[17]

Despite the effectiveness of the Mixed Commission, the working agreement was abrogated by the League, September 1, 1926.[18] The reason for the abrogation is not to be sought in any disagreement within the Mixed Commission, but in deep differences between the ICRC and the League on the question of the organization of the IRC. 1925 is the year of the failure of the "Study Commission"[19] entrusted with finding a solution to this problem, and also the year of the 13th International Conference called by the ICRC against the will of the League.

As of 1926, the League undertook its "first independent relief action"[20] and organized, thereafter, at least fifteen relief actions in favor of victims.[21] Following their "reconciliation" in 1928, however, the ICRC and the League worked out a draft agreement (March 1929) "concerning their joint relief actions and their relations with the International Relief Union"[22] but it foresaw only the issuing of joint appeals.[23] The two first joint appeals were to be issued in December 1938, in favor of Spanish and Czech refugees.[24]

The League and the ICRC *de facto* divided up the area of assistance, the former acting in case of catastrophes, the latter in case of conflicts, without

[16] This Commission organized significant assistance for the Russian people suffering from famine caused by the years of civil war. The Commission stood out at the time as a "leader in the area of international relief" (*Ibid.*, p. 176).

[17] *1919-1963, 1963-1969. Grandes dates de l'histoire de la Ligue des Sociétés de la Croix-Rouge.* Geneva, League, no date, year 1923.

[18] DUNNING, *op. cit.*, p. 45.

[19] *Ibid.*, p. 44.

[20] In favor of Greek and Turkish refugees in Bulgaria. *Grandes dates,* 1926-1927.

[21] *Grandes dates,* 1930-1933.

[22] DUNNING, *op. cit.*, p. 51. Concerning the Union, *cf.* PERRUCHOUD, *Les résolutions des Conférences,* pp. 247-249. The Union, a rather ineffective organism, "recognized the preponderant role of the International Red Cross in matters of assistance". The ICRC and the League, which belonged to several organs of the Union, withdrew in 1948 (*Manuel,* 1971, p. 501).

[23] *Cf.* Doc. 24 bis, p. 4, 14th Conference, Brussels, 1930.

[24] *Grandes dates,* 1938. Durand, however, only speaks of appeals issued by the ICRC concerning Spanish refugees (p. 271).

this division of labor being formalized in the IRC Statutes and without there having been any formal agreement between the two institutions. The Spanish Civil war was therefore the first relief action in a conflict in which the ICRC "coordinated with the League".[25] The League assisted the ICRC in its efforts by taking charge of the purchase of relief materials and by obtaining facilities for the expedition of equipment to Spain.[26] Coordination of the action, distribution and control remained entirely in the hands of the ICRC.

During the Second World war, the ICRC and the League were to create the "Mixed Relief Commission"[27]–made up of two members of each organism and one "neutral" person–whose statutes were adopted July 23 1941.[28] The task of the Mixed Relief Commission consisted in the organization of relief actions "which need to be given to an organism distinct from the ICRC and the League, in favor of civilian populations–more specially women and children–victims of the war".[29]

The Mixed Relief Commission was dissolved in 1946,[30] as soon as other more powerful organizations created in order to provide relief to civilian populations (Allied governments, UNRWA, etc.) had been put or were about to be put into place.

5.2. 1952-1980

Here too, once the Second World war had ended, the question of principle, present since the League's creation in 1919, was raised: does a uninational humanitarian organization such as the ICRC still have its place in a world whose multinational vocation is even more clearly affirmed by the new system of collective security embodied in the UN? Should it not effect a simple transfer of responsibilities to the League and consider its historic mission as accomplished, its role as ended?

Once again, the answer to this rhetorical question of its survival is given: the ICRC continues to have its role to play, an essential one, alongside other organs of the Red Cross Movement, and in particular the League. It is, in fact, precisely its uninationality which guarantees its indispensable neutrality, in an era of the increased politicization of the international system and its division into rival blocks. Once this general answer had been given, the

[25] DURAND 2, p. 271.

[26] DUNNING, *op. cit.*, p. 56.

[27] In November 1940. *Grandes dates*, 1940.

[28] According to DUNNING (p. 61), the Commission's Statutes are based on Article 9 of the IRC Statutes (1928).

[29] The Commission's Statutes (DURAND 2, p. 403).

[30] On October 31. *Ibid.*, p. 558.

problem was to be that of a clearer distribution of roles, and, mainly, of an effective coordination of activities among the two organizations.

As for coordination, its bases are laid down by the existence of the Permanent Commission and by the International Red Cross Conference which in principle takes place every four years. In addition, the two organizations produce reports which depending on the theme, may be separate or joint, and which are intended to increase transparency and narrow differences.

It is, of course, during the period between International Conference that the need for ensuring coordination in the theoretical, but especially practical, field, is most problematic.

Conscious of the survival of a certain ambiguity in the respective attributions of the two organisms, despite the principles set down in the Red Cross Statutes (Art. 6 for the ICRC and 7 for the League), the League and the ICRC concluded the agreement of December 8, 1951.[31]

By this agreement, the ICRC and the League attempted to harmonize their respective activities in cases where they might be carried out simultaneously. They likewise attempted, in their relations with the National Red Cross Societies, to avoid overlapping work and confusion.

The agreement essentially deals with relief, the domain where both organizations are implicated. But Article 3 stipulates that actions in favor of refugees and legal assistance to them are the responsibility of the ICRC and the League, and notes that "where the two institutions are equally competent, they shall agree as to which of them shall assume the direction and execution of a specific operation"[32], something which is not specified for all of their common activities, but which is understood given the reference to the need to study potential problems "by joint agreement, taking into account the situation and, where necessary, the particular character conferred upon the International Committee by its right of initiative confirmed by the Geneva Conventions".[33]

The 1951 agreement, as a whole, attempts to single out the underlying particularities of each of the two institutions even in those cases where their activities would be similar or overlap. Thus the dominant characteristic of the ICRC, particularly for relief which it can deliver in case of conflict, is and remains its neutrality, which defines its responsibilities where that quality is essential (Art. I.A.1., I.A.3., I.A.4.); whereas the League is the privileged partner of the National Societies which compose it, and, for this very reason, "qualified to ensure the coordination of relief operations undertaken as the result of an appeal addressed by it to the National Societies on behalf of one of their sister Societies" (Art. I.A.2.).

---

[31] *Handbook of the International Red Cross*, Geneva, 1953, Annex 9, pp. 610-615.

[32] *Op. cit.*, p. 613.

[33] *Ibid.*, p. 611.

Protection remains the responsibility of the ICRC (Art. V) and it also preserves responsibility for making legal pronouncements, interpreting the Geneva Conventions and establishing agreements and analogous documents (Art. VI).

Clearly, previous experiences in the field and, in particular, certain difficulties which had been encountered, dictated the tone of the accord which attempts better to delineate responsibilities but most of all to call in all cases for conciliation, which is in the fundamental interests of the victims.

5.2.1. Joint, Concerted and Parallel Actions

The difficulties in question were due to the rise of National Societies and to their role in the more active policy of the League.

This had led to a certain rivalry between the ICRC and the League, the latter demanding a more important role in activities in favor of victims, especially in cases of internal conflicts.

In Palestine, for example, the League and the ICRC had launched a simultaneous, but not joint, action. Upon the request of the UN and with its financial support, the two organizations as well as the American Friends Service Committee, had agreed on a geographic distribution of their relief efforts, the League taking charge of refugees in Transjordan, Iraq, Syria and Lebanon, whereas the ICRC did the same in Israel and the West Bank of the Jordan, and the American Friends Service Committee in the Ghaza strip. This approach was a simultaneous one, but coordinated only thanks to its overall sponsorship by the UN. Without the generosity of the latter's financing, difficulties could have appeared.

The Korean war and the rather fruitless efforts of the two organizations in favor of its refugees and prisoners, is another example of a separate approach, whereas the possibility of carrying out a joint action is illustrated by the repatriation, in 1949-1950, of Greek children residing in various countries due to the Civil war.

It was, as we have stated, practical experience which led the two organizations to recognize the need for codification, of which the aforementioned 1951 agreement is a first formulation. Later on, coordinated actions were to be more numerous as well as concerted actions and, from 1970, truly joint actions.

The action in 1956 in favor of Hungarian refugees was a concerted one. Its execution partakes of the same principle as the 1949-1950 Palestine action, with a distribution of responsibilities among the two organizations according to geographic criteria, the ICRC being active in Hungary itself, and the League taking charge of refugees in neighbouring countries, Austria and Yugoslavia.

During the Algerian war, and especially between 1957 and 1963, the respective actions of the ICRC and the League were partially concerted, the

ICRC becoming involved in Algeria and the League taking care of refugees in Morocco and Tunisia, according the distribution of tasks which had become habitual.

But the experiences of the 1960s, in particular those of Vietnam[34] and Nigeria, which were long and complex conflicts, convinced the Committee and the leadership of the League that yet more precise codification of their relations in the field was necessary. Once again, it was especially in the area of relief distribution that problems arose.

Whereas the mission of protection is entirely in the domain of the ICRC, whereas circumstances have meant that in case of conflict the ICRC cannot divest itself of relief distribution, the League has nonetheless a role to play, if only as mobilizer of resources. It was therefore essential to specify the distribution of tasks.

It was also impossible to ignore the fact that the National Societies, particularly the Nordic Societies, tended to intervene with the League Secretariat to galvanize it if necessary. If they desired to do more in case of conflict, it was because they were in turn subjected to the pressure of their supporters, who called them to account.

Tensions between the ICRC and the League therefore rose. They were to be all the greater during the Nigerian conflict, in that the Red Cross Movement as a whole felt "threatened" by the competition of numerous charitable agencies and the Churches, which had engaged themselves demonstratively and passionately in what had at a certain moment become a battle between "humanitarians in search of victims". The ICRC was able to impose itself for awhile as the coordinator of the Red Cross action and of the charitable agencies–a coordination which was ensured thanks to specific organs–due to the openness of spirit of some who, a the League and in the National Societies, accepted to serve as members of a team.[35] With the Churches, on the other hand, that is to say with some of their activist chiefs, there was not any agreement, and this had regrettable results in terms of the cause being defended.

The problems resulting from the Vietnam and Nigerian wars therefore imposed the negotiation of a new accord signed April 25, 1969. In order to avoid any ambiguity, it was stipulated from the outset that the ICRC "shall assume the general direction of the Red Cross international action" in case of conflict (Art. 2). The 1951 agreement had only indicated that it was the duty of the League to "get in touch with the International Committee of the Red Cross in order to make sure that its relief operation is in no way, prejudicial to the primary, specifically neutral, role incumbent on the

---

[34] Where the ICRC had been eliminated from relief actions and replaced by the South Vietnamese and American Red Crosses as well as the League. *Cf.* FREYMOND, *Guerres, révolutions, Croix-Rouge*, pp. 151-152.

[35] *Cf.* the Preface to the *Annual Report* for 1968, concerning coordination by the ICRC.

latter". (Art. I.A.3.). On the other hand, it is stipulated in 1969 that the ICRC may reach agreement "with the League with a view to associating it with the relief action or even handing over to it the entire responsibility" (Art. 2). Reciprocally, in peacetime, it is the League which is to coordinate relief actions, with the proviso that if the intervention of a specifically neutral interlocutor were to become necessary, it would call on the ICRC (Art. 3). So as to be prepared for any contingency, the 1969 agreement calls for the establishment of an organism of coordination for each situation requiring their common intervention, an organism which is to include representatives of the ICRC, the League and the National Societies (Art. 4). The 1969 agreement thus goes into detail in a way which is intended to avoid any disagreement, any ambiguity, any friction (Art. 5 to 7 specify the composition of the organs of coordination, the modalities for launching appeals, and the exact distribution of respective tasks in the field).

The consciousness of the need to maximize the degree of coordination, in the very interest of the victims, led the ICRC and the League in 1973 to draft the document "International Relief Operations", a document which specified some of their respective responsibilities (ratified by the ICRC in 1974). In this document, it is clearly indicated that one of the main motivation of the two parties, but also one of the possible roots of problems, resided in the fact that active participation, at the place of action, in the emotion of the moment, appeared to a certain number of National Societies as a condition for preserving the sympathy of public opinion in their country and, therefore, its financial support, which was in turn the guarantee "of their independence" from their government.[36]

This explains their desire to be present in the field, especially in times of crisis with a strong public impact.

The document shows what are the means for better using the resources of the National Societies, but also the limits which they must not go beyond. It is thus recalled that the ICRC may not delegate the mandates which are expressly granted to it by the Geneva Conventions.[37] But it especially emphasizes that "another lesson to be drawn from recent operations is... the slowing of a united front by the Red Cross in international operations",[38] and that *preparation* and the observation of a few rules are essential, notably the establishment of the coordinating body called for by the 1969 Agreement. Contingency planning is important, so as "to reduce impro-

[36] Note from the League and the ICRC to the National Red Cross Societies, Geneva, 18 September 1974: "Interpretation of the Agreement between the ICRC and the League, of 25 April 1969, for the purpose of specifying some of their respective functions", in *Compendium of Basic Reference Texts*, Geneva, 1983, p. 41.

[37] *Ibid.*, p. 44.

[38] *Ibid.*, p. 45.

visation to the utmost in both integrated and co-ordinated Red Cross operations".[39]

Truly joint actions had in fact taken place since 1969. The first of these, limited in its framework and in its duration, appeared exemplary precisely because of its short duration: an intervention in Jordan, following the events of September 1970. It was directed by a representative of the League, and the two organizations, as well as the National Societies concerned, were able to cooperate properly.

Such was not to be the case during the relief operation launched beginning in 1971 in favor of the new State of Bangladesh. The ICRC and the League became involved separately, the former because of the armed conflict, the other in the wake of floods. Thereafter, during the first months of 1972, they acted in concert. But the ICRC is finally "brutally expelled".[40] This fiasco was to precipitate the drafting of the new document interpreting the 1969 agreement, which we have just quoted.

The drafting of the 1973 document concerning international relief operations was prepared by a series of discussions, for the crisis which had arisen during the action had created an uproar. Neither of the two institutions could allow itself to compromise the authority of the Red Cross Movement by quarrels for prestige. The importance of the problem posed by the conduct of humanitarian action in a turbulent world elicited criticism with respect to the ICRC and the League and even questions which turned into doubt. A strong current of opinion in favor of a reevaluation and reform of the role of the Red Cross took shape. These discussions led, through the so-called "Cannes study", to setting up the Tansley Commission, which the ICRC, as jealous as it may be of its independence and conscious of the particular nature of its mission and status, could not afford not to associate itself. 1972 was to be a key year. In addition to the nearly permanent exchanges between the League Secretariat and the ICRC administration there were discussions at the level of what political scientists call decision-makers: Montreux Conference in April, during which the members of the International Committee were to meet the leaders of the League; the more modest meeting in October in Copenhagen at the initiative of the leaders of the Scandinavian National Red Cross Societies, to examine the international role of the National Societies, their capacity for initiative, their relations with the Committee. It is from this conference, in particular, which the project for joint action in Vietnam was to emerge, a project considered so important and so urgent by the Scandinavian Societies that they would not

---

[39] *Ibid.*

[40] Freymond, *op. cit.*, p. 154.

await the return of the ICRC representatives to Geneva before proposing it.[41]

The most important integrated operation was therefore without any possible doubt the Indochina Operational Group (IOG), established in 1972. "The creation of the IOG must therefore be understood both as an authentic desire to bring aid to populations overwhelmed by war and as a new demonstration that the International Red Cross furnished its own justification to those who support it. Its absence would have been inexcusable."[42] Despite the multiplicity and delicacy of material and political problems, the IOG was successful. It was prolonged until 1975, its direction being at first in the hands of the Director of the Swedish National Society, and then (during IOG–II, from April 1974 to March 1975) of the League's Relief Office. From April 1975 to June 1978, the operation was called INDSEC (Indochine Secours), and the ultimate responsibility was given to the ICRC. Since 1978 and beyond 1980, the liquidation of the program has been underway, and it can only be considered as the greatest success of relief coordination between the various organisms of the Red Cross Movement.

Since the setting up of the IOG and with the exception of this prolonged action in Southeast Asia, there have not been any more important actions jointly undertaken by the League and the ICRC. On the other hand, the 1970s, at least after the experience of Bangladesh and the effort culminating in 1973 clearly to delimit respective responsibilities, were marked by a more harmonious division of labor. The Tansley Report asks that such cooperation be yet reinforced, going so far as to propose that the two organizations locate themselves in the same building. But whether at the summit, the intermediary levels, or in the field, relations are often good.

True, some friction was to occur when the new President of the League took office, resulting from differences in the interpretation and the application of the principle of neutrality. The incidents, for, one would hope, they were mere incidents, will at least have served to remind all the members of the Red Cross Movement that humanitarian policy and diplomacy cannot be conducted without discretion. The good Samaritan does not make speeches, he testifies through action.

---

[41] *Cf.* on this question the letter of October 23 by the President of the Danish Red Cross to the President of the ICRC, which constitutes a report on the Copenhagen meeting of October 17-18. The document as a whole is interesting, but particularly the following passage: "It was mentioned that deficiencies in Red Cross operations have had an adverse effect upon national Red Cross Societies activity in the field of public involvement in the humanitarian field. The importance of the preplanning of operations was stressed by several speakers. The urgent need for preplanning of joint Red Cross operations in Vietnam at the end of hostilities was stressed repeatedly. It was decided to single out this specific matter for immediate action." We shall add that, in November 1972, a new Conference was organized in Stockholm at the initiative of the same Scandinaviens.

[42] *Ibid.*, pp.159-160.

CHAPTER 6

Financial Contributions – Governments and National Societies

In the first part of our study, which was devoted to problems which the evolution of the international system had posed for the ICRC, we devoted a chapter to the increase in the volume of expenditures. In this second part, where we analyze the effects of the evolution of activities on the structure of the institution and its policy, we must examine the measures taken by the ICRC to ensure receipts. This chapter belongs to the second part of the analysis of the financial policy of the ICRC.

6.1. Financing of the Ordinary Budget (Tables 25-28)

The ICRC is an "independent institution" (IRC Statutes, 1969, Art. 6.1), whose principal "assets shall be the contributions of National Red Cross Societies and of Governments, such gifts and bequests as it may receive and the proceeds of the sale of its publications" (ICRC Statutes, 1969, Art. 11.)[1]

Up until the end of the Second World war, the contributions of the National Societies and the governments were made on a strictly voluntary basis. The amount of the contribution and its date varied according to the wishes of National Societies and governments. This system of financing was judged to be "totally inadequate" by the ICRC in 1948.

6.1.1. The Financial Contributions of States

The States in turn reaffirmed their moral commitment during the 1949 Diplomatic Conference by recognizing the need to give the ICRC regular financial support (Resolution 11, Final Act, 1949).[2] By this Resolution, the

---

[1] The governments, cited in second place in the Statutes, are, in fact, the principal sources of ICRC financing.

[2] Whereas the Geneva Conventions require the International Committee of the Red Cross to be ready at all times and in all circumstances to fulfill the humanitarian tasks entrusted to it by these Conventions, the Conference recognizes the necessity of providing regular financial support for the International Committee of the Red Cross. In *International Red Cross Handbook*, 1971, p. 229.

governments therefore recognized that the regular financing of the ICRC concerned all of them.

Important though it was, the Resolution did not provoke any miracles. Governmental contributions (including that of the Swiss government) prior to 1964, covered barely 40% of expenditures and, between 1954 and 1964, those contributions represented hardly any more than half of the *receipts* of the ICRC!

Resolution 13 of the 20th International Conference (Vienna, 1965), clearly blames governments for a major portion of "the constant lack of balance" between the ICRC's resources and needs, since it is "in the first place incumbent on governments... to furnish the ICRC with the financial resources essential to it in the fulfilment of its obligations". The Resolution, similar to Resolution 9b of 1957, issues an "urgent appeal to all Governments of States parties to the Geneva Conventions that they include in their budgets a voluntary annual contribution to the ICRC".

Since then, considerable efforts have been made by governments. Beginning in 1966 they covered more than 50% of the ordinary budget and, after 1971, the percentage of governmental contributions fluctuated between 68% and 84%.

As a result, the ICRC has no longer had major difficulties in balancing its ordinary budget.

The period 1968-1971, however, requires more detailed analysis. In 1968 and 1969, the ICRC was conducting four simultaneous major actions: in Yemen since 1963, in Vietnam since 1964, in the Middle East (resurgence in 1967) and the Nigerian action which, beginning in 1968, dominated all the others. The sudden increase in the expenditures of the ordinary budget led the Swiss Federal Council to grant the ICRC, on its request, a credit of 10 million Swiss francs.

Despite this additional sum, the ordinary budget remained unbalanced until an extraordinary grant from the USA of 1.432 million Swiss francs made it possible, in 1971, to balance it once again. The balance which had been achieved in 1968 for the first time since 1947 had been impossible to maintain in 1969 and 1970.

Portion of Contributions From the Swiss Confederation and the Other States

During the period 1951-1961, the Swiss portion represented approximately 40% of governmental contributions. From 1962 to 1971, it amounts *de facto* to about two-thirds of the governmental contributions to the ordinary budget.

Formally speaking, the Swiss part was made up of its regular contribution and special contributions to the ordinary budget.[3] For a few years, the

[3] For details, *cf.* Table 27.

Swiss government thought it could retrieve what it had advanced as credit. Later on, it realized the irreversible nature of the evolution of the ICRC and decided to transform the credits into subsidies. The main reason was probably that "the modernization of the ICRC organization and the extension of its permanent activities in more distant regions of the world did not leave much hope for seeing the situation modified in the short or medium term".[4]

It is for the same reasons that the Confederation increased its annual contribution to 7.5 million Swiss francs starting in 1972 (and opened a complementary line of credit of 5 million Swiss francs, to which the ICRC can resort in case of need, "notably for the hiring of personnel called upon to strengthen its delegations abroad".[5] The ICRC was to use the credit up every year (until the end of 1980).

From 1968 to 1978, Switzerland therefore furnishes more than half of the regular resources of the ICRC, and more than three quarters of governmental contributions. The structure of financing of the ICRC by governments therefore fundamentally differs from that of the International Organizations of the UN family. For the latter, the maximum quota of a State (that is to say that of the USA) was fixed at 33 percent, then reduced to 25 percent.

This does not mean that the institution is dominated by the Swiss government. The latter has no right to oversee the use of its contributions. Furthermore, the ICRC turned over its financial supervision to a private fiduciary Genevan company and, since 1968, the supervision of its management to a British charter accountant.

As of the beginning of the 1970s, however, the ICRC, wishing to remain international, sought to ensure that the total of other governmental contributions would be equal to that of Switzerland.

With an eye to developing a strategy for attaining the objective of 50 percent, the ICRC made a study (July 1978) of the effects of the possible application of a system of scaled contributions.[6] In order to reach the objective of 14.5 million, which had been the 1978 level of Swiss contributions, the total governmental contributions would have had to have been trebled, since their level was 4.56 million. According to the study, 106 countries would have had to increase their contribution.

Those countries may be divided into three groups: first, those possessing a planned economy; their contribution was only 1.5 percent of what it would have had to be according to the scale. Secondly, the majority of industrialized countries and, in particular, the big ones, such as the US, Canada,

---

[4] DICK, Jean-Pierre. *Le Comité international de la Croix-Rouge.* Etude comptable et financière (1967-1971). Genève, Université de Genève, 1973, p. 85.

[5] *Ibid.*

[6] *Projet No 1.* "Contributions des gouvernements au budget ordinaire du CICR", July 1978, 30 p.

the FRG, France, Japan, etc., which would all have had at least to double, or probably to treble, their contribution. The third group is that of the third world countries, especially those in Asia and Latin America, and, to a lesser extent, Africa.

On the other hand, thirty-one countries pay 60 percent "too much" in case of the application of a scale, given that it could not be coercive.

The study also revealed that it would henceforth be necessary somewhat to modify the image of a totally "Western aligned" ICRC. For the financing of its ordinary budget, the ICRC does not depend on the great industrial powers. An important part of its resources come from medium-size European and Middle-Eastern countries.

6.1.2. The Financial Contributions of the National Societies

In order to remedy the insufficiencies, the ICRC, at Stockholm in 1948, proposed that the 17th International Conference "accept the principle of obligatory financial aid to the ICRC and to all other organs of the International Red Cross" (A.X. 1, p. 3). The National Societies would in particular, according to this proposition, have had to assume towards the ICRC the same financial obligations as towards the League. The Conference did not formally accept this principle, but it recognized the need for the ICRC to be able to count on the regular financing of its activities and, by voting Resolution 8, 1948, established a Commission for the financing of the ICRC which was to decide what was the best method to be applied in order to guarantee such regular financing.

The Commission for the financing of the ICRC established a schedule of quotas, based on that of the UN, and recommended that the National Societies respect it. These appeals had very little effect. The National Societies' contributions progressed only very little (A. 48, p. 7).

The decision of the Commission, in 1949, to ask the National Societies to make an overall contribution representing approximately one third of the total foreseeable expenses of the ICRC (A. 48, p. 2) aimed too high. Total governmental *and* National Society contributions, for 1950 and 1951, did not even cover one-third of the expenditures of the ordinary budget.[7] The contributions of the National Societies even decreased slightly after 1952. The Report of the Commission for the financing of the ICRC in 1957 indicates that the scale set up to distribute contributions is "of purely indicative nature and, likewise, the annual quotas proposed for the Societies" (D. 7, p. 4). This is a discrete allusion to its ineffectiveness. The 19th International Conference (New Delhi, 1957), adopted a text which

[7] The NSs financed 7 and 9% of those expenditures, the governments (including Switzerland) 16 and 22%. *Cf.* also Table 24.

went one step beyond the simple recognition of the principle of regular financial aid. Resolution 9b states "that each National Red Cross Society accepts its obligation as a member of the International Red Cross, to pay regular, voluntary, annual contributions to the International Committee" (G. 13 a/1, Annex III).

By this resolution, the National Societies placed themselves, without any coercion, in the obligation of making an annual contribution. This is probably the primary meaning of the term "voluntary".[8] The term might also mean either that the National Society is to fix its own level of contribution, or that it is free to accept or not to accept the proposed scale.[9]

Following that Resolution, the Commission felt (as expressed in its session of September 25, 1959) that the National Societies should accept to give to the ICRC "half of what the League asks of them".[10]

This method of distribution has since then been regularly recommended to the National Societies at International Conferences, but the formula has never been formally approved.[11]

If the scale of "half-quotas" resulted in nearly constant slight increase in total National Societies' contributions, the relative overall volume does not rise until 1967. It even falls by half beginning with the Nigerian action.

At the 24th International Conference in 1981, in Manila, a new system of financing was adopted, by which the National Societies were asked for a total contribution equivalent to 10% of the expenditures of the preceding year's regular budgetary expenditures. The distribution of the 10% among National Societies was to be made according to the scale applied by the League for its own contributions.

While it cannot be denied that, during the 1960s and 1970s, some National Societies made a real effort to increase their contributions, the importance of the effort should be measured in relation to what the ICRC would have the right to expect according to the rule recommended by the Commission for the financing of the ICRC.

The reading of table 24 shows that the effort made by the National Societies was more or less constant (the 52% for 1967 might be seen as an exception): it is situated around 43%. As a comparison, the percentage of contributions made to the League is of 95.8% as compared to the scale set down during the same period. In other words, more than four times as

---

[8] Interview accorded by Mr. Edmée Regenass, June 4, 1981.

[9] According to recent discussions at the Manila Conference, the use of the term "voluntary", signifies, in the eyes of the NSs, that they remain free to decide whether or not they wish to make an annual contribution to the ICRC.

[10] The League in 1959 set up a Permanent Scale of Contributions Commission, which every two years examines the formula for the financial participation of the NSs (League Statutes, Art. 34).

[11] 1969: P 10/1, p. 9. 1973: D 4b.d.e., p. 20. 1977: CD 5/1, p. 16.

much, since contributions to the League are twice those of the ICRC. The number of National Societies contributing to the ICRC varies over the period; half or more participate in the regular financing of the ICRC (50% to 60%; for the League, 83% to 89%). This is the major explanation for the phenomenon. A second one is that the National Societies which do contribute, in particular those of the USA and the USSR, give considerably less than the "half-quota" proposed by the Financing Commission. Finally, one should also mention the financial difficulties of certain National Societies.[12]

In conclusion, a kind of "zero growth" of National Society contributions is the dominant characteristic which emerges from the analysis of the period.[13]

24. Expected[14] and Received[15] National Society Contributions (cf. Table 28)

	50% of Total Contributions by the NSs to the League (in Sw. Frs.)	Contributions Received by the ICRC	%	Number of NSs
67	1 115 000.–	581 000.–	52,1	65
68	1 550 000.–	612 000.–	39,4	63
69	1 550 000.–	690 000.–	44,5	60
70	1 700 000.–	738 000.–	43,4	58
71	1 838 000.–	836 000.–	45,4	64
72	2 010 000.–	858 000.–	42,6	59
73	2 215 000.–	929 000.–	41,9	–
74	2 761 000.–	1 124 000.–	40,7	66
75	3 095 000.–	1 246 000.–	40,2	60
76	3 705 000.–	1 482 000.–	40,0	68
–	–	–	–	–
80	5 100 000.– approx.	2 100 000.– approx.	41,0	69

[12] DICK, *op.cit.*, p. 72 ff.

[13] The 1976 *AR* (p. 50) displays a certain myopic optimism when it characterizes as "overall... positive results" the fundraising efforts which yielded an increase of 0,23 million Swiss francs as compared to 1975. In percentage terms, overall contributions remain constant (40%).

[14] "A Short History of the Work of the Permanent Scale of Contributions Commission", Annex II, Geneva, League of Red Cross Societies, July 1977, 5 p. – Annex I-III.

[15] One should not forget that we are comparing an *obligatory* contribution (to the League) to a *voluntary* contribution.

Portion of Contributions Made by States and National Societies

If we now proceed to a comparison of governmental contributions (excepting that of Switzerland) and those of National Societies we can make the following observations:

– Over the entire period 1967-1979, the evolution of contributions is similar. From 1967 to 1972, one observes a decline in the proportional curve. In other words, the effort at expansion and reorganization on the part of the ICRC, and the costs which derive from it, are nearly totally borne by the Swiss government.

– Beginning in 1974, the increase in contributions is slow but constant. This means, not a reduction on the part of the government, which maintains and increases its effort, but a tendency towards a better equilibrium of contributions.

– The difference between contributions within these two categories of donors is therefore not to be situated in their tendency, but in their annual rate. Whereas that of the National Societies is of a nearly linear constancy (variations inferior to 5%), that of governments is very irregular (cf. Table 26). A detailed study of contributions shows that there are two types of reasons for that: on the one hand, extraordinary contributions on the part of States, whether as gifts or as voluntary payment of late dues,[16] on the other hand, the decline of the dollar.[17] Another reason is that the ICRC, during the 1970s, applies more pressure on governments than on National Societies.

Making abstraction of the Swiss contribution, one notes that National Society contributions, over the whole 1967-1979 period, represent one-third[18] of governmental contributions. This begins to approach the directive proposed by the Financing Commission in 1948: that the National Societies furnish one-third (and governments two-thirds) of the ICRC's resources. Seen in this global perspective, the National Societies' effort is therefore more important than it as first seems.

---

[16] 1971: extraordinary grant by the USA of 1.432 million Swiss francs.

1973: extraordinary contributions by Saudi Arabia and the United Arab Emirates, of respectively 0.81 and 0.315 million Swiss francs.

[17] 1976: the USA reduces its contribution by 0.26 million Swiss francs as compared with 1975.

1978: the USA reduces its contribution by 0.32 million Swiss francs as compared with 1977.

[18] Between 6.9% and 20.5% of total receipts.

6.1.3. *Fundraising Policy of the ICRC.*

The evolution of activities influenced donors individually. The first expansion (beginning in 1960, weak in relation to that which was to take place in the fall of 1967) provokes a reaction of governments (excluding Switzerland) which double their contributions, while the National Societies increase theirs by nearly 50%. From 1968 to 1980, governmental contributions quadruple, those of the National Societies are multiplied by three.

But the evolution of activities also changed the attitude of the ICRC in the area of financing.

After an ICRC offensive, notably in 1948 and 1949, which was crowned with success on the legal level by Resolutions 8/1948 and 9/1949, it would seem that the institution was somewhat discouraged by the feeble response of donors. The ICRC's fundraising efforts during these years thus consists in sending appeals by mail[19] and in seizing the occasion provided by International Conferences to exhort the participants, with much circumspection, to honor their commitment:

"The Committee firmly hopes that... it will be possible for it–in a future which it hopes will be very near–to consider that the question of its financing has been definitively resolved."[20]

Worse, in December 1952, the Financing Commission even has to ask the ICRC to prepare a report on its financial activities and position, including its estimated figures for 1953, to be sent to the National Societies. Such a degree of passivity in the area of fundraising (donors are not even spontaneously informed as to needs) went hand in hand with a spirit of parsimony in the management of funds.

It must here be repeated that the ICRC disposed of a credit from the Swiss government of 7.5 million Swiss francs, of which 4.5 million remained (as of 1946), which it did not touch during the 1950s. Furthermore, in 1961, it even reimbursed 3 million advanced by the Confederation during the first term of 1946.

Out of a concern for healthy management, the ICRC gradually reduces its expenses by two-thirds between 1951 and 1957. If receipts double during the same period, this is not due to greater efforts at fundraising, but to able management. The increase in receipts is only partially attributable to government contributions. More than 40% of recepts, in 1956, came from various donations, revenues from investments, reimbursements and various receipts.

The policy of appeals by letter was perhaps enough to ensure constant financing, but was certainly not a way of favoring increased contributions.

[19] Direct appeals to governments, appeals through the Financing Commission to National Societies.

[20] "Financement du CICR." Report presented by the ICRC at the 18th International Conference (Toronto, 1952), p. 2.

Since there is no legal provision forcing the States and National Societies to contribute to the financing of the institution, the ICRC must convince its donors as to the usefulness of its activities.

Since 1972, the ICRC has seconded more systematically its written appeals with visits, where it explains to government representatives, and if possible to those responsible for the question, the actions underway and the projected actions of the ICRC.

This fundraising policy was reinforced in 1974 by the creation of a section on fundraising responsible to the Director of the Finance Department.

During the 1950s, the ICRC reduced its expenses rather than modifyed its insufficient financing policy.[21] It began to spend more hardily in 1962, and it was only starting with the Nigerian action that it really became aware of the importance of fundraising.

Today the ICRC figures the minimal resources which it will need and bases itself on that figure to specify its needs. In a word, the ICRC is trying to give itself the means of its policy, whereas before it pursued the policy permitted by its means.

25. Ordinary Budget Receipts and Expenditures

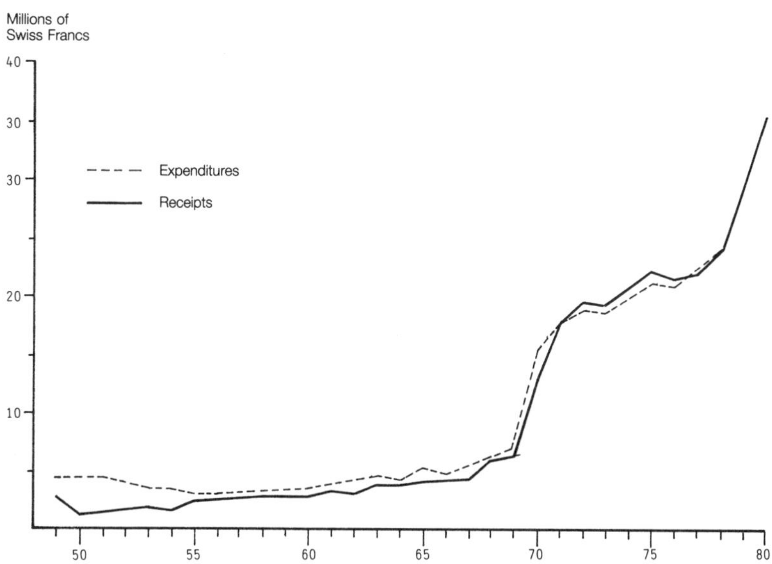

[21] Conclusion of the study by Professor Probst in 1962 (mentioned by Mr. E. Regenass during an interview).

26. Governmental Contributions to the Ordinary Budget

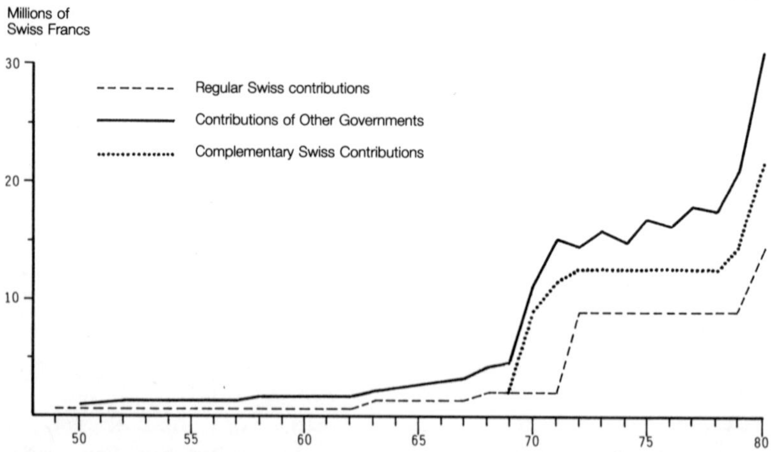

27. Credits from the Swiss Government

(Supplementary Contributions 1945-1971)

		Sw. Frs.
1) 1945	Open Credit, Federal Decree Dec. 19, 1945	5 000 000
1946	Advances for Expenses Resulting from the Second World War	− 3 000 000
	Balance, End of March 1946	2 000 000
	New Margin of Credit Accorded by Federal Decree, April 5, 1946	+ 2 500 000
	Balance, End of April 1946	4 500 000
1961	Reimbursed by the ICRC, May 24, 1961	+ 3 000 000
	Balance, End of May, 1961	7 500 000
1962	Nepal Mission	− 1 500 000
1963	Yemen Mission	− 750 000
1964	Yemen Mission	− 1 400 000
1965	Yemen Mission	− 750 000
1966	Reimbursed by the Technical Cooperation Service, which takes over Expenses for the Nepal Mission (Concerns Equipment Taken from the ICRC by the Confederation)	+ 188 862

1967	Vietnam, Yemen, Middle East Missions and School Manual		– 2 135 000
	Balance, End of 1967		1 153 862
2) 1968	Opening of Credit, Federal Decree March 13, 1968		10 000 000
	Middle East	400 000	
	Yemen	1 020 000	
	Vietnam	400 000	
	Nigeria	930 000	
	Vietnam	250 000	
	Middle East	250 000	
	Greece	270 000	
	Nigeria	2 230 000	5 750 000
1969	Yemen	900 000	
	Middle East	2 000 000	
	Vietnam	600 000	
	School Manual	250 000	3 750 000
1971	Middle East, Aden, Yemen, Greece Missions		500 000
	Exhausting of Credit		10 000 000

Source: Dick, *op. cit.*, p. 26 f.

28. Contributions of Red Cross National Societies to the Ordinary Budget

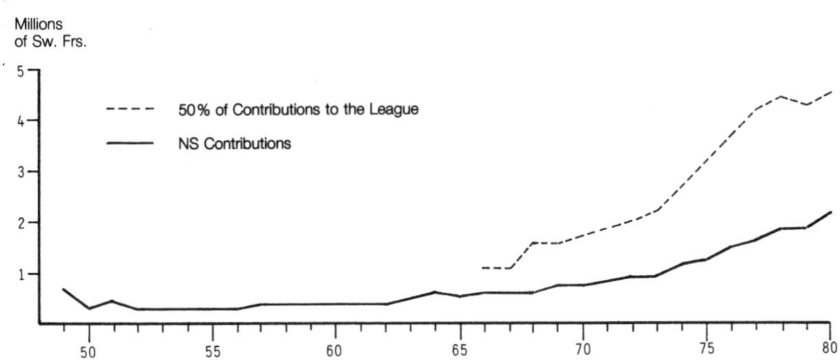

6.2. Financing of the Extraordinary Budget (Tables 29-34)[22]

Like most organizations intervening in the framework of crises, whether the latter be natural, economic, political or military, the ICRC disposes of an extraordinary budget of which we have often spoken, since it is always greater than the ordinary budget and sometimes much greater (Cf. Expenditure Tables, Nos. 7, 9 and 10).

The existence of such a budget is explained because of the unforeseeable nature and dimensions of crises, which may require rapid and considerable expenditures of funds. This makes it possible on the one hand to face such crises while on the other hand preventing the organization as a whole from being paralyzed by the needs of a single action.

6.2.1. 1949-1967

The post–war period is divided into two parts. One goes from 1949 to 1967 (cf. Table 30). During this period, almost one-half the receipts of the extraordinary budget (40 to 50%) remained unspent, if one excludes the funds disbursed for Hungary, Nepal and Nigeria.

One should also note the origin of funds during this first period. They mainly come from the Swiss national collection (cf. Table 31), receipts from which are entirely free for expenditure on any needed task. This campaign, between 1949 and 1967, was one of the main resources of the organization, except in the face of crises of exceptional dimensions and suddenness.

The end of the first period is announced by the experiences of Nepal and Yemen, which result in considerable deficits, and force the organization to draw on its financial reserves in order to pay its debts, thus causing serious reflection as to the means of financing.

6.2.2. 1968-1980

It was the war in Nigeria which led to decisive change in terms of extraordinary receipts. The institution, thanks to the experiences of that crisis, changed its policy, and decided to invert its procedure. Upon the outbreak of a conflict, the ICRC first decides whether or not to commit itself, and once engaged, launches an appeal for funds. This approach is much more active than that of the preceding period.

Another important change: from the early 1970s on, the internal structure of the organization accords an important role to fundraising. There is now an office which does nothing else, and which must maintain permanent contact with important donors.

---

[22] One must today understand the term as a collective singular, meaning that there is now an extraordinary budget for each action, and not one single one for all of the ICRC's extraordinary activities.

The contrast with the previous period is striking, when the ICRC quite passively awaited the arrival of funds, before deciding whether it would be possible to carry out a given action. There were of course advantages to non-earmarked donations: they gave the organization greater freedom of action. But that advantage was more than offset by the lower level of revenues.

After 1967, on the other hand, despite the fact that there is a certain inconvenience linked to earmarked gifts, the Committee is able to carry out major actions, whereas before, while freer, it could only intervene in a limited way.

In the same way, the percentage of extraordinary budget receipts from the Swiss national collection declined after 1967. It must be recognized that the policy of the ICRC concerning that drive did not evolve along with its general policy. The way of issuing the annual appeal to the Swiss people has remained close to that which prevailed in 1949. It is launched in general terms, which appear somewhat abstract, and is not based on immediate events in the outside world, which alone are capable of mobilizing in the present era.

The main contributions to the extraordinary budget during the present period come from governments and Red Cross National Societies, and no longer from the Swiss people alone (cf. Table 34). Among the donors, governments give the most (cf. Table 32). But one can observe as of 1978 the relative and absolute increase of donations by National Societies which, in 1980, furnish approximately one-quarter of all extraordinary receipts (cf. Table 34).

Among governments, the main donors are in North America and Western Europe (cf. Table 32). One likewise observes that there are sporadically important gifts from certain other donors, when a given crisis breaks out. The governments of Asia and Oceania, for example (especially Japan and Australia) gave more during the Bangladesh and Indochinese actions. The Middle Eastern countries, and especially the Arab governments, gave considerable sums for the ICRC's action in Lebanon (1976), and the percentage coming from these governments undergoes an across-the-board increase beginning in 1979.

Within the North-American region the US, since 1969, has furnished a significant portion of extraordinary receipts, although Canada often gives as much in terms of GNP and sometimes in absolute terms (for example in 1973, 1975 and 1977). The US portion tends to stabilize around 20% of the total budget for the recent period as a whole, excepting the years 1968-1969 during which, because of the Nigerian action, it furnished 64% of total receipts, and 1976 when its contribution, because of the Lebanese action, was 58.1%.

The portion of the principal European donors remained stable during recent years (cf. Table 33), with the exception of Switzerland's. In this connection it must not of course be forgotten that the Swiss government furnishes a large part of the ordinary budget. The latter progressively but irregularly reduced its contribution to the extraordinary budget, which had been, during the first period, relatively important. In 1980, it furnishes 2.7% of the total.

The volume of the extraordinary budget thus increases significantly beginning with the Nigerian crisis, and during the entire 1970s (cf. Table 10) it tends to rise in regular fashion.

29. Extraordinary Budget
(excluding AICR Indochina)
(In thousands of Swiss Francs)

	Expenditures	Receipts	%
1949	?	?	
1950	?	?	
1951	?	?	
1952	?	872	
1953	1 690	928	−45
1954	1 372	?	
1955	1 562	1 270	−19
1956	1 978	3 236	+64
1957	9 264	8 959	−3
1958	2 484	1 926	−22
1959	1 403	1 369	−2
1960	1 127	1 314	+17
1961	3 030	2 991	−1
1962	3 666	2 044	−44
1963	1 923	1 240	−36
1964	2 883	1 892	−34
1965	1 927	1 768	−8
1966	1 796	1 890	+5
1967	7 221	6 798	−5
1968	39 209	39 898	+1,8
1969	113 451	106 884	−5,8
1970	4 434	4 390	−1,0
1971	3 492	3 667	+5,0
1972	17 620	17 332	−1,6
1973	12 635	12 890	+2,0
1974	14 588	16 435	+12,7
1975	16 209	13 469	−16,9
1876	24 348	34 299	+40,9
1977	22 610	13 216	−41,5
1978	27 415	32 023	+16,8
1979	71 394	77 378	+8,4
1980	107 453	98 645	−8,2

Extraordinary Budget:

30. Receipts from the General Account of Actions Underway 1949-1967

(In thousands of Swiss Francs)

	Non-earmarked	%	Earmarked
1949	935		?*
1950	920		?*
1951	962		–
1952	872		–
1953	928		–
1954	650		–
1955	630	49,6	640
1956	648	20,0	2 589
1957	572	6,4	8 387
1958	575	29,9	1 351
1959	579	42,4	789
1960	624	47,5	690
1961	695	23,2	2 297
1962	736	36,1	1 307
1963	767	61,9	473
1964	754	39,9	1 138
1965	849	48,0	920
1966	846	44,7	1 045
1967	828	12,2	5 969

* Palestine Action.

31. Swiss National Collection

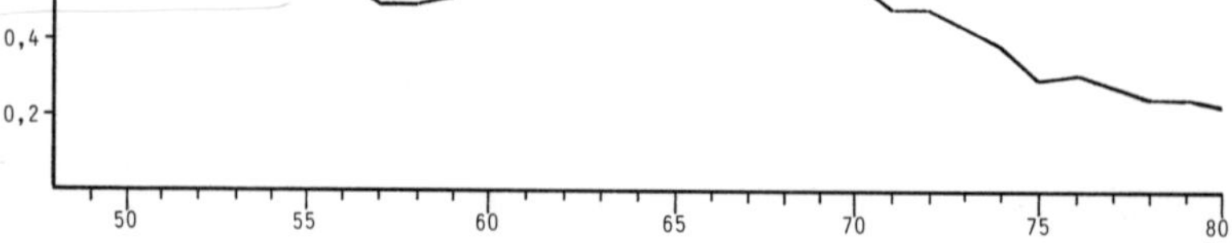

32. Contributions of Governments and National Societies to Special Financing (Excluding RCIA)

(In Thousands of Sw. Frs)

	Africa	Latin America	Asia Oceania	Europe North-America	Middle East	Total Governments	National Societies
1968 1969[1]	350	103	811	136 172	—	137 436	8 609
1970	—	—	23	1 187	—	1 210[2]	1 031
1971						? (500)	? (329)
1972	—	—	179	11 465	42	11 686	3 237
1973	1	—	3 342	4 500	315	8 158	1 577
1974	1	2	492	8 815	411	9 721	579
1975	—	4	1 039	7 953	38	9 034	1 365
1976	17	12	53	28 783	1 384	30 249	1 264
1977	5	—	8	6 629	421	7 063	1 441
1978	—	—	—	23 396	30	23 426	5 343
1979	—	—	7 961	45 091	1 075	54 127	8 400
1980	4	12	4 437	52 663	1 633	58 749	19 230

[1] In 1969, the governments gave 84.7 million Sw. Frs (cf. *AR*, 1969, p. 116). The rest was given in 1968 (approx. 36 million, cf. *AR*, 1969), in 1967 and in 1970.
[2] Jordan.

33. Special Financing–Most Important Government Contributions Over a Decade

(In thousands of Swiss Francs)

	1968/69	1970/71	1972	1973	1974	1975	1976	1977	1978	1979	1980
USA											
Nominal Value	94 081		3 750	630	2 390	2 369	19 040	1 499	7 307	15 869	17 528
% of Special Financing	64,1		25,3	6,0	18,1	21,4	58,1	13,5	23,7	20,8	18,0
Canada											
Nominal Value	1 402		1 021	585	498	2 182	2 336	1 107	4 090	5 379	6 903
% of Special Financing	1,0		6,9	5,6	3,8	19,7	7,1	10,0	13,3	7,1	7,1
United Kingdom											
Nominal Value	11 848		1 853	1 184	543	254	1 183	30	2 514	4 692	7 362
% of Special Financing	8,1		12,5	11,3	4,1	2,3	3,6	0,3	8,2	6,2	7,6
Scandinavian Countries											
Nominal Value	2 079		1 409	1 122	1 016	576	2 677	1 746	4 312	7 345	7 223
% of Special Financing	1,4		9,5	10,7	7,7	5,2	8,2	15,7	14,0	9,5	7,4
Netherlands											
Nominal Value	3 971		168	174	1 131	701	1 469	1 798	2 312	3 820	4 605
% of Special Financing	2,7		1,1	1,7	8,6	6,3	4,5	16,1	7,5	5,0	4,7
Switzerland											
Nominal Value	9 671		2 220	767	1 475	1 100	500	200	1 150	3 820	2 630
% of Special Financing	6,6		15,0	7,3	11,2	10,0	1,5	1,8	3,7	5,0	2,7

34. Contribution of National Societies and the Swiss People to the Extraordinary Budget

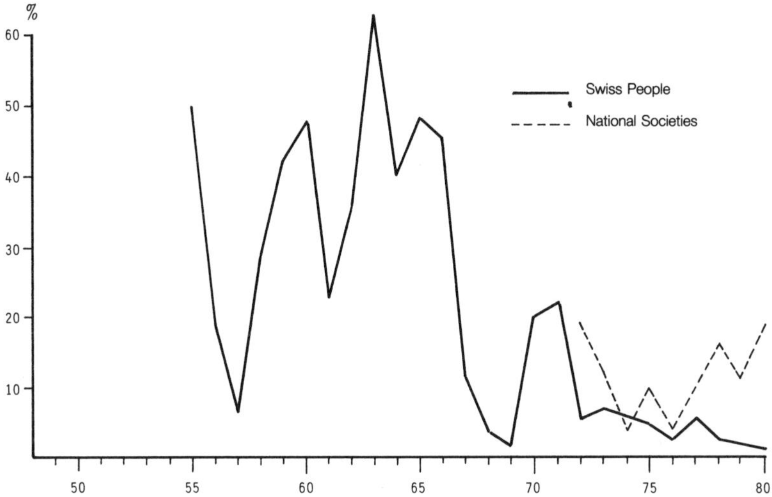

CHAPTER 7

Relations with the States (Tables 33-35)

The States belong to the International Red Cross Movement. They take part in the diplomatic Conferences which create humanitarian law and are parties to the Conventions. Their governments participate in the financing of the ICRC's ordinary budget and its extraordinary actions and entertain direct relations with it and with the National Red Cross Society they have recognized. Signature of the Geneva Conventions is the main (necessary and sufficient) condition for their participation in the Red Cross Movement, for their participation at International Red Cross Conferences.

Not all States have yet acceeded. The evolution of accessions has not automatically kept pace with the proliferation of new States, and it is not identical to that of admissions to the UN.

7.1. Admissions to the UN. Accession to the Conventions. A Tentative Comparison

It seemed interesting to us to compare the movement of admissions of new States to the UN with that of adherence to the Conventions. Different though the *organization* of the United Nations and the Red Cross *Movement* might be, they are comparable in some respects.

Period 1945-1949

"We, peoples of the United Nations determined to save succeeding generations from the scourge of war... have resolved to combine our efforts..." (Preamble of the UN Charter). This political will was expressed by the adoption of a UN Charter and the creation of an international organization. The first goal of the organization is "maintain international peace and security, and to that end: to take effective collective measures..." (Art. 1/1), in particular through the intermediary of a special organ, the Security Council, whose main responsibility is precisely "the maintenance of international peace and security" (Art. 24/1), and as well through the International Court of Justice and the General Assembly.

The chapters of the UN Charter to which the Security Council can refer are the Pacific settlement of disputes (Chapter 6) and, in case of failure, Action in case of threats to the peace, breaches of the peace and acts of aggression (Chapter 7). The Charter of the United Nations, signed June 26, 1945, was ratified the same year by fifty-one States out of the seventy-six which made up the international community.

It would be quite naive to claim that, given such a strong will to do away with war once and for all, the Geneva Conventions which apply "in all cases of declared war or of any other armed conflict..." (Art. 2 in common to the Conventions) no longer had any reason to exist.

Practice proves the contrary. Between 1946 and 1949, six States[1] adhered to the 1929 Convention for the improvement of the lot of the sick and wounded. Even more, the need to improve and enlarge the provisions for protection in case of war is so generally felt that the ICRC, as of October 1945, organized a series of consultations in view of revising them. The work led to the adoption of new Conventions, on August 12, 1949.

We cannot here analyze the reasons for this parallel development of two international legal systems, nor indulge in a detailed comparison of their origins, objectives and parallel evolution. Let us nonetheless note a few simple facts:

– The UN Charter is maximalist. It proclaims not only the maintenance of peace and the prevention of war–which is in itself more ambitious a program than that of the Conventions–but also collaboration in every domain. The Conventions, on the other hand, represent the minimal consensus between opposed States.

– In 1945, the fifty-one States linked by the UN Charter belong apparently to the camp of the victory. The Charter is the expression of their political will. The 1929 Convention on the sick and wounded also binds together fifty States in 1945,[2] but they are not the same ones. In 1949, the UN is made up of sixty States. Sixty-one States sign the Geneva Conventions, among which one quarter (fifteen States) are not, at that moment, UN members. The majority of that quarter is composed of States which sought as best they could to remain neutral during the Second World war. The Community of States parties to the Geneva Conventions is therefore qualitatively more universal.

– The codification of crimes against peace and against humanity which the UN wanted to undertake came up against the political problem which is the definition of peace. This is why, as Michel Virally observes, "The

[1] Israel, Lebanon, Monaco, Pakistan, the Philippines and Transjordan.

[2] Seven States, among which Germany and Austria, were dissolved for having lost the war.

development of humanitarian law, under those conditions, had to be pursued outside the framework of the United Nations: that of "Geneva law" (August 12, 1949 Conventions)".[3]

Period 1950-1955 (December 14, 1955: Admission of Sixteen States to the UN)

During the cold war, the difference between procedures of admission to the UN and procedures for adherence to the 1949 Conventions played an important role in the evolution of the two systems. In both cases, the States must take the initiative for accession or request for admission.

In the framework of the UN, however, the States must, in order to be accepted be judged capable of fulfilling the obligations of the Charter through the two political organs of the organization, the General Assembly and the Security Council (Art. 4).[4] As to the Conventions, the State simply deposits the instruments of ratification or accession with the Swiss government which notifies the other contracting States.

One-third of the States notified their ratification or adherence to the Convention before being admitted to the UN (16 out of 48).[5] The majority had taken the necessary steps before the UN, but had been victims of the blocking tactics practiced by the two superpowers during the cold war.

To become parties to the Conventions was, for these "outsider" States, a means of manifesting their will to be an integral and equal part of the international community and, in more limited fashion, to be recognized by it. The most significant examples are those of Austria in 1953, while it still possessed the status of an occupied State, of South Vietnam in 1953 and, in 1956, of the People's Republic of China.

These examples and those States of Eastern and Western Europe confirmed the vocation of the Conventions which was, in a time of serious tension, to be the political expression of the minimal consensus of the international community.

Period 1960-1965

During this period, the rhythm of signatures of the Geneva Conventions fell significantly behind that of admissions to the UN. This is the period when the African States became independent.

When the old colonies became independent, the first concern of the new States was to be admitted to the UN. They succeeded, with a few

[3] VIRALLY, Michel. *L'organisation mondiale*. Paris, Armand Colin, 1972, p. 303.

[4] *Ibid.*, p. 256.

[5] Date of the first ratification: 1950.

exceptions, the very year in which they became independent. This was the case for sixty-eight States, or 44%, out of the 157 members States on March 31, 1983. Only fifteen of those States simultaneously[6] adhered to the Geneva Conventions.

The main reason is doubtless political. The young State derives many tangible benefits from its presence in the UN. Another, less important, reason, resides perhaps in the doctrinal position which the ICRC had adopted on the question of colonies acceding to independence during this period.

The ICRC's interpretation was that "newly independent States are implicitly bound by the participation of the State to which they succeed, unless they explicitly repudiate these Conventions".[7]

The ICRC therefore invited these States, not to adhere to the Conventions, but to make a "declaration of continuity" in order to manifest their respect for the Conventions.[8] We will not here discuss the legal justification for this position. We are simply stating that this might explain the delay. Why would a young State be in a hurry to notify its declaration of continuity when it was already bound? As for the heart of the question, was it not to lessen the importance of the *will* of the independent State to participate in the Conventions?

The ICRC has recently had to revise its position on this point so as to take into account that of the Convention on State succession to treaties by the United Nations Conference in Vienna, 1978.

The 1980 Annual Report thus notes that:[9]

"The Convention made it clear that the international community did not consider a successor State to be a party to a treaty by which its predecessor had been bound, unless such a successor formally expressed it intention to accept the obligations of the treaty."

Period 1970-1972

Twice, in 1970 and 1972, an equal number of States are members of the UN and parties to the Conventions. With sixteen exceptions, they are the same ones.[10] During this period, the Conventions achieve their highest degree of universality. (Cf. Table 35).

---

[6] We have arbitrarily fixed the parameter at twelve months beginning with the date of admission to the UN.

[7] *AR*, 1965, p. 53.

[8] Some States have nonetheless preferred to notify their accession to the Conventions; for example Somalia, Uganda, Mali, Kenya, Zambia, Malawi.

[9] *AR*, 1980, p. 68.

[10] Eight are only members of the UN and eight only parties to the Conventions.

Period 1975-1980

The Conventions lose some of their attractiveness. Few micro-States manifest their interest in adhering to the Conventions. Furthermore, the Portuguese ex-colonies of Africa[11] and Zimbabwe have not yet decided to adhere to the Conventions.

General observations

Over the entire period, we can observe a chronic advance of admissions to the UN over accessions to the Conventions. This should not, however, be interpreted as an opposition of principle to the Conventions.

The date of ratification of or adherence to the Conventions is determined by several factors, the most important among which is that of the internal situation of a State.

Another factor which explains the discrepancy is the fact that both the old and the new States already feel bound by Geneva law. The old ones are in their great majority linked by the 1929 Conventions which are applicable for each contracting State, as long as it does not adhere to the new Conventions. The 1929 Conventions are thus still valid today, since one contracting State, Burma, did not adhere to the new Conventions. One must here stress the fact that Burma, as well as a number of States having somewhat put off their adherence to the Conventions, nonetheless manifested their support for the ICRC by contributing to the financing of the ordinary budget.

In conclusion, one notes that the 1949 Conventions presently approach universality. Out of a total of 168 States, 154 are parties to the Conventions (157 are UN members) on March 31, 1983.

In this respect, it might be interesting, for purposes of comparison, to examine the state of ratifications, accessions, etc. of a certain number of other international human rights instruments, as of January 1, 1980.[12]

The 1948 Convention for the Prevention and the Repression of the Crimes of Genocide had been ratified by seventy-nine States, the 1951 Convention on the Status of Refugees by seventy-six States and the 1954 Convention on the status of Stateless Persons by twenty-four States. Likewise, the two great international pacts concerning economic, social and cultural rights and civil and political rights of 1966 were only adhered to by respectively fifty-two and forty-nine States.

There are several explanations for this considerable discrepancy between the participation of States in the instruments of human rights and the Conventions which, let us recall, at the same date bound one hundred and

[11] Except Guinea-Bissau.

[12] Source: *Droits de l'Homme. Instruments internationaux.* Signatures, Ratifications, Adhérences, etc. January 1, 1980, Geneva, United Nations, 1980, p. 13.

forty-four States. The instruments cited are not more coercive than the Conventions, but one cannot ignore the proliferation of legal instruments within the UN. There are nineteen pacts, conventions, protocols, etc., only in the area of human rights. This inflation has surely slowed down a movement which must develop an ideal. But the main reason for the difference is that most States perceive an immediate interest in being parties to the Geneva Conventions (the protection of their citizens, civilians, wounded or military, in the hands of the enemy in case of armed conflict) whereas most of the agreements concerning human rights impose obligations upon them with respect to their own citizens, without reciprocal advantages to be drawn from other States.

The International Red Cross Movement propagates the humanitarian ideal, of which the Conventions are the legal instrument. But the diplomatic Conference on the Reaffirmation and Development of International Law (1974-1977) was unable to avoid dividing its results into two additional Protocols, precisely because the second created obligations for States in the specific area of internal conflicts, where States like to feel as free as possible.

The success of the additional Protocols of June 8, 1977 must be evaluated, on the one hand, in terms of the present state of international law, and on the other hand in comparison with that which existed at the time of the 1949 Diplomatic Conference on Humanitarian Law and finally in terms of the contents of the various texts. The proliferation of States and the progressive complexity of international law are responsible for the fact that a consensus on a general question is more and more difficult to obtain. In 1949, sixty-one States out of sixty-four that were present (among which five observers) had signed the Conventions within six months.[13] Of the one hundred and two States which signed the Final Act of the Diplomatic Conference in 1977, only sixty-two and fifty-eight States had signed Additional Protocols I and II within eighteen months.

States presently hesitate in the face of a *formal* commitment. The rhythm of accessions is therefore significantly slower (two or three times as slow relatively speaking) than after the Second World war. But the main reason for the hesitation of States to ratify the 1977 Protocols is the inclusion in the latter of elements of so-called "The Hague" law. Whereas the Geneva Conventions, from 1864 to 1949, limited themselves to protecting the enemy when he was out of combat (wounded, sick, shipwrecked, prisoner, civilian), the additional Protocols contain rules concerning the very conduct of hostilities, the observation of which has a much more direct influence on military behavior. Respecting a soldier who surrenders has never resulted in losing a war, on the contrary. Making it illegal to attack civilians as such (the

[13] The rhythm of ratification of the UN Charter is characterized by the same speed and quasi-unanimity.

main humanitarian gain of the Protocols) poses certain concrete problems to military personnel charged with fighting and winning. Furthermore, the applicability of Protocol I to so-called wars of liberation poses political problems for certain States and causes them to hesitate to ratify the text.

Finally, Protocol II is–wrongly–considered too constraining in civil wars by the third world States.

7.2. Active Collaboration

Accession to the Conventions by a State implies the legal recognition of the ICRC and obligates it to accept its services in international conflicts. A State may of course allow the ICRC to conduct activities on its territory without having adhered to the Conventions, just as the ICRC may offer its services to a State which is not a party to the Conventions. The Conventions foresaw such situations in Article 9 which stipulates that:

"The provisions of the present Convention constitute no obstacle to the humanitarian activities which the International Committee of the Red Cross or any other impartial humanitarian organization may, subject to the consent of the Parties to the conflict concerned, undertake for the protection of wounded and sick, medical personnel and chaplains, and for their relief."

This right of initiative, also applicable in case of civil war (according to Art. 3.2. common to the Conventions) and in case of internal disturbances (according to the Statutes of the International Red Cross, Art. 5, Paragraph 5) is, in the eyes of the ICRC, of capital importance, for it "allows the ICRC to operate, even in matters not coming within the scope of the Conventions".[14]

The ICRC is therefore an organism whose existence and activities are reinforced by a legal system, but whose independence, not only inside, but even outside of the framework of the Conventional system, is approved and sanctioned by the system.

The history of the ICRC's activities shows that it has in fact taken the initiative in areas and in situations which are totally unmentioned in the Conventions. The column "Active Collaboration of States with the ICRC"[15] also shows us that forty-one States, or more than a third (approximately 37%) of States which once (or several times) accepted the services of the ICRC, did so without having at that time adhered to the Conventions.

This shows that the ICRC's action is not simply a function of the legal relationship, but just as much, if not more, of the humanitarian and political aspects of a problem. The legal framework reinforces the action of the institution if need be. The institution itself acts within the framework of the Conventions, but without necessarily referring to them explicitly.

[14] *AR*, 1949, p. 35.

[15] *Cf.* Table 36.

35. The International Community – UN Members – Accessions to the Geneva Conventions

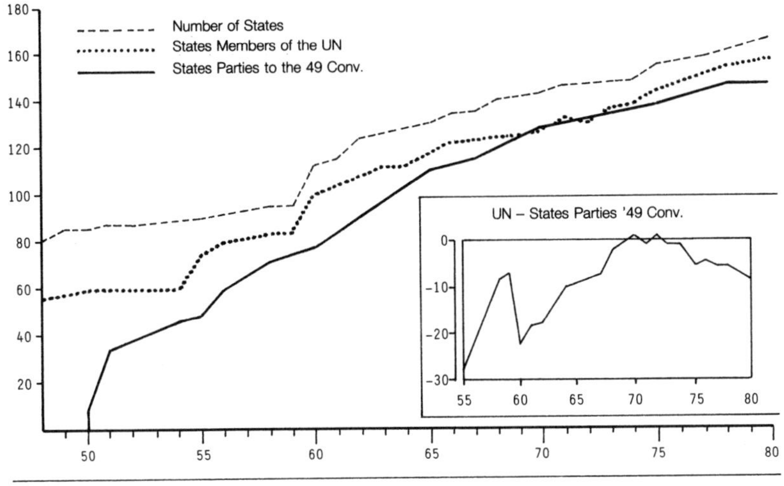

36. Relations of the ICRC with States Making Up the International Community

Situation as of December 31, 1980.

Legend

* State Independent Before the Creation of the UN.

= State Admitted to the UN the Same Year as its Accession to Independence.

Date: Year of Independence.

r State Having Expressed Reservations Concerning Certain Dispositions of the Conventions.

A State Having Adhered to the Conventions Before Being Admitted to the UN.

S State Having Adhered to the Conventions in the 12 Months Following its Admission to the UN.

R Regular Contributions.

R+X Contributions Made Before Accession.

R−X Number of Years During Which Contributions Were Not Made.

Active Collaboration:

States having accepted the ICRC's presence for

- an action (opening a Delegation),
- a mission (visit to a place of detention, repatriation operation, etc.),
- aid to detainees and their family,
- aid to the National Society,

The visits to governments and National Societies as well as diffusion actions are not registered.

AA State having accepted the services of the ICRC before its accession to the Conventions.

= State having accepted the services of the ICRC the same year as accession to the Conventions.

Date: First collaboration since 1949.

States	Admission to the UN	Accession 4 Geneva Conventions	Governmental contribution to ICRC ordinary budget	Active collaboration with the ICRC
Afghanistan	19.11.46 *	29.09.56	SP	1975
Albania	14.12.55	26.05.57 r	–	–
Algeria	08.10.62 =	20.06.60 A	– (1×)	1955
Angola	01.12.76 75	–	–	1966 AA
Argentina	24.10.45 *	18.09.56	–	1963
Australia	01.11.45 *	14.10.58	R +8	1952 AA
Austria	14.12.55 =	27.08.53 A	R +1	1956
Bahamas	18.09.73 =	11.07.75	–	1976
Bahrein	21.09.71 =	30.11.71 S	R from 74	–
Bangladesh	17.09.74 71	04.04.72 A	– (2×)	1971 AA
Barbados	09.12.66 =	10.09.68	–	–
Belgium	27.12.45 *	03.09.52	R =1	–
Benin	20.09.60 =	14.12.61	– (1×)	1973
Bhutan	21.09.71 *	–	–	–
Bolivia	14.11.45 *	10.12.76	–	1969 AA
Botswana	17.10.66 =	29.03.68	– (1×)	1977
Brazil	24.10.45 *	29.06.57	R +6	1964
Bulgaria	14.12.55 *	22.07.54 r A	R from 63	1964
Burma	19.04.48 =	–[16]	R from 53	1949 AA
Burundi	18.09.62 =	27.12.71	R from 76	1962
Byelorussian SSR	24.10.45 *	03.08.54 r	–	–
Canada	09.11.45 *	14.05.65	R +14	–
Cape Verde	16.09.75 =	–	–	–
Central African Rep.	20.09.60 =	01.08.66	SP (4×)	1973
Chad	20.09.60 =	05.08.70	–	1969 AA
Chile	24.10.45 *	12.10.50	R –2 from 54	1971

[16] Accession to the 1929 Conventions in 1937.

States	Admission to the UN	Accession 4 Geneva Conventions	Governmental contribution to ICRC ordinary budget	Active collaboration with the ICRC
China	24.10.45 *	28.12.56 r	– (1×)	1949 AA
Colombia	05.11.45 *	08.11.61	R +11	1969
Comoros	12.11.75 =	–	–	1978
Congo	20.09.60 =	30.01.67	–	1970
Costa Rica	02.11.45 *	15.10.69	R from 77	1955 AA
Cuba	24.10.45 *	15.04.54	–	1958
Cyprus	20.09.60 =	23.05.62	R from 67	1955 AA
Czechoslovakia	24.10.45 *	19.12.50 r	–	1961
Dem. Kampuchea	14.12.55 53	08.12.58	(from 61 to 66)	1966
Dem. Yemen	14.12.67 =	25.05.77	–	1966 AA
Denmark	24.10.45 *	27.06.51	R from 52	–
Djibouti	20.09.77 =	06.03.78 S	?	1976 AA
Dominica	18.12.78 =	–	–	–
Dominican Rep.	24.10.45 *	22.01.58	(from 58 to 61)	1965
Ecuador	21.12.45 *	11.08.54	R +2 (–2)	1970
Egypt	24.10.45 *	10.11.52	R –1 from 53	1949 AA
El Salvador	24.10.45 *	17.06.53	R –1 from 60	1969
Equatorial Guinea	12.11.68 =	–	–	1971 AA
Ethiopia	13.11.45 *	02.10.69	–	1973
Fiji	13.10.70 =	09.08.71 S	R from 77	1975
Finland	14.12.55 *	22.02.55 A	R +5	–
France	24.10.45 *	28.06.51	R	–
Gabon	20.09.60 =	20.02.65	–	1973
Gambia	21.09.65 =	11.10.66	SP	1972
German Dem. Rep.	18.09.73 49	30.11.56 r A	R –1 from 66	1950 AA
Germany, Fed. Rep. of	18.09.73 49	03.09.54 A	R from 62	1950 AA
Ghana	08.03.57 =	02.08.58	SP	1973
Greece	25.10.45 *	05.06.56	R +6	1949 AA
Grenada	17.09.74 =	–	–	–
Guatemala	21.11.45 *	14.05.52	–	1954
Guinea	12.12.58 =	–	–	–
Guinea-Bissau	17.09.74 =	21.02.74 r A	–	1965 A
Guyana	20.09.66 =	22.07.68	R –1 from 71	1971
Haiti	24.10.45 *	11.04.57	(+3; +2)	1971
Honduras	17.12.45 *	31.12.65	R from 67	1969
Hungary	14.12.55 *	03.08.54 r A	R –3 from 58	1956
Iceland	19.12.46 *	10.08.65	R from 66	–
India	30.10.45 *	09.11.50	R	1949 AA
Indonesia	28.09.50 49	30.09.58	R +7 (–3)	1949 AA
Iran	24.10.45 *	22.02.57	R +2	1955 AA
Iraq	21.12.45 *	14.02.56	R +1 (–3)	1954 AA
Ireland	14.12.55 *	27.09.62	R +9	–
Israel	11.05.49 48	06.07.51 r	R –3 from 53	1949 AA
Italy	14.12.55 *	17.12.51 A	R	–

States	Admission to the UN		Accession 4 Geneva Conventions			Governmental contribution to ICRC ordinary budget	Active collaboration with the ICRC
Ivory Coast	20.09.60	=	28.12.61			R –2 from 63	1970
Jamaica	18.09.62	=	17.07.64			R –1 from 67	1972
Japan	18.12.56	*	21.04.53	A		R from 60	1956 1950 AA
Jordan	14.12.55	46	29.05.51	A		R –4	1949 AA
Kenya	16.12.63	=	20.09.66			–	1957 AA
Kuwait	14.05.63	61	02.09.67	r		R	–
Lao People's Dem Rep.	14.12.55	54	29.10.56		S	– (1×)	1953 AA
Lebanon	24.10.45	*	10.04.51			R from 60 (–3)	1949 AA
Lesotho	17.10.66	=	20.05.68			–	1970
Liberia	02.11.45	*	29.03.54			R –1 from 69	1973
Lybian Arab Jamahiriya	14.12.55	51	22.05.56		S	–	–
Luxemburg	24.10.45	*	01.07.53			R +2	–
Madagascar	20.09.60	=	13.07.63			(from 61 to 73)	1972
Malawi	01.12.64	=	05.01.68			–	1966 AA
Malaysia	17.09.57	=	24.08.62			R –4 from 63	1956 AA
Maldives	21.09.65	=	–			–	–
Mali	28.09.60	=	24.05.65			–	1973
Malta	01.12.64	=	22.08.68			R from 70	–
Mauritania	27.10.61	60	27.10.62		S	– (2×)	1973
Mauritius	24.04.68	=	18.08.70			– (1×)	1973
Mexico	07.11.45	*	29.10.52			R +1	1969
Mongolia	27.10.61	46	20.12.58	A		R –2 from 65	–
Morocco	12.11.56	=	26.07.56	A		R –2 from 58	1955 AA
Mozambique	16.09.75	=	–			–	1962 AA
Nepal	14.12.55	*	07.02.64			R from 68	1960 AA
Netherlands	10.12.45	*	03.08.54	r		R from 55	–
New Zealand	24.10.45	*	02.05.59			R +9	–
Nicaragua	24.10.45	*	17.12.53			(from 59 to 71)	1955
Niger	20.09.60	=	16.04.64			–	1972
Nigeria	07.10.60	=	09.06.61		S	(from 61 to 70)	1967
Norway	27.11.45	*	03.08.51			R from 52	–
Oman	07.10.71	51	31.01.74			– (1×)	–
Pakistan	30.09.47	=	12.06.51	r		SP	1949 AA
Panama	13.11.45	*	12.02.56			–	1969
Papua-New Guinea	10.10.75	=	26.05.76		S	–	–
Paraguay	24.10.45	*	23.10.61			– (1×)	1972
Peru	31.10.45	*	15.02.56			–	1969
Philippines	24.10.45	*	06.10.52			R –6 from 54	1957
Poland	24.10.45	*	26.11.54	r		R from 56	1961
Portugal	14.12.55	*	14.03.61	r		R +9	1962
Qatar	21.09.71	=	15.10.75			–	–
Romania	14.12.55	*	01.06.54	r A		– (1×)	–
Rwanda	18.09.62	=	21.03.64			R from 76	1964 =

States	Admission to the UN	Accession 4 Geneva Conventions	Governmental contribution to ICRC ordinary budget	Active collaboration with the ICRC
Saint-Lucia	18.09.79 =	–	–	–
St-Vincent and				
Grenadines	16.09.80 79 –	–	–	
Samoa	15.12.76 62	–	–	–
Sao Tome				
and Principe	16.09.75 =	21.05.76 S	–	–
Saudi Arabia	24.10.45 *	18.05.63	R +13; –8	–
Senegal	28.09.60 =	23.04.63	SP	1972
Seychelles	21.09.76 =	–	–	–
Sierra Leone	27.09.61 =	31.05.65	SP	1972
Singapore	21.09.65 =	27.04.73	– (1×)	1975
Solomon Islands	19.09.78 =	–		–
Somalia	20.09.60 =	12.07.62	–	1976
South Africa	07.11.45 *	31.03.52	R	1967
Spain	24.12.55 *	04.08.52 A	R –2 from 58	1955
Sri Lanka	14.12.55 48	28.02.59	R +8 (–1)	1958 AA
Sudan	12.11.56 =	23.05.57 S	– (1×)	1968
Suriname	04.12.75 =	13.10.76 S	–	–
Swaziland	24.09.68 =	28.06.73	–	1972 AA
Sweden	19.11.46 *	28.12.53	R +1	–
Syrian Arab Rep.	24.10.45 *	02.11.53	SP	1949 AA
Thailand	16.12.46 *	29.12.54	R +1	1959
Togo	20.09.60 =	06.01.62	SP	1972
Trinidad				
and Tobago	18.09.62 =	24.09.63	R –1 from 68	1971
Tunisia	12.11.56 =	04.05.57 S	R from 59	1957 =
Turkey	24.10.45 *	10.02.54	(from 53 to 68)	–
Uganda	25.10.62 =	18.05.64	SP	1965
Ukrainian SSR	24.10.45 *	03.08.54 r	–	–
Emirates	09.12.71 =	10.05.72 S	R –2 from 73	–
United Kingdom	24.10.45 *	23.09.57	R +7 (–1)	1971
United Rep.				
of Cameroon	20.09.60 =	16.09.63	R –3 from 67	1972
United Rep.				
of Tanzania	14.12.61 =	12.12.62 S	R –2 from 63	D64
Upper Volta	20.09.60 =	07.11.61	SP	1972
Uruguay	18.12.45 *	05.03.69 r	– (1×)	1972
USA	24.10.45 *	02.08.55 r	R from 65	–
USSR	24.10.45 *	10.05.54 r	–	–
United Arab				
Venezuela	15.11.45 *	13.02.56	R +3 (–2)	1966
Viet Nam	20.09.77 *	28.06.57 r A	SP	1949 AA
Yemen	30.09.47 *	16.07.70	–	1966 AA
Yugoslavia	24.10.45 *	21.04.50 r	R –1	1959
Zaire	20.09.60 =	20.02.61 S	(from 68 to 74)+1×	1960 AA
Zambia	01.12.64 =	19.10.66	–	1970

States	Admission to the UN	Accession 4 Geneva Conventions	Governmental contribution to ICRC ordinary budget	Active collaboration with the ICRC
Zimbabwe	25.08.80 =	–	–	1959 AA
Popular Rep. of Korea	– *	27.08.57 r A	–	1950 AA
Rep. of Korea	– *	16.08.66 r A	R +7	1950 AA
Liechtenstein	– *	21.09.50 A	R	–
Monaco	– *	05.07.50 A	R from 63	–
San Marino	– *	29.08.53 A	– –2 from 59	–
Holy See	– *	22.02.51 A	–	–
Switzerland	– *	31.03.50 A	R	–
Tonga	– 70	13.04.78 A	–	–
Kiribati	– 79	–	–	–
Nauru	– 68	–	–	–
Tuvalu	– 78	–	–	–
Vanuatu	– 80	–	–	–

37. List of States Parties to the Geneva Conventions (August 12, 1949)

	Western	Socialist	Latin Amer. (and Caribb.)	African	Afro-Asian Asian
1950 7	Switzerland Monaco Liechtenstein	Yugoslavia Czechoslovakia	Chile		India
1951 10 (17)	Holy See Denmark France Norway Italy				Philippines Lebanon Jordan* Pakistan Israel
1952 6 (23)	South Africa* Spain Belgium		Guatemala Mexico	Egypt	
1953 9 (32)	Luxemburg Austria San Marino* Sweden		El Salvador Nicaragua		Japan* Syria S. Vietnam*
1954 14 (46)	Netherlands F.R. of Germany	USSR Romania Bulgaria Bielorussia Hungary Ukraine Poland	Cuba Equador	Liberia*	Turkey Thailand
1955 2 (48)	USA Finland				
1956 12 (60)	Greece	German Dem. Rep.	Panama* Venezuela Peru Argentina	Libya* Morocco*	Iraq* Afghanistan Laos* People's Rep. China

1957 9 (69)	United Kingdom	Albania	Haiti* Brazil	Tunisia* Sudan*	Iran Dem. Rep. Vietnam* Pop. Rep. of Korea*
1958 6 (75)	Australia	Mongolia*	Dominican Rep.*	Ghana*	Indonesia Cambodia*
1959 2 (77)	New Zealand				Ceylon
1960 1 (78)					Algeria*
1961 7 (85)	Portugal		Paraguay Colombia	Congo (Leopoldv.)** Ivory Coast** Upper Volta** Nigeria**	
1962 7	Cyprus* Ireland			Tanganika** Dahomey** Togo** Mauritania**	Malaysia
1963 6 (98)			Trinidad & Tobago*	Senegal** Somalia* Madagascar** Cameroons**	Saudi Arabia
1964 5 (103)			Jamaica**	Niger** Rwanda** Uganda**	Nepal
1965 6 (109)	Canada Iceland*		Honduras	Gabon** Mali* Sierra Leone**	
1966 5				Central Afr. Rep.** Kenya* Zambia* Gambia**	Rep. of Korea
1967 2 (116)				Congo (Brazzav.)**	Kuwait

1968 6 (122)	Malta**		Guyana** Barbados**	Malawi* Botswana** Lesotho**	
1969 3 (125)			Uruguay Costa Rica*	Ethiopia	
1970 3 (128)				Chad*	Yemen Arab. Rep. Mauritius**
1971 3 (131)				Burundi**	Fiji** Bahrein*
1972 2 (133)					United Arab Emirates Bangladesh*
1973 2				Swaziland*	Singapore* (South Viet. PRG)
1974 2 (137)				Guinea-Bissau*	Oman*
1975 2 (138)[1]			Bahamas*		Qatar*
1976 4 (142)			Surinam**	Sao Tomé & Principe*	Papua-New Guinea**
1977 1 (143)					Dem. Pop. Rep. of Yemen*
1978 2 (145)				Djibouti**	Tonga**
1979 – (145)					
1980 – ( )					

(No asterisk): Signatory State. Date of Ratifications

* Accession

** Declaration of Succession: The State having acceded to independence declares that the treaties concluded by the colonial power maintain their full and entire value in its eyes.

[1] Reunification of Vietnam in 1975.

CHAPTER 8

Principles and Law

The Statutes chosen by the International Committee of the Red Cross stipulate, in Article 4, that the ICRC has as its role in particular the perfecting of international humanitarian law, and the promotion, diffusion and development of the Geneva Conventions. This competence is confirmed by the 1952 Statutes of the International Red Cross (Art. 6, Par. 7).

Perfecting, comprehension, diffusion, development: the task is a heavy one. It essentially falls upon what the ICRC calls the General Affairs Directorate which, after the regroupment of services we have spoken of and which the Tables of Contents of the Annual Reports single out better than we could have, is today divided into two departments: The Department of Principle and Law, the Information Department.

The legal function clearly plays an essential role if one keeps in mind the fact that the years 1949 to 1980 encompass two major events: the 1949 Diplomatic Conference which drew up the four Conventions requiring application and enforcement; the 1974-1977 Diplomatic Conference, the intellectual and diplomatic preparation of which required a considerable effort over more than a decade. The ICRC was not content with diffusing the Conventions and seeing that their spirit was understood. It had to ensure their development so as to have them apply as nearly as possible to the reality, that is to say to situations experienced in the field. The ICRC legal experts did not only have to state the law, to define, for their colleagues engaged in operations, the legal framework of their action, to furnish interpretations of the articles of the Conventions, and thus to determine in what conditions one or another should be invoked. They are not only the advisers of delegates or of those who, at headquarters, assume a direct responsibility in the conduct of humanitarian diplomacy. They must also–and this should be one of their daily tasks–attempt, on the basis of their observations in the field and experiences accumulated through the permanent confrontation between legal norms and lived reality, to make propositions aimed at causing humanitarian law to progress. They are not alone in taking on this problem, which all of the people working at the ICRC, from the delegate to the Committee member, deals with from his own perspective. Whoever observes the life of the institution with sustained interest knows that all are guided by a concern not to be led by opportunism, something which is only possible thanks to a systematic comparison between applicable and desirable law. The legal function therefore plays a key role.

It is not possible, in the framework of this study, to go into detail concerning the activities of the Legal Division of the Department of Doctrine and Law. The problems posed by the application of humanitarian law and its evolution have spawned an abundant literature and, in particular, several doctoral theses. One may also refer to publications of the legal service of the ICRC, those of Jean Pictet whose commentaries are still authoritative, of Claude Pilloud, René-Jean Wilhelm, Jean de Preux, Jacques Moreillon, Yves Sandoz, Michel Veuthey and of the new team of collaborators.

We will therefore be satisfied to point to directions in which reflections have gone and research undertaken in the spirit of deepening and developing humanitarian law or, in other words, adapting it to new forms of war.

8.1. From the 1947 Rules Project to the Ban on the Use of Certain Weapons.

The 1949 Diplomatic Conference was mainly marked by the experiences of the decade from 1929 to 1939 and, even more, by those of the Second World war, which explains, as everyone knows, the attention given to the elaboration of a Convention, the fourth, aimed at ensuring the protection of civilian population. This also explains some of the dispositions introduced in the three other Conventions and, in particular, Article 3 common to the four Conventions. But even if the Hiroshima bomb provoked a shock, the new fact created by the use of a nuclear weapon in war was too recent, too unique, too terrifying to be able, at that early date, to evaluate its implications and consequences for humanitarian policy. There was something of a repulsion to imagine the unimaginable and hope was maintained that an accord will be reached on the international control of nuclear energy. When the USSR, in turn, demonstrated, in early 1949, its capacity to make a nuclear bomb, the problem suddenly became acute: one could no longer exclude the eventuality of the recourse to a nuclear weapon in an international conflict. And the unease caused by that hypothesis could only grow with the intensification of the cold war, the outbreak of the Korean conflict and the new arms race in Europe. Hence the question posed with even more insistence than during the years when the rules of The Hague were worked out in the interwar years: how to protect civilian populations from arms of mass destruction?

The ICRC set about working on the problem as of 1952, and prepared a study which it submitted to a Conference of Experts. Encouraged by a

Resolution of the League's Council of Governors in Oslo in May 1954, it drafted a *Rules Project Concerning the Protection of Civilian Populations* which, in the summer of 1955, it submitted to the National Societies. From the analysis of the observations it elicited, an examination carried out by a new commission of experts sent by a few National Societies,[1] was to emerge a new Rules Project which was presented to the 19th International Red Cross Conference, held in 1957 in New Delhi. The members of the Committee were conscious of the boldness of their step. It was clear that in the eyes of the Western governments, nuclear weapons offered an extremely important means of deterrence, since they offered them the means for correcting the disequilibrium in conventional weapons. The UN was also dealing with the problem. There was to be no question of entering an area which is reserved to that body. That is why the ICRC avoided taking sides in the debate on the banning of nuclear weapons. "The Red Cross, according to Frédéric Siordet, spokesman for the Committee at the New Delhi Conference, is not a political institution; it has no competence in the art of war and still less in nuclear science. It does not have to concern itself either with the manufacture of armaments or with the elaboration of strategy. Its only anxiety is, and should remain, the protection of non-combatants *and the giving* of relief....

"The ICRC therefore considered that a solution should not be sought in drawing up a catalogue of authorised or prohibited means of warfare, but rather in making out a list of principles ensuring the safety of those who must, by general consent, be protected from attack. Now, these principles have long existed. Though they are often forgotten and are stated in the ancient rules of the law of nations in a form which may appear out of date in this age of aviation and atomic energy, innumerable manifestations of public opinion and even the opinion of States–such as the signature of the Geneva Conventions of 1949–show that they are still living in the public conscience. We therefore considered that it was both necessary and sufficient to reaffirm these rules in a form which takes into account the developments of modern science. Indeed, there can be found in our Draft Rules nothing but:

"a reaffirmation of the principle that the civilian population must be left outside the sphere of armed attacks;

"the consequent obligation on the parties to the conflict to take every precaution to ensure that attacks on military objectives do not harm the civilian population which is to be removed from the vicinity of threatened objectives;

"the consequent obligation to abstain from the use of methods of destruction, the effects of which may escape from the control of the person using them, thus endangering the civilian population.

---

[1] *AR*, 1957, pp. 51-54.

"It is not the selection of a particular weapon which may make it lawful to destroy human life. We are, therefore, very desirous of the principles stated in the Draft being valid in all circumstances, whatever the weapon used and whether it is already known or yet to be invented".[2]

The Rules Project was to be much praised. The International Conference of the Red Cross voted an encouraging resolution which concludes with an invitation to the ICRC to transmit the Project and the notes of the Conference's deliberations to the governments. The problem raised was too complex and burning, the resistance on the part of some governments too strong for the Conference to go beyond a declaration of principles.

It was in fact a failure which the ICRC registered regretfully, without being discouraged by it. The governments were, in 1958, presented with the Rules Project and deliberation notes which it had drafted in New Delhi. In the years which followed, the Legal Division pursued what one might call a policy of erosion: since it was not possible to obtain from governments a commitment to renounce the use of massive and therefore indiscriminate weapons of destruction, it tried to reinforce the immunity of the so-called "civil defense" organizations and the civilian medical personnel whose intervention in favor of civilians must be promoted. This does not mean that the ICRC abandoned the principal objective: the formal recognition by governments of the distinction which must be made at all times between combatants and non-combatants, which may mean the renunciation of the use of mass destruction weapons. The 20th International Red Cross Conference, held in Vienna in 1965, made it possible to take a step forward. A resolution was voted there, which was to be called the "Vienna Declaration" reminding governments that:

- "The right of the parties to a conflict to adopt means of injuring the enemy is not unlimited;
- it is forbidden to launch attacks against the civilian population as such;
- distinction must be made at all times between persons taking part in the hostilities and members of the civilian population to the effect that the latter be spared as much as possible;
- the general principles of the law of war apply to nuclear and similar weapons."[3]

This Vienna Declaration is considered positive by the ICRC, by the very fact that it emanates from a Conference in which governmental delegations participate. Efforts were therefore to be pursued in the following years with a view to imposing in practice an effective protection of civilian populations

[2] *Cf. AR*, 1957, pp. 84-85.

[3] *AR*, 1965, p. 52.

against arms of mass destruction. Attention is no longer concentrated on nuclear arms, but rather on the engagement of conventional weapons, likely to have indiscriminate effects or to cause useless suffering.[4] The ICRC thus consciously penetrates in even greater detail into the area of what is called the law of The Hague. If it does so, it is because it is encouraged to, but also because the observation it makes in the field demonstrates that the technical progress accomplished since 1907 in the art of killing one's neighbor urgently imposes an updating of the law of war.[5] It devoted itself to that cause resolutely, in a permanent dialogue with governments intended to provoke general debate.[6] In the end its efforts were crowned with success. The 1974-1977 Diplomatic Conference set up an ad hoc commission on conventional weapons which studies propositions or documents furnished by governments. Two Conferences organized by the ICRC on indiscriminate weapons were held at Lucerne in 1974 and Lugano in 1976.

The results of these Conferences, in the opinion of the very people who organized them, were not as positive as they would have wished, given the strong resistance of governments. But it cannot be said that the tactic of "erosion", consisting in returning ceaselessly to a bothersome theme, failed. The successive meetings made it possible at least to identify in a precise manner certain concrete problems needing resolution and, finally, to obtain, in the UN framework, the establishment of Protocols limiting the use of certain weapons inflicting needless harm or having indeterminate effects.[7] This effort mainly made it possible, through the permanent debate instituted by the ICRC, to remind the parties, as noted by its representative in New Delhi, that if "peace and war are a matter for governments" and if "in a conflict the preservation of a country's safety may face it with harsh necessities", the mission of the ICRC and the Red Cross is "to proclaim and ceaselessly reaffirm the fact that humanity also has its necessities".[8]

---

[4] On September 18, 1968, the General Assembly of the UN, through its Resolution 2444 (XXIII): "Respect of Human Rights in a Period of Armed Conflict", adopted the first three principles of the "Vienna Declaration", which is a tribute rendered by the political institution to the humanitarian organization, but also a recognition of the fact that the problems posed by nuclear weaponry cannot be resolved in the framework of the law of war.

[5] *Cf.*, in this respect, the vigorous exposé-program that Jean Pictet presented at a meeting of National Red Cross Societies in Geneva, 1968. In *AR*, 1968, pp. 65-66.

[6] *Cf.* the 1967 "Memorandum" addressed to governments. *AR*, 1967, pp. 63-64.

[7] *Cf.* SANDOZ, Yves. "Interdiction ou restriction d'utiliser certaines armes classiques". Conférence des Nations Unies sur l'interdiction ou la limitation de l'emploi de certaines armes classiques. Acte final. *IRRC*, 1981, vol. 63, pp. 3-19.

[8] *AR*, 1957, p. 85. It must be noted that the ICRC has pursued its efforts. One might even say that the signature, in April 1981, by 34 governments, of the text of a Convention on the banning and limitation of certain classical weapons, prepared in the framework of a UN Conference, is to an extent the result of the ICRC's action.

8.2. Internal Conflicts

In a lecture before the National Red Cross Societies in 1968,[9] Jean Pictet, stressing the need for the revision of humanitarian law and the law of war, brought up the problem of internal conflicts and guerilla war, an important problem if ever there was one, for the ICRC which is by its statutes obligated to act, in its quality as a neutral institution, especially in case of war, of civil war, of internal unrest, so as to protect and assist military and civilian victims (cf. Art. 4, Par. 1, letter d and Art. 6, Par. 5). It was the President of the ICRC, Léopold Boissier, who in his Preface to the 1955 Annual Report noted that the ICRC has, "with the assistance of legal experts... studied the question of the application of humanitarian principles in the event of internal disturbances, of assistance to political detainees...".[10]

The groups of experts he referred to had met in October 1955, in order to answer certain questions submitted to it by the Committee:

(1) "Is it possible to define the idea of an "armed conflict", so as to determine the moment when Article 3 of the Fourth Geneva Convention of August 12, 1949, becomes applicable in law, in the event of internal disturbances?

(2) So long as the said Article is not applicable in law, is it consistent with the interests of humanity and the standards of civilisation for the humanitarian safeguards defined by the Fourth Convention to be applied, in particular in the case of persons (citizens or subjects) detained by their own Government for political reasons?

(3) Would not the International Committee be justified, by virtue of its traditions, the Statutes of the International Red Cross and its own Statutes, in offering its services to the Governments responsible for law and order?

(4) What should the conditions be for its action to be exercised, and what should be the limits of such action?"[11]

These were fundamental questions to which the ICRC legal experts were to attempt to obtain positive answers from the governments concerned and which their colleagues in operations regularly face in their activities.

The experts consulted in 1955 gave a nuanced but positive answer: while they recognized that it is difficult to include "internal disturbances" in the field of application of Article 3, they nonetheless felt that "such situations"

[9] Passage referred to above. Cf. *AR*, 1968.

[10] *AR*, 1955, p. 3.

[11] *Ibid.*, p. 48.

(internal disturbances) tend to become more and more frequent and that it is important "to meet them, in so far as possible, by applying the humanitarian principles upon which the Geneva Conventions are based". The State, they recalled, "has full liberty to judge which measures it shall take" and "humanitarian action should never include any intrusion on the legal plane".

On the second question, the commission "did not hesitate":

"It does, indeed, appear consistent with the interests of humanity as well as with the standards of civilization that the humanitarian safeguards, as defined more particularly by the Fourth Convention, should be applied to persons at strife with their own government on political or social grounds."

As for points 3 and 4, the commission felt that the ICRC was justified in basing its action, not only on "its general mission to alleviate human suffering", but also on the right of initiative which is recognized by the Conventions. In these conditions, the experts concluded, it is difficult to see what objections could be directed against the action of the ICRC in case of "internal disturbances', if it "remains strictly on the humanitarian plane which is its own".[12]

The answer of the 1955 experts was encouraging. But what the ICRC can deduce from it is that humanitarian policy like war is an art based entirely on its application. It is therefore through actions undertaken in the field, as we have already noted, and through a discrete diplomacy which is careful not to challenge the sovereignty of States, that the ICRC was to be able, in certain regions of the world and at certain periods, to extend its protection to victims of internal disturbances and to political detainees.[13] But the efforts which it made to obtain legal approval for new situations created by its interventions did not obtain results to match its ambitions.

These efforts were nonetheless considerable and regular. It is enough to consult Annual Reports in order to note that year after year, the Committee returned to the theme, that it frequently consulted experts, launched bilateral and multilateral negotiations. Every one of its interventions in situations of so-called internal unrest, every one of its failures, rekindled the debate with the institution: is there no lesson to be drawn from the experience? Is the moment not approaching when governments, having understood that the intervention of a humanitarian institution like the ICRC, far from threatening their security, could contribute to reducing the internal unrest which they fear, will accept the principle?

The calling of a new Conference for the Reaffirmation and Development of International Humanitarian Law–such was at least the hope nourished in

---

[12] *Ibid.*, pp. 76-80.

[13] *Cf.* Chapters 2.2. and 3.3.

Geneva at the time when its convening was being planned–was to make it possible to consolidate the results already obtained. But the hope declined as the meeting approached, because it became perceptible, in Geneva, that there was a change in the international climate accompanying the modification of the structure of the world system. The international community was undergoing a mutation. New actors had appeared. Would they be sensitive to the importance of humanitarian law in the relations between States and within societies? A considerable effort was made, in agreement with the League–an effort intensified as the years go by–to deepen the understanding of the Conventions and their implications, to make them known. But it was not possible, before the Conference, to foresee the reception which would be reserved for the ICRC's propositions.

It was all the more difficult to predict the outcome of the Conference in that the work of the ICRC's legal experts was, correctly, oriented towards what one might call the updating of humanitarian law. Experiences in the field since 1949 in application of the Conventions had revealed numerous failings which needed to be repaired.

But the indispensable enlargement of the range of dispositions which needed to be introduced in the Additional Protocols in order to adapt humanitarian law to new types of war, to new forms of combat, to the fallout from technical progress, the detailed work implied by a deepening of humanitarian law, had as their consequence the "levelling" of the problems to be resolved. Even if the outlawing of indiscriminate attacks and the application of the Conventions in case of internal unrest remained the fundamental objectives whose realization would represent a significant development in humanitarian law, the reinforcement of the protection of victims of conflicts imposed an examination of the totality of measures to be taken.

Numerous examples of observed gaps can be cited: the increasing recourse to aerial transport for the evacuation of the wounded made it necessary to introduce provisions guaranteeing the security of aircraft; contemporary conflicts, civil wars, national liberation wars, as well as the Vietnam war, had made more urgent the recognition of the status of guerilla war (the Nigerian war, among others, imposed the reexamination of conventional provisions concerning blockades). Particular situations were examined such as that of mercenaries; the increasing concern with ensuring the protection of the civilian population made it necessary to consider additional guarantees to be furnished to those who carry out the protection (medical personnel, civil defense corps). In short, there was so much to do in order to adapt humanitarian law to the reality experienced since 1949, that preparatory work was to result in detailed propositions being made, so detailed that the objectives considered essential were as drowned in the totality of measures to be taken.

The provisions of the two Protocols were of course a valid constitution to humanitarian law. A careful reading of the Additional Protocols shows that the Diplomatic Conference in fact adopted most of the propositions submitted to it by the ICRC.

Protocol I, in particular, contains extremely important provisions which the ICRC can justifiably view as the reward for its efforts spanning several decades. Article 48, for example, stipulates that:

"In order to ensure respect for and protection of the civilian population and civilian objects, the Parties to the conflict shall at all times distinguish between the civilian population and combatants and between civilian objects and military objectives and accordingly shall direct their operations only against military objectives."

A principle is thus clearly stated, a rule to be observed in the conduct of war is imposed, whose field of application is specified by Article 49. The outlawing of "indiscriminate attacks" which is pronounced by Article 51 includes a definition of "indiscriminate" precise and concrete enough to be applicable: those responsible for military operations must, before the engagement of their means of destruction–and Article 57 on precautionary measures stipulates how this is to be done–evaluate the relative importance of the military objective and the losses and destructions which may result for the civilian population and their possessions. Notable progress has therefore been made in the definition of criteria of behaviour, and this represents a breakthrough in one of the two main axes and a stage in the development of humanitarian law.

One may even consider that Protocol I, by including in its field of application armed conflicts in which people struggle against colonial domination and foreign domination, took into account–even more perhaps than those who had insisted on the inclusion of the clauses–new types of war existing in the world. If the mention of colonial domination and that which one finds later on of the struggle against racism reflect the climate of a historic period, the reference to foreign occupation and the right of self-determination made in the same Paragraph 4 of Article 1, has a general and permanent application. The same is true of Article 44 which *de facto* accords guerillas the status of combatants who have the right to protection in international conflicts. But the provisions we have just quoted, and others included in Protocol I, cover, not explicitly but in practice, situations belonging to the category of internal unrest. In the troubled world in which we live, war in its many forms does not know any borders and neither does humanitarian action. One can therefore not say that the Diplomatic Conference of 1974-1977 represents a failure.

To the very extent to which the distinction between armed, international and non-international, conflicts is declining, Protocol II is losing its usefulness to the point where it is even something of an obstacle. The events which took place after 1977 revealed that the pressure of circumstances, by shaking the barriers of sovereignty, forced the ICRC to make use of its right of initiative.[14]

As for Protocol I, which confirms in detailed texts the imperatives of the protection of civilian populations which the Vienna principles had summed up, it represents, in the long march begun in New Delhi, pursued without interruption through the "Vienna Declaration" and Resolution 2444 of the UN, an important stage in the development of international humanitarian law.

8.3. Information

Information was long considered by the ICRC as a non-priority or even marginal, task. It was enough, the Committee felt, to make actions and the principles that guide them known to a few governments with which the ICRC had relations. The informing of public opinion was not desired and great discretion surrounded the activities of the institution. It is therefore not surprising that the ICRC should have in time created the image of a self-enclosed organization, one revelling in its taste for secrecy. This attitude, which was still the rule during the 1960s, was no longer possible from the time the ICRC was to engage in a policy of intensifying its involvement in the world.

The Nigeria-Biafra war was, as in other areas of ICRC activity, the decisive turning-point and it provoked a profound mutation in the information policy of the ICRC. The emotion caused by the drama in world public opinion, the vast material and human means employed for the operation, the observations made by delegates in the field that essential rules of humanitarian law were totally ignored by the combatants, were as many elements which caused the ICRC totally to review its information policy.

Beginning in 1970, efforts were launched in two directions:

8.3.1. Operational Information

The rapid development of means of mass communication considerably modified the ICRC's conditions of intervention, and those of other large charitable organizations, in that the pressure of public opinion has today become a reality which the Committee can no longer ignore. Thanks to the development of telecommunications, everyone is now able to follow day to day, if not hour after hour, the evolution of the great international crises and

---

[14] The results obtained at the Diplomatic Conference will be found in the "Report on the Diplomatic Conference on the Reaffirmation and Development of International Humanitarian Law Applicable in Armed Conflicts", presented by the ICRC at the 23rd Red Cross Conference at Bucharest, in 1977. Geneva, ICRC, 1977, 34 p. *Cf.* also the *AR*s, particularly those for the years 1975, 1976, 1977, as well as the July 1975 and October 1977 issues of the *International Review of the Red Cross.*

the human dramas which they engender. Who can remain insensitive in the face of television pictures showing the horrors of war?

The Committee has thus understood that, in order to obtain financial, material support indispensable to the conduct of its operation, it had to make its action and the principles which guide it better known, not only among directly concerned governments, but also among National Red Cross or Red Crescent Societies, as well as the mass media whose influence on public opinion, and through it, on governments, is often decisive.

The ICRC therefore strongly reinforced its Press Division beginning in 1970. At the time, other than its chief (who essentially carried out the functions of spokesman), it only included a press attache, mainly responsible for publishing the monthly *The ICRC in Action.* Ten years later, the Division includes a dozen professionals charged with diffusing operational information among the international media and also National Red Cross Information Services. It is interesting to note that an important portion of the information is orally communicated, as a function of the needs and interests of the interlocutors of the Division. The fact that the service is "personalized" explains that, during the past twelve years, the ICRC has given few press conferences, whereas, nearly every day, one or another of the media referred to its action. Likewise, the ICRC reserves its press communiques mainly for the publication of its reactions to an event or a situation rather than the presentation of the details of its actions, the press attaches being charged with this task in the framework of their daily contacts with the media and information services of the National Red Crosses.

It became apparent, as of 1970, that information diffused in Geneva was no longer sufficient, that the ICRC had every interest in sending its message from the field, from the very theater of operations. It has been noted that once a major conflict breaks out, the representatives of the press, radio and television come from the entire world to "cover the event". The ICRC therefore found it indispensable, as quickly as possible, to establish on the spot contacts with the representatives of the international press, so as to make its action and, even more, the principles which guide it, better known. That task of "expatriate" spokesman is by its very nature a delicate one: the press attache, who lives in a climate of extreme tension, where emotions generally overpower reason, must be able quickly to react and even anticipate, inspiring himself not only by his own experience but even more by the spirit of the Conventions and international humanitarian law. His essential preoccupation must be to bring people whose attention is concentrated on the event, to understand the concern for coherence which guides the ICRC in its action.

It is, finally, interesting to note that in addition to its task of information directed towards the outside public, the Press Division has, ever since the beginning of the 1970s, played an essential role in the area of the search for information necessary to the Committee and to the Operations Department for the conduct of its action. This involved mainly the reading, selection and treatment of the cables of two large press agencies (AFP and Reuters) and of articles from the international press (dailies and weeklies). This press documentation, classed according to precise criteria of selection (by country and by subject) today constitutes a very precious working tool.

The task, in terms of operational information, is not easy. Due to the very fact that the ICRC must work with discretion, while mobilizing as large a portion of public opinion as possible for a humanitarian venture. It is therefore not surprising that the ICRC's information policy has been the object of frequent criticism. It is only slowly, through internal debates, on the basis of experts' reports and above all under the pressure of circumstances, that a global information policy has been defined, not only at the world level at which the ICRC's activities are carried out, but also at the national and local levels. This makes it possible for very different people to follow and understand the ICRC's action: to understand not only operations underway which cannot be presented in their every detail, but mainly the spirit in which the institution works, the mission which it bears and the objectives which it pursues. The Press Division, in this way, played just as useful role in the preparation of the Diplomatic Conference as in the explanation of the actions underway in the Middle East and in Cambodia. And if it obtained modest but appreciable results such as an increase in specific references to the International Committee in press communiques and articles, it was because the Committee itself consented to make public relations effort, because the credibility of the ICRC, it was understood, depended on its ability to ensure an essential coherence between principles and law on the one hand, and operations on the other. It is first and foremost through information that the agreement–or disagreement–between tactics and strategy can be observed.[15]

8.3.2. The Dissemination of Red Cross and International Humanitarian Law Principles

As we have seen, the ICRC had, by the end of the 1960s, concluded that it was necessary to make better known and understood throughout the world, not only its actions and guiding principles, but also the rules which it had elaborated for the purpose of protecting the civilian and military victims of armed conflicts. This task–an immense one, since it is exercised at a

[15] The *Annual Reports* make it possible to grasp the evolution of the information policy and the change which took place in the conduct of public relations as a function of the transformation of societies and methods. *Cf.* also MODOUX Alain. "Les problèmes du Comité international de la Croix-Rouge en matière de relations publiques", *IRRC*, Nov.-Dec. 1978, pp. 207-217.

planetary level–could only progress on condition that the Red Cross and Red Crescent movement as a whole were associated with the effort. True, the ICRC, from the beginning of the 1970s, has opted for the opening of regional Delegations in Latin America, Africa and Asia. But it was also necessary for National Societies, each one in its country, to put themselves to work and collaborate to that end with the international institutions of the Red Cross.

The ICRC, together with the League and the Henry-Dunant Institute, had fixed for itself a dual objective for the 1970s: on the one hand, to inspire the creation in each country of an "interministerial Committee" for dissemination, with which the concerned National Society was to be associated; on the other hand, to organize, on a regional basis, seminars on international humanitarian law intended to sensitize certain leaders of the National Societies, the armed forces and the academic community to the importance of the Geneva Conventions, in the hopes that those leaders would pursue the effort in their own country.

Whereas it can be said that the second objective was realized, a dozen regional seminars having been organized since 1977, it is not certain that the hoped-for multiplier effect occurred. Several participants in these seminars went home with the firm intention of pursuing the task at a national level, but many others were content to emit pious hopes. As for the creation of "interministerial committees", it was only realized in a limited number of countries, mainly in Western Europe, as well as Australia and New Zealand.

The regional delegations which were opened in Africa, Asia and Latin America did of course contribute to making the ICRC better known in those regions. But it rapidly appeared that due to various conflicts and tensions which proliferated on those three continents, the regional delegates were absorbed by daily tasks.

At the beginning of the 1980s a new approach is being elaborated. Since the National Societies, in most countries, in particular those of the third world, encounter many difficulties in carrying out alone what is a kind of teaching, the ICRC has decided to train among its own delegates, specialists in the area whom it will send to the various delegations throughout the world. The beginnings were modest and difficult, since the first efforts are being attempted in countries engulfed by violence and where the Red Cross emblem is either ignored or abused. The countries involved are those of southern Africa (Rhodesian conflict) and El Salvador. The two experiences demonstrate the necessity for reaching not only members of elite socio-professional groups (armed forces, government and academic communities), but also the civilian population within which the guerilla forces clandestinely move about. The action of "dissemination on the battlefield" has a double purpose: on the one hand, to obtain, by making them known, greater respect for the essential rules of humanity so as to protect persons not or no longer participating in hostilities; on the other hand, to protect the mission of the Red Cross, in particular those who are charged with carrying it out, by making the aims, actions and principles of the institution known.

While it is not easy to evaluate the results of these actions, testimony received on the spot, both among ICRC delegates and from leaders and volunteers of the concerned National Societies, are very encouraging, so that, in future, any operation of the ICRC which takes place in a context of internal conflict is to be systematically supported by a reminder of the principles which guide it. Such is the case in Pakistan (Afghan conflict), Poland, Lebanon, Nicaragua, the Philippines.

The development of the ICRC's activity, as can well be imagined, encounters serious obstacles. But nobody can deny the need, through concrete engagements, for a sustained effort to make governments, combatants and public opinion understand the pacifying and peaceful value of a humanitarian strategy.

Conclusion

Conclusion

We have, in the course of this study, attempted to define the nature of problems which the evolution of the international system had posed to the International Committee of the Red Cross, and also to see to what extent it had been able to face up to them.

Given the complexity of problems posed by the extension of the political and diplomatic arena to the entire planet, as well as the interaction of interests and the instantaneous globalization of emotions, there could be no question of treating all the manifestations of the ICRC's activity. We therefore deliberately concentrated on what, from the point of view of Geneva headquarters, is called the field, that is to say the world's battlefields. The ICRC, it cannot be emphasized enough, is an international "operational" institution, whose objective is the protection of victims of armed conflicts. That mission and the role assigned to it of guardian of the Conventions, oblige it to develop in peacetime the legal apparatus on which its intervention in favor of victims will be based during wartime. An important part of its activity is therefore oriented towards the development of humanitarian law as a result of observations made in the field and conclusions that may be drawn from them in order to consolidate the legal basis of humanitarian policy. But it is not enough to consolidate. One must also educate, diffuse the Red Cross message, teach at all levels, from that of Chief of State to that of primary school pupil, without neglecting the armed forces and–something more and more important–police forces as well as those services, which are becoming dangerously ubiquitous, charged with ensuring the security of the State. Hence the importance of the role played within the ICRC by the Department of Principles and Law.

If we did not develop the analysis of the activities of the Department of Principles and Law, it is because–as we said–the subject has been treated by numerous studies on the part of legal scholars, and the Diplomatic Conference for the Reaffirmation and Development of International Law inspired an abundant literature. It is also because the Conference yielded results which are only significant for our study in one area: the demonstration they provide of the rigidity of institutional structures and behavior.

Governments–and, as a result, those who are charged with representing them–are not disposed to make commitments limiting through time their freedom of action. They are all the more zealous in the defense of what they call their sovereignty when their independence has been freshly acquired. The very people who have just triumphed through a "national liberation" struggle or revolution, and who affirm their solidarity with a few other movements yet engaged in an analogous struggle, have a tendency to show themselves particularly resistant to any intervention in their internal affairs, even when it is proposed in the name of the principle of humanity.

But the refusal to make commitments in favor of the protection of victims, which might have consequences not only for the exercise of State sovereignty in general but, more specifically, for dispositions put in place to assure their security, in the jumble of transnational conflicts, does not necessarily create an insurmountable barrier to any humanitarian intervention. Sovereignty, like political borders, is a barrier with doors which the States are obliged to open in order to preserve their relations with their neighbors. One cannot protect it from humanitarian contraband, that is to say that multitude of individual actions undertaken in order to save lives and in the face of which even the most stubborn governments are sometimes forced to close their eyes.

It is therefore through the development of its activities in the field that we had to grasp the reaction of the ICRC to the evolution of the contemporary world. It is through its delegates that the International Committee perceives change. The delegate plays a capital role, not only through what he does, the way in which he behaves in the field, but through that which he reports to Geneva, the quality of his testimony, the precision of his accounts. That is why a direct debriefing of a delegate freshly arrived from the field of operations on the part of members of the Committee in plenary council or in executive committee, is decisively important, not only for the measures to be taken in a given situation, but for the elaboration of the long-term policy of the institution and, finally, for the evolution of international humanitarian law. It is through the experience accumulated by men engaged in the field, through the multiplicity of experiences undergone in various parts of the world, in contacts with regimes of all natures and political leaders representing the entire range of possible behavior, from the sometimes open cynic with well-constructed arguments to the falsely generous type incapable of respecting a commitment, it is in this permanent exchange of views, this confrontation between the "humanitarian warrior" and those on whom rests the strategy of the long battle for humanity that, progressively, a vision of the war emerges, a perception of forces in play, of their relative intensity, and that are defined the orientation and the contents of the policy to be followed as well as the necessary diplomatic manoeuvers. Those are the discussions, which in fact constitute a permanent internal negotiation, in which problems such as access to political detainees, the policy to adopt concerning torture and disappearances, are broached. This is where the junction is progressively made in the minds of the ICRC between the activities carried out in the framework of the Conventions and those by which the Committee enters into the domain of the protection of human rights.

The road travelled, from intervention in armed international or non-international conflicts, towards that aiming at protecting human rights, is considerable. It is difficult to evaluate its importance from the outside because that type of activity, to which governments are particularly sensitive, imposes extreme discretion. But the little we know of it leads us to say that, in fact, the ICRC is one of the international non-governmental organizations whose action in the protection of political detainees is not only one of the most effective but exemplary from the point of view of method.

The Geneva Conventions furnish a sufficient legal framework so that, by using its right of initiative, the ICRC can pursue and intensify its action in the area and, more particularly, in the struggle against torture in which concrete results have been obtained. It is only through discrete diplomacy bearing on specific cases and through operations limited in time that results can be obtained.

This in no way diminishes the role played by those of the intergovernmental or non-governmental international organizations whose action is oriented towards the mobilization of public opinion and which have sometimes brought governments to make concessions. A division of labor has been tacitly set up, which functions to a certain extent, and without all too apparent coordination.

The enumeration of the ICRC's activities and its role in the protection of victims should not be interpreted as praise without criticism. The institution has had failures often due to the resistance of governments or to its own errors. Even if most States have adhered to the Conventions, governments reserve the freedom to interpret them according to the vision they entertain of their interests. The diversity of philosophies or of ideologies to which the parties to international or internal conflicts refer creates as many obstacles to the development of a humanitarian policy. The international system is not only shaken by crises. It tends to disintegrate. Universalism is placed on the defensive by the centrifugal impact of nationalism, but also of factions and religions. The temptation of the regionalization of the Red Cross Movement periodically appears. The quarrel concerning the protective emblem is in this respect significant. What is just as serious is the fact that national communities are also threatened by disintegration due to ethnic, sectarian, ideological conflicts, that power tends to dilute itself, that certain countries are sliding into anarchy and are becoming ungovernable. And the ICRC can only ensure its mission of protecting victims if it finds valid interlocutors, governments or chiefs able to offer its delegates guarantees of security. When the conditions of security are not fulfilled, it is forced to retire from the scene, thus regretfully abandoning the victims to the arbitrary treatment of warring chiefs. And the zones in which unrest escapes all control tend to be expanding, which limits the practical influence of the ICRC and gives a blow, not so much to its prestige as to the cause which it embodies.

But despite past failures and the proliferation of unresolved problems, it is clear that the authority and influence of the ICRC have not ceased to grow. A good number of governments better understand the importance of its role in the international system and, even if they always tend to transform it into an instrument of their policy of the moment and ignore it when it bothers them, even if the appeal to humanitarian institutions such as the ICRC is often a mere consequence of their incapacity to take the risk of imposing political solutions, even if, to give only one example, their incapacity to make the collective security system function in the Indochinese peninsula or the Middle East has contributed to multiplying the number of victims of wars, they have nonetheless progressively learned to respect the ICRC which has managed, until now, to preserve its independence, its reputation of impartiality and the specific character of its neutrality, distinct from Swiss neutrality.

One can therefore conclude that, within the limits of its modest means, the ICRC has been able to face up to the demands of a world in transformation, that it has even managed to give itself the means for responding to demands, that it has been able to mobilize the manpower and the funds which it required by providing for their commitment at the needed moment. The instrument, whatever may be its deficiencies and inevitable failures, is used effectively. Let us stress in this regard that an aspect of the effectiveness is the speed of reaction to crisis situations, which is the result of the flexibility of the organization and, ultimately, of the decision-making capacity of its leaders. And if leaders can make rapid decisions, it is not only due to the quality of the men, but also to the acquired experience and to the uninational character of a Committee whose members decide without having to consult governments; they are also in a position to arbitrate interests in the course of discussions which can sometimes be difficult but which take place in a small circle and whose duration is limited by external circumstances, namely the conflict underway.

This brings us, at the end of our study, to the reiteration of a point we have already made: despite numerous debates concerning structures which have wracked the ICRC and the Red Cross movement, the Huber reform was preserved in its essential aspects, and the distinction among the three decision-making levels was maintained.

In fact, the ICRC Statutes were drafted in terms sufficiently general and with a long-term vision of its mission, so that they constitute a solid base for undertaking long-lasting activities.

It is to the extent that they are content to define principles, rules of behavior, working methods, that they have facilitated the adaptation of the institution to a world which is doubtless changing, but without bringing about change in the behavior of human beings. The parameters of the problems which the members of the International Committee of the Red Cross have to resolve in the contemporary period are not totally different from those of their predecessors of the 19th century, so that the institutional framework put in place during the last century remains valid.

Bibliography

1. SOURCES

Action du CICR en Angola. Geneva, ICRC, 1975, 15 p.

Action du CICR à Chypre. Geneva, ICRC, 1974, 13 p.

L'action du CICR dans le monde arabe, 1955-1979. Geneva, CICR, 1979, 49 p.+ annexes.

Action de secours en faveur de réfugiés d'Algérie en Tunisie et au Maroc. 1959-1962. Geneva, League, 1963, 39 p.

Assistance médicale au Congo. Rapport sur l'action de la Croix-Rouge internationale. Geneva, ICRC, League, 1961, 29 p.

Le CICR et le conflit algérien. Geneva, ICRC, 1962, 23 p.

Le Comité international de la Croix-Rouge et le conflit de Corée. Recueil de Documents. 2 vol. Geneva, ICRC, 1952, 255+159 p.

Le CICR et le conflit du Yemen. Geneva, ICRC, 1964, 34 p.

1919-1963, 1963-1969. *Grandes dates de l'histoire de la Ligue des Sociétés de la Croix-Rouge*. Geneva, League, no date, 36 p.

Historique succinct des GMI (Groupes pour missions internationales). Berne, GMI, 1980, 6 p.

Manuel chronologique pour l'histoire générale de la Croix-Rouge, 1863-1899. Geneva, ICRC, 1900, 30 p.

Handbook of the International Red Cross. 11th Ed., Geneva, ICRC, League, 1971, 637 p.

Rapport sur l'action en Hongrie, octobre 1956-juin 1957. Genève, CICR, 1957, 61 p.

Activity Reports 1947-1980, International Committee of the Red Cross.
Annual (Biannual) Reports. Geneva, League.

Various ICRC Reports and Joint ICRC-League Reports to International Red Cross Conferences:

XVIIth – Stockholm – 1948

XVIIIth – Toronto – 1952

XIXth – New Delhi – 1957

XXth – Vienna – 1965

XXIth – Istanbul – 1969

XXIIth – Teheran – 1973

XXIIIth – Bucharest – 1977

* *Rapport final sur l'opération de secours en Jordanie*, 1970. Geneva, ICRC (no date), 16 p.

Rapport général d'activité du Commissariat pour l'aide aux réfugiés en Palestine. 4 vol. (1.1.1949-30.4.1950). Geneva, ICRC (1952?).

GONARD, Samuel A. *Rapport de mission en Afrique équatoriale et centrale.* Geneva, ICRC, 1962, 91 p. (Internal document).

GONARD, Samuel A. *Rapport de mission en Algérie.* Geneva, ICRC, 1963, 65 p. (Internal document).

Report of the ICRC Medical Mission to the Brazilian Amazon Region. Geneva, League, 1970, 70 p.

II. WORKS

BERGER, Jean-François. *L'action du Comité international de la Croix-Rouge en Indochine,* 1946-1954. Montreux, Corbaz, 1982; 95p.

BOISSIER, Léopold. "Le CICR et ses interventions dans les conflits politiques". *Annuaire Suisse de Science Politique,* vol. V, 1965; pp. 7-14.

BOISSIER, Léopold. "La Croix-Rouge et l'Assistance aux détenus politiques". *Politique étrangère,* vol. XXIII, No. 1, 1958; pp. 5-24.

BOISSIER, Pierre. *Histoire du Comité international de la Croix-Rouge, de Solférino à Tsoushima* (Revised Edition). Geneva, Henry-Dunant Institute, 1978; 512 p.

BOSSHARDT, Werner. *Zur Effektivität des Kriegsvölkerrechts.* Möglichkeiten empirischer Forschung. Zürich, Universität Zürich, 1973; 34 p. Collection "Kleine Studien zur politischer Wissenschaft", No. 21.

BOUTHOUL, Gaston et CARRERE, René. *Le défi de la guerre, 1740-1974.* Deux siècles de guerres et de révolutions. Vendôme, PUF, 1976; 224 p.

*BUGNION, François. *L'emblème de la Croix-Rouge.* Aperçu historique. Geneva, ICRC, 1977; 85 p.

BUTTERWORTH, Robert. *Managing Interstate Conflict, 1945-1974.* Data with Synopsis, Pittsburgh, UCIS, 1976; 535 p.

CHAIX, Emile. "Le théâtre des guerres contemporaines de la Croix-Rouge". *Bulletin international des Sociétés de la Croix-Rouge,* No. 107, juillet 1896; pp. 168-178.

DICK, Jean-Pierre. *Le Comité international de la Croix-Rouge.* Etude comptable et financière (1967-1971). Geneva, Geneva University, 1973; 124 p. (ronotyped).

DJUROVIČ, Gradomir. *L'Agence Centrale de Recherches du Comité International de la Croix-Rouge.* Geneva, Henry-Dunant Institute, 1981; 295 p.

*DUNANT, Henry. *Un Souvenir de Solférino,* 1862. Berne, Croix-Rouge Suisse, 1963; 147 p.

DUNNING, H. W. *Eléments pour l'histoire de la Ligue des Sociétés de la Croix-Rouge.* Geneva, League, 1969; 105 p.

*DURAND, André. *Le Comité international de la Croix-Rouge.* Lausanne, Centre de Recherches Européennes, 1980; 88 p. (Durand 1).

* Durand, André. *Histoire du Comité international de la Croix-Rouge de Sarajevo à Hiroshima.* Geneva, Henry-Dunant Institute, 1978; 590 p. (Durand 2).

Forsythe, David. *Humanitarian Politics.* The International Committee of the Red Cross. Baltimore, Johns Hopkins U.P., 1977; 298 p.

* Freymond, Jacques. "Le Comité international de la Croix-Rouge dans le système international". *IRRC,* 1972, vol. 54, pp. 267-289.

Freymond, Jacques. *Guerres, Révolutions, Croix-Rouge.* Réflexions sur le rôle du Comité international de la Croix-Rouge. Geneva, IUHEI, 1976; 222 p.

Hentsch, Thierry. *Face au blocus.* Histoire du Comité international de la Croix-Rouge dans le conflit du Nigéria, 1967-1970. Geneva, Droz, 1973; 307 p.

Historique succinct du GMI (Groupe pour missions internationales). Berne (GMI), 1980; 6 p.

Huber, Max. *La pensée et l'action de la Croix-Rouge.* Geneva, ICRC, 1954; 376 p.

Jacobson, Harold. *Networks of Interdependence*: International Organizations and the Global Political System. New York, Alfred A. Knopf, 1979; XXIV+486 p.

* Modoux, Alain. "Les problèmes du Comité international de la Croix-Rouge en matière de relations publiques". *IRRC,* 1978, vol. 60; pp. 307-317.

Moreillon, Jacques. *Le Comité international de la Croix-Rouge et la protection des détenus politiques.* Geneva, Henry-Dunant Institute and l'Age d'Homme, 1973; 303 p.

* Moreillon, Jacques. "La Croix-Rouge: protection et assistance". *IRRC,* 1981, vol. 63, pp. 267-272.

Nobs, Marguerite. *Les collaborateurs bénévoles et le CICR.* Geneva, ICRC, 1954; 18 p. (Internal Document).

Perruchoud, Richard. *Les résolutions des Conférences internationales de la Croix-Rouge.* Geneva, Henry-Dunant Institute, 1979; 469 p.

Rosas, Allan. *The Legal Status of Prisoners of War.* Helsinki, Suomalainen Tiedeakatemia, 1976; 523 p.

Ruegger, Paul. "L'organisation de la Croix-Rouge internationale sous ses aspects juridiques". *Recueil des cours de l'Académie de droit international de La Haye,* vol. 82, I, 1953, pp. 373-585.

* Schindler, Dietrich. "Le CICR et les droits de l'homme". *IRRC,* 1979, vol. 61, pp. 3-15.

Schindler, Dietrich. "Übergangsformen zwischen Krieg und Frieden". *Schweizer Monatshefte,* 1960, pp. 113-124.

* Tansley, Donald. *Rapport final: Un ordre du jour pour la Croix-Rouge.* Réévaluation du rôle de la Croix-Rouge+les 6 documents de références. Geneva, Henry-Dunant Institute, 1975; 139 p.

Veuthey, Michel. "Les conflits de caractère non international et le droit humanitaire". *Current Problems of International Law,* ed. by A. Cassese Milano, Guiffrè, 1975; pp. 179-266.

* Veuthey, Michel. "La Croix-Rouge et les conflits non-internationaux". *IRRC,* 1970, vol. 52; pp. 467-480.

Veuthey, Michel. *Guérilla et droit international humanitaire.* Genève, Henry-Dunant Institute, 1976; 431 p.

Virally, Michel. *L'organisation mondiale.* Paris, Armand Colin, 1972; 587 p.

Zacher, Mark. *International Conflicts and Collective Security, 1946-1977:* The United Nations, OAS, OAU and Arab League. New York, Praeger, 1979; x+297 p.

* English version available